THE
BATTLE
FOR
MOSCOW

BY

COL. ALBERT SEATON

SARPEDON
New York

Published by
SARPEDON

For any additional information, contact:

Sarpedon Publishers
166 Fifth Avenue
New York, NY 10010
(212) 741-9538 / Fax (212) 633-1036

ISBN: 0-9627613-2-X

10 9 8 7 6 5 4 3 2

Book and cover design by Libby Braden

MANUFACTURED IN THE UNITED STATES OF AMERICA

ACKNOWLEDGMENTS

THE AUTHOR wishes to thank the Director General, Imperial War Museum for kind permission to reproduce all the photographs in this book, except *Mud and the German panje wagon* and *German motorized troops,* which are reproduced by permission of Keystone Press, and *A main road in April 1942* by permission of Planet News; and Arthur Barker Ltd for permission to make use of certain passages from the author's *The Russo-German War 1942–1945.*

MAPS

CONTENTS

INTRODUCTION

In JUNE 1941, when Hitler attacked the Soviet Union, the strength and equipment of the Red Army were inferior to none, yet in terms of leadership, training, experience, and efficiency it ranked much below both the German and the Japanese Armies. German ground troops, with their powerful Luftwaffe tactical support, at that time made up the most formidable fighting machine in the world, and during the summer and autumn of 1941 could attack and destroy a Soviet enemy three times more numerous.

On 3 October Hitler broadcast that the Red Army was finally defeated and would never rise again, and, when several days later nearly three-quarters of a million Soviet prisoners were taken near Vyazma on the Moscow highway after only the briefest of resistance, it looked as if his words were no idle boast. The gateway to Moscow seemed to be wide open and Red Army resistance coming to an end. This was the view of many Muscovites, who saw with it the rapidly approaching disintegration of the Soviet Union.

London was shocked. The British had given too much credence to the exaggerated claims of Russian war propaganda and the successful defensive battle Soviet Marshal Timoshenko was said to have fought near Smolensk. It was believed at that time that the German High Command had called off its August attacks eastwards towards Moscow because of its very high casualties, and had gone southwards into the Ukraine in search of easier laurels. On 10 October 1941 a BBC London radio commentator gloomily gave news of the new German Vyazma offensive as "the most successful yet in the whole of the war. It had always been believed that the door to Moscow had been firmly barred. That obviously was not the case."

These words were monitored by German radio intercept and recorded with satisfaction by the war diarist of von Bock's Army Group Center.

There were virtually no Red Army troops in front of Moscow. In the capital itself there was widespread looting and panic-stricken flight.

Yet, over six weeks later, von Bock had still not reached the Russian capital. By the New Year, in a most remarkable change of fortune, Army Group Center was in retreat and appeared to be threatened with imminent encirclement and destruction, a catastrophe of unheard-of dimensions. This Soviet success was the first victory of the Second World War over an enemy who had come to be regarded as invincible.

This book is intended to describe how this change came about.

The sources for the material on which this book is based will be apparent both from the bibliography and from the notes. In the writing, constant reference has been made to General Burkhart Mueller-Hillebrand's *Das Heer,* Wolf Keilig's *Das Deutsche Heer,* and Dr. Georg Tessin's *Verbände und Truppen der Deutschen Wehrmacht und Waffen SS.* Numerous divisional histories have been used, and in particular that excellent account, *Kampf und Ende der Fränkisch–Sudetendeutschen 98. Division,* by General Martin Gareis, one-time regimental and later the divisional commander of that formation. To these authors I express my thanks.

I owe a great debt to Dr. Friedrich-Christian Stahl and the staff of the Bundesarchiv-Militärarchiv for the use in Freiburg of the unpublished diaries of von Bock and von Weichs, and the war diaries of the principal German higher formations of Army Group Center. I should also like to thank the Director General of the Imperial War Museum, the Librarian and staff of the Institute of Contemporary History and Wiener Library, and the Librarian and staff of the Royal United Service Institution for loaning or making available to me published works.

Once more I would like to thank most warmheartedly Mr. D. W. King, the Chief Librarian of the British Ministry of Defence Library (Central and Army), and Mr. C. A. Potts, the Librarian in charge of the Library's Historical Section, for placing at my disposal a great store of English, German, and Russian published material, and for their patient and expert assistance, so willingly given.

Finally my thanks are due to my wife, who has assisted me in much of the German research and who has undertaken the typing of the manuscript and the reading and pageproof checking.

A. S.

CHAPTER ONE
THE PANZER GENERAL

O N 10 A U G U S T 1940, Field-Marshal Wilhelm Keitel, the Chief of
the German Armed Forces High Command (OKW), returned to the
temporary Reich Chancellory headquarters at Berchtesgaden in the
Bavarian Alps from the leave which he had spent on his Hanoverian
estate at Helmscherode, where he had, for the last time, played the part
of *Gutsherr,* the gentleman farmer. For Keitel was miscast in his role as
a soldier.

The simple-minded field-marshall already knew that Adolf Hitler
had no intention of invading the United Kingdom that autumn, even
though there was no other way of overcoming Britain. On the first day
of his return to duty, Keitel was sent for by the Führer and instructed
to explore other means of forcing the British out of the war. The
Italians, thought Hitler, might be assisted in the Mediterranean by
allotting German Army and Luftwaffe formations to that theater. Then,
almost as an aside or afterthought, he told the startled Keitel of the
possibility of a new war against the Soviet Union.

Keitel was not gifted with either a quick brain or clarity of vision.
Burly and corpulent, monocled and handsome, the fifty-eight-year-
old field-marshal had a very imposing presence, and he struck such
arrogant attitudes that Hitler found it convenient to take him round
Europe with his retinue as a show piece, so that Keitel might impress
foreign dignitaries and statesmen with his haughty bearing; when
Keitel was admitted to a conference he could be counted upon to echo
his master, for he idolized the dictator. Behind this majestic exterior
there was nothing except physical bravery. For Keitel had neither
character, intelligence, moral courage, nor professional ability, and he
owed his rapid advancement to the fact that he was useful to Hitler; any
difference of opinion between the Führer and his generals could always

1

be settled by bringing in Keitel to weigh down the scales. So Keitel earned himself the sobriquets of "the lackey," "the blockhead" and "the nodding ass."

Yet the thought of this new war made Keitel uneasy and raised doubts in his mind as to why it was necessary to go to war at all. During that night he was troubled, so he returned the next day to the Führer's Berghof home to put the question directly to the dictator.

Hitler was direct and frank. A clash between Germany and communist Russia was inevitable, he said, because of their diametrically opposed ideologies; Stalin had as little intention of abiding by the 1939 von Ribbentrop–Molotov Pact as he had himself. The new war could not be avoided, and it was better that he (Hitler) should shoulder this onerous responsibility now, rather than bequeath it to his successor. But in any case, he added, merely to calm the troubled Keitel, no irrevocable steps had yet been taken. All that he had decided upon was precautionary planning.[1]

In fact, although Keitel had not been told at the time, at the end of June 1940, only a few days after the French had laid down their arms, Hitler had already turned his eyes eastwards and given directions for plans to be drawn up to destroy the USSR. Although, for the sake of form, he left the final decision open, he had made up his mind on what he called the new campaign (*Feldzug*), in spite of the fact that he had once promised never to engage in a war on two fronts.

It is doubtful whether Hitler ever seriously intended to invade the British Isles at this time partly because of the grave risks which it would have entailed and partly because he regarded the destruction of the Soviet Union as the easier task. So he turned his armies towards Russia while he made a half-hearted attempt to patch up some form of peace with Britain. Such was his optimism that he even gave some thought to the possibility of striking down the USSR by a lightning attack in the autumn of 1940.[2]

Since 1934 Hitler, as Führer, had been in effect both President and Chancellor of the German Reich, and in 1938, when General von Blomberg, the last Minister of War, had been obliged to resign, Hitler had himself taken over the appointment as Commander-in-Chief of all the Armed Forces. That year he had retired a number of worthy

EASTERN EUROPE 1940

senior officers whose ideas and loyalties he regarded as too traditional and of the old school, as being *zu preussisch oder zu kaiserlich,* and he openly began to favor younger generals with avant-garde views, particularly the officers of the newer arms, the Luftwaffe and the panzer troops. The German Army Commander-in-Chief, Colonel-General von Fritsch, was ousted from his appointment by a conspiracy, the Führer's nominee to replace him being General of Artillery von Brauchitsch, the General Officer Commanding *Gruppenkommando 4* in Leipzig.

Von Brauchitsch, who was a firm supporter both of the Führer and of National Socialism, had been promoted by Hitler to the rank of colonel-general. In the summer of 1938 his first wife divorced him and within three months this fifty-eight-year-old officer had remarried. The match was an unfortunate one, for his new wife, an admirer of Hitler, encouraged von Brauchitsch in his blind obedience to the Führer. Like Keitel, von Brauchitsch was an upright, imposing looking man, square-jawed and of confident bearing, in outward appearance what might have been thought a typical Prussian officer, reserved in manner and exacting towards his subordinates.

Yet in truth von Brauchitsch was irresolute. Although it was probably not Hitler's intention at this time to personally control the German Army through a mouthpiece and a puppet, in the final outcome this is what happened. For the unfortunate von Brauchitsch, who was under an obligation to Hitler for financial assistance to cover the expenses of his divorce, lost composure and often his wits when in the dictator's presence.

From 1938 onwards Hitler began to meddle directly in German Army matters even to the extent of altering operational plans, and in September 1939, although he had little cause to do so, he interfered with von Brauchitsch's handling of the Polish War. Although the Führer refused to accept von Brauchitsch's offer of resignation, he still continued to be dissatisfied with his Army Commander-in-Chief throughout 1940, and he took upon himself von Brauchitsch's responsibilities when he decided on the detail of the strategy of the French campaign. This he did by listening to the views of relatively subordinate officers, Colonel-General Guderian, the Commander of 19 Corps, and Lieutenant-General von Manstein, the Chief of Staff of Army Group A, supporting their ideas against those of von Brauchitsch and the General Staff.

The rapid overrunning of France took all, Hitler included, by surprise. Yet much of the credit properly belonged to the Führer, since the victory was based not only on an unusual and daring strategy but on the use of concentrations of tanks in mass, supported by a heavy weight of tactical air power, a departure from the accepted role of tanks at that time. Since Germany had begun to re-arm only recently, from 1935, it had assumed a plentiful stock of new armaments of modern design; for this, too, Hitler was responsible. The Nazi propaganda machine saw to it that the Führer was given almost the entire credit for the victory, and the German press and public joined in the adulation.

Hitler's personal military circle was not a healthy one. Keitel, the head of the Armed Forces High Command (OKW), was a pompous nonentity, an administrator convenient to his master to telephone orders. The able General Jodl, Chief of Staff and Hitler's principal executive within the OKW, was, as Albert Speer has said, as subservient to Hitler as was Keitel. Colonel Schmundt, Hitler's military aide, and later Colonel Scherff, the historian, were enthusiastic proselytes of the Führer and these and many senior generals, both in command and on the staff, joined in the exaltation, calling the Führer the greatest general of all time. He, not unnaturally, eventually began to believe it. For Hitler's vanity knew no bounds and the most fulsome flattery was demanded as no more than his due.

Instead of accepting the credit for Germany's victory, the Führer would have been better advised to examine critically the reasons for the Polish and the French defeats. Both countries were weaker than the Reich in military potential, in manpower and in industrial and economic strength; neither had armed forces which were so well equipped or so well led and trained as those of Germany. But the main cause of their defeats lay in the air and in the employment of tank forces. It was of course to follow that when Germany's hoard of armaments had been used up and when the enemies of the Reich, singly or in coalition, produced more aircraft and tanks than German industry could, and those of equal or better quality, then the control of the air and with it the victory on the ground would pass from Germany's grasp forever. Drunk with heady success, however, Hitler was far removed from such sober reflections. He had already become convinced that nothing was impossible for him or for his troops, whose success appeared to underline the Nazi teaching of the superiority of the German race. The victory over France was in fact Hitler's undoing.

It is very doubtful whether Hitler could ever have been considered a great general, but he certainly had military aptitude. He had many qualities which would have stood him in good stead had he been a professional soldier: restless energy, an inquisitive and active brain, great will-power, a clear memory and a good head for detail and technicalities. He was intensely interested in army matters, particularly the waging of war, and, although he had no military experience other than that of a regimental runner in the First World War, by attending demonstrations and exercises he soon acquired the necessary military vocabulary and a grounding in war planning. He checked and crosschecked the information and opinions given to him by his advisers, and was not above encouraging ambitious or disloyal officers to criticize their absent seniors.

In this way he soon amassed a fund of knowledge the better to confound his generals, the weaker and more naïve of whom were to credit the Führer with genius, for he always produced the views of others as his own. There seems to be some evidence, too, that he was particularly influenced by officers of the panzer arm, Guderian among them. Hitler was fascinated, not merely by the concept of armored warfare and by the technicalities of tank design, but more especially by the way in which these officers envisaged campaigns being based on the capabilities and characteristics of massed panzer formations.

The waging of war, as the Germans and Russians saw it at the time, was echeloned into four separate levels of command. The highest of these was at government level—foreign policy, propaganda, home morale, the war economy (including the administration of all resources such as manpower, industry and raw materials) and the overall conduct of the air, land and sea battle at home and abroad; this activity was the province of the head of state and war cabinet and their military and civil advisers and staffs. Then came grand strategy, the waging of war at the highest military level in the air, at sea or in the field, conducted by war ministers, commanders-in-chief, chiefs of general staff and by the commanders of theaters. Below strategy was the field of *operations* or the operative art, generally centered on the activities of army groups and armies. The lowest activity in the waging of war, that below *operations,* was tactics, the close engagement of the enemy, usually from the level of corps downwards. The dividing line between *operations* and tactics was in fact a fine one and depended also on the depth of the battle area.

The ability of military commanders, even of the most competent professional soldiers with the service of a lifetime behind them, obviously varies widely. The strength of some lies in tactics, that of others in *operations* or strategy, the reason for this difference lying not only in experience and education but more particularly in natural bent and cast of mind. This has long been recognized for, as von Clausewitz once said, many a distinguished field-marshal would be lost if placed at the head of a regiment. A few officers, the gifted, are equally at home in all military fields, but these are rare. Even Napoleon was a better strategist than tactician.

Although Hitler himself would have been most loath to admit it, it appears that his military ability lay only in the field of *operations,* for he showed that he had great flair for the direction of ground formations at about army group and army level. Such ability is rarely innate. It is more likely that the dictator's mind was conditioned to this particular level by his talks with the leading officers of the panzer troops, most of whom, because of their training and the characteristics of their arm, were proponents of this operative art.

Hitler had concentrated all power and all activities of state in his own person. There was no collective responsibility of Cabinet, which in any event had ceased to meet since 1937. Hitler was in effect President and Chancellor; but he was also Party leader, industrialist, economist, War Minister, Commander-in-Chief and, as the influence of von Ribbentrop declined, Foreign Minister, this arrangement of responsibilities suiting the Führer's temperament and character. He was morbidly distrustful and averse to any decentralization, for, as he once told Kurt Ludecke, his guiding principle was "to say what must be said only to him who must know it, and then only when he must know it." This tenet he imposed on the German Armed Forces.

In early 1940, following the loss of the most important secret plans covering the proposed invasion of the Netherlands, Hitler decreed in his *Basic Order No. 1* the principle that none of his ministers, staffs or commanders should be given any information other than that which was strictly necessary for the performance of his duties. Since it was already an offense to listen to the enemy radio or read the foreign press, Nazi officials and German generals became rapidly isolated, not only from world affairs, but also from the true conditions inside Germany. Since only the Führer saw all and heard all, he maintained that he alone knew all, and he demanded from his subordinates blind obedience. In this phenomenon lay much of the unreality of the German plan to conquer the USSR.

The Soviet Union had for long been under the heavy hand of the dictator Joseph Stalin. Stalin was neither President nor Prime Minister and had retained for himself only the post of Secretary-General of the Communist Party, for he was anxious to preserve the façade of collective and democratic governmental responsibility. This deception was taken to such lengths that he always described himself as *having been instructed* by his colleagues to do this or do that. Yet he alone ruled the whole Soviet Empire through his Prime Minister and spokesman, Molotov; Stalin was the sole arbiter of policy.

In the Politburo Stalin demanded absolute submission and whoever dared to disagree with him was doomed to moral degradation and death. His government was made up of mere underlings, not one of whom had been truly elected or was controlled from below. Stalin was not accountable to people or to Party (thirteen years had elapsed between the Eighteenth and Nineteenth Party Congresses), politics had been substituted for morality, and force and astuteness for law. Propaganda fomented national prejudices and misled the Soviet people, the whole of the USSR being effectively isolated in order to conceal from its inhabitants what was happening in the outside world.

The NKVD secret police system made it impossible for Stalin to have remained long in ignorance of the activities of his ministers, should these have been contrary to his orders or interest, for the dictator's power was maintained by the police file, the pitiless system of hostages, the concentration camp and the NKVD death cellar.

Although Stalin appeared to identify himself with the people, he was remote and unknown, for he shunned any contact with them. He was a poor speaker and rarely broadcast, and he was never seen in public. And yet, he who had initiated the cult of Lenin perpetuated the cult of Stalin and had history rewritten, attributing to himself all the virtues. As Trotsky said, the untutored Asiatic cast of Stalin's mind made it obligatory that the press should praise him extravagantly each day, publish his portraits and refer to him on the slightest pretext. The novel, the opera, the cinema, art, literature and agriculture all had to revolve around Stalin.

The nineteen-thirties showed Stalin in clear relief for what he had always been: able and, within the limits of his dogma, essentially practical. He said little, and that often to disguise his true thoughts. When he so pleased, he was a good listener. He knew how to use people by deceit and trickery and, when it suited him, by flattery — this applying particularly to influential foreigners. He displayed oriental deviousness and dexterity in intrigue and unscrupulousness. He had a nervous, mercurial, highly strung temperament and he was irritable by nature. He was capricious and cynical and had a biting, sarcastic tongue; he never admitted to an error. Brutal and harsh, a hypocrite and a liar, he scorned human decency and human life, exploiting for his own purpose only the lower instincts of human nature, by provocation, terror, demoralization, corruption and blackmail.

By 1938 the government of the Soviet Union had acquired those destructive characteristics which could be attributed directly to Stalin's personality and control, and this was particularly apparent in its foreign policy. Strong elements of caution, mistrust, malice, brutality and treachery could be discerned there, together with a capacity for mischief-making. For Stalin was a man who never took direct action when he could instigate others to do his work for him. There is, for example, a parallel between Stalin's conduct during his early life in a Tsarist prison when he is said to have secretly incited hot-tempered desperadoes against those who opposed him, but himself kept out of the fighting, and what was to emerge as Soviet foreign policy in the years between 1938 and 1941.[3] The similarity appears too strong to be fortuitous.

For, in 1938, there was more than a hint of suspicion that Stalin caused his Foreign Minister Litvinov and the Moscow-trained Czech communist Gottwald to make imprecise offers of Soviet help to Czecho-Slovakia, encouraging that nation to withstand by force of arms German demands. Again, Maisky, the Soviet Ambassador in London, at that time coldly treated by the Chamberlain Government, was directed by Stalin to court Churchill, then without government responsibility, presumably in an effort to use the British politician as a sounding board or as a nucleus of a pressure group having as its aims more direct action by Great Britain against Germany.

Although Chamberlain harbored a deep distrust of Stalin, he had eventually been forced by political opinion to send a military mission to Moscow. This did not suit Stalin, who appears to have changed his ground, for it was, in his own words, no part of his policy that the Soviet Union should embroil itself in war for the sake of others.[4] The opposite was in fact the case, since the dictator found it more attractive that Britain and France should go to war with Germany over Hitler's demands on Poland, because such a war, according to the communist doctrine, would benefit the USSR. It is possible, too, as Trotsky said in 1940, that Satlin's venomous nature and his hurt pride found balm in revenging himself on Chamberlain, for he never forgave an affront.

Immediately after the British and French missions arrived in Moscow, secret parallel Russo-German negotiations were opened in Berlin, probably at Stalin's instigation, and on the night of 23 August, while the talks with the British representatives were still in progress, von Ribbentrop and Molotov (recently appointed Soviet Foreign Minister), in Stalin's presence, signed the Russo-German Pact and the secret protocol. By this secret protocol, and the one that followed a month later, Poland was to be partitioned between Germany and the USSR, and the Baltic States, Finland, Bessarabia and South-East Europe were to be regarded as the Soviet Union's sphere of interest.

Stalin's schemes might of course have come to nothing if Poland, in spite of its new alliances with Britain and France, had, like

Czecho-Slovakia, declined to fight the German aggressor. Such a situation would have proved an embarrassment, for Stalin intended to occupy by armed force the eastern regions of Poland, populated predominantly by White Russians and Ukrainians (who have no closer racial affinity to the Russians than the English and Dutch have to the Germans), under the pretext that he was the protector of the *Russian* peoples; he could hardly do this unless war were to break out. Since there is a suspicion that his political aim was the involvement of Germany in war with Britain and France, Poland's armed resistance to Germany was essential. So he ordered Marshal Voroshilov, his Minister for Defense, and the Soviet Ambassador in Warsaw to inform the Polish Government, in confidence, of the Soviet Union's benevolent neutrality and to offer Poland Soviet arms and war supplies.[5]

Hitler's rapid victory over France was unexpected by Stalin and little to his taste, since Germany had come out of the French campaign unscathed and stronger than it was before. So Stalin immediately ordered the occupation and annexation of the three Baltic States, Bessarabia and adjoining North Bukovina, before Hitler could move formations from Western Europe to Germany's eastern frontier. Stalin took what consolation he could in the fact that Great Britain, relying on United States material support, was still in the war. The jeers and sneers at the British which had been a daily feature in the Soviet press suddenly ceased, and Moscow reported more objectively the air war which was being fought over the United Kingdom, both British and German claims being reproduced without Soviet comment.

But Stalin did not intend to entangle himself with the British, and his natural caution made him cold-shoulder London and the newly appointed Ambassador in Moscow, Sir Stafford Cripps. Above all he feared openly to affront Hitler.

Yet this did not prevent him from fishing in other troubled waters which he had come to regard as his own, allocated to him by the von Ribbentrop-Molotov protocol. Finland was put under heavy pressure from Moscow, and Stalin tried to extend his hold on the Balkans by setting them aflame, presumably since this might afford the pretext for the Red Army to interfere. Hungary and Bulgaria were encouraged to make territorial demands on Rumania, which was itself menaced by

Stalin, these hazarding one of Germany's principal sources of oil. Turkey was assured of Moscow's benevolent neutrality should it feel itself compelled to go to war against Germany. Stalin was even bold enough to sanction the signing of an open Treaty of Friendship with Simovich's anti-German Yugo-Slav Government, making verbal promises of military aid through Molotov, promises which were immediately repudiated by Vishinsky, the Deputy Foreign Minister, "as a misunderstanding" when Hitler invaded Yugo-Slavia.[6] Stalin, the young Koba of the Bailov prison, had not altered the tactics of his youth.

Stalin had endeavored to extend the Soviet hold on the Balkans as far as the Dardanelles and the Aegean, and failed only because he was barred by German diplomacy; for, since the victory over France, Eastern and Central Europe had become of paramount importance in Hitler's eyes as a jumping-off area for the new war which he was preparing against the Soviet Union.

The bedrock of the Führer's foreign policy had always been the destruction of both communism and the Soviet Union.[7] To Hitler the 1939 Russo-German Pact and secret protocol had been only an arrangement of convenience aimed at preventing an Anglo-French-Russian coalition, and at serving as a deterrent which, the dictator hoped, would keep Britain and France out of the Polish War. But the Führer's attitudes towards Russia and the many peoples which made up the population of the USSR were entirely negative. The Soviet peoples were not to be offered any form of freedom under an alternative political system, but were merely to become the slaves of Greater Germany, directly ruled from Berlin through German commissioners. For this cataclysmal policy Hitler's insane racial fantasies were responsible.

Hitler was interested primarily in the permanent occupation of the Ukraine, the vast black earth area between Russia and the Black Sea, rich in industry, coal and grain, and in the seizure of the oilfields of the Caucasus; he wanted the Soviet Union excluded from the Baltic and from Finland, in order to safeguard the shipment of Finnish nickel and Swedish iron and food to the Reich; Belorussia, the land immediately to the east of Poland, was to be held merely as a buffer state. His political aims in going to war, which in themselves were never very clear, probably even to himself, centered, not as he said, on the liquidation of the Soviet Union as a political and military force, but rather on the seizure of the Baltic, Western Russia, the Ukraine and the Caucasus.

Hitler's character was full of contradictions and he was of course in many respects ill-equipped for the position he held. He was poorly educated. His brain was keen yet clogged with useless trivia; he could be far-sighted on scarcely relevant matters, yet on subjects vital to the Reich he often could not see the wood for the trees. He lacked the mental discipline to apply himself to problems of real importance and come to dispassionate and logical conclusions; decisions were too often given in haste, the circumstances leading to them being shrouded in secrecy. He would have been too proud to ask for advice and was too arrogant, too convinced of his own infallibility and destiny, to be guided by it.

For Hitler already regarded those around him, his ministers, commanders and staffs, with something akin to contempt. A few of these, including *Freiherr* von Weizsäcker of the German Foreign Office, Admiral of the Fleet Raeder, the Naval Commander-in-Chief, and Colonel-General Halder, the Chief of General Staff, had expressed some doubts as to the necessity for going to war at all.

Hitler, however, was in his element. He was a *Feldherr,* in a field gray tunic of his own design without badges of rank and with his much prized Iron Cross First Class dangling from his left breast; black or field gray trousers, Party pattern leather calf boots and a German Army forage cap completed his uniform. As at the time of the Polish crisis, when his only fear was that someone would come forward with a mediation proposal, he was determined to fight.

In retrospect it can be said that Hitler's defects as a war leader became apparent during the autumn of 1940, although this was not realized at the time either in Germany or abroad. His decision to engage in a war on two fronts was obviously a wrong one. Yet, apart from this, Hitler showed little inclination to fulfill his proper function as a war leader, a function which encompassed politico-economic and higher military strategy in all its aspects.

He did admittedly foil Soviet efforts to intimidate Finland and Rumania when he guaranteed their integrity and put German troops into those countries. He had also safeguarded his vulnerable Balkan flank by the Vienna Award of 1940, which temporarily patched up the quarrel between Rumania on the one side and Hungary and Bulgaria on the other. Bulgaria had subscribed to the Tripartite Pact, and Yugo-Slavia and Greece had been subdued by force of arms. But these were just manifestations of the mailfisted *Machtkampf,* scarcely the diplomacy expected of a war leader and world statesman of first rank. It might be thought that United States benevolence, British neutrality and the active participation of the Japanese were essential preliminaries before a new war could be entered upon. Some preparation, too, might have been made to subvert or reeducate the Soviet population and loosen the draconian grip of the Georgian dictator.

Yet Hitler showed little interest in these matters or in the true economic or military strength of the Soviet Union, a state which had a standing army of five million men, comprising 303 field divisions, 24,000 tanks and 7,000 combat planes, with a production capacity of 12,000 tanks and 21,000 aircraft a year.[8] Sober estimates of the United States' industrial potential, capable of turning out nearly 100,000 combat aircraft a year, Hitler dismissed as pure humbug.

Little constructive thought had been given to the German war economy for, although its enemies did not know this, the war industries of the Reich were organized in breadth but not in depth and were not on a war footing. Plant was working on a single shift system, there was no restriction on consumer goods, and no direction of labor. The armed forces were merely living on the stocks amassed before 1940 and, in the event of a long war of attrition, current production capacity was insufficient to fill the Wehrmacht needs. German armored production in 1941 was only 2,800 tanks against a 1944 output, after Speer had reorganized the industry, of 18,000 tanks a year.[9] The British aircraft industry, rapidly making up for lost time, had by 1941 already outstripped that of Germany.

When Hitler instructed von Brauchitsch to begin war planning against the Soviet Union he gave him no strategic direction as to higher politico-economic or military aims, except that the USSR was to be

knocked out in a short summer campaign and that Western Russia was
to be dismembered.

The Führer Order caught the office of the Chief of General Staff
by surprise. No planning for a possible war against Russia had taken
place for decades. Lieutenant-General Friedrich Mieth, the same Mieth
who was to die four years later in the close-quarter fighting on the
Berlad in Rumania, was the *Oberquartiermeister I,* responsible for war

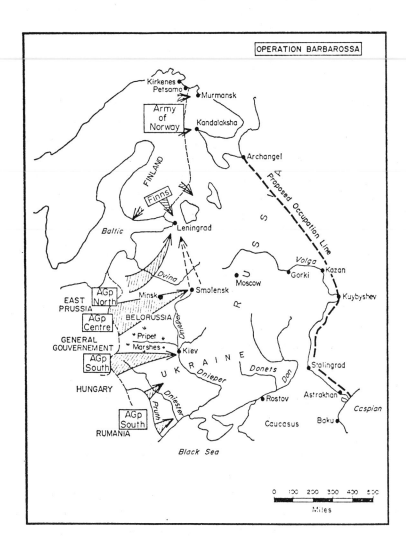

planning. But Mieth had been detached to supervise the Armistice Commission in France. His replacement, Lieutenant-General Paulus, would not become available until September. So Halder called in Major-General Erich Marcks, in spite of the fact that he was *persona non grata* with Hitler because he had once been the press officer for von Schleicher, murdered in 1934 in the Night of the Long Knives. Marcks, whose wire-rimmed spectacles and thoughtful manner gave him a learned, professorial air, temporarily left his appointment as Chief of Staff of 18 Army in East Prussia to prepare a preliminary draft of the plan for the invasion of the Soviet Union.

The draft produced by Marcks on 5 August 1940 is of particular interest since it came to be used as the basis for the final orders for the invasion, known first by the code name of *Fritz* and then *Barbarossa*. Marcks, lacking precise political and higher strategic direction, assumed that it would be necessary to occupy the Ukraine, European Russia and the Caucasus as far east as a line from Archangel to Astrakhan, since this line was thought to be far enough to the east to safeguard Germany against Soviet bombing and, it was wrongly assumed, would take in the greater part of the war industry of the Soviet Union.[10]

In due course Hitler accepted Marcks's premise and from that time onwards devoted his energies to the narrow field of planning the military campaign in the western area of Russia and the Ukraine, to a depth not very much greater than that of the French Republic. For Hitler's military inclinations and his main strength lay, as we have said, in the field of *operations* and he tended to view the new war from very much the same command level as Guderian and Hoepner, both colonel-generals of panzer troops. He was little interested in the sea war on the Baltic and Black Sea flanks, and for him air operations were mainly confined to the tactical support of the ground battle.

Planning continued on these lines, the main aim being to destroy those Red Army formations known to be in the West Ukraine and Belorussia, and it came to be tacitly assumed that when this was done the war would be virtually over.

Apart from those who had doubts as to the need to go to war, only the sixty-year-old, elegant, tall and spidery Field-Marshal von Bock seems to have openly questioned Hitler's political and strategic aims.

Formerly an officer of the Kaiser's foot guards and a man whose main military ability appeared to be in the field of strategy, von Bock was arrogant, aloof, cynical, vain and unbending. Yet he was on good terms with Hitler, of whom he stood a little in awe. When, on 3 December 1940, the Führer visited the sick von Bock to congratulate him on his birthday, the field-marshal learned for the first time of the dictator's intention to attack the Soviet Union. He immediately voiced his fears. Russia, von Bock said, was an enormous country and its military strength was unknown; he believed that such a war might be difficult even for the Wehrmacht. These opinions were unwelcome to Hitler who, much offended, became cold and stiff in his manner and sharp in his replies.

Von Bock saw the Führer again for about an hour on 2 February 1941, and the conversation covered the same ground as that two months earlier. But this time Hitler was breezily optimistic and regarded the early collapse of the Red Army as a foregone conclusion, going so far as to say that the Soviet Union would think that a hurricane had hit it. Von Bock brought up once more the question of strategic aims, and remained unconvinced by Hitler's answers; the Soviet Union stretched for several thousands of miles to the east of Archangel and Astrakhan and von Bock was curious to know what the Führer intended to do when he had arrived on the line, particularly if the Soviet Union was still in being and still in the war. It is perhaps doubtful whether this thought had ever occurred to the Führer but, after a moment's reflection, he replied stoutly that in such an eventuality he would advance again another 800 miles to the east as far as the Urals.[11] There the matter was left.

Belorussia and the Ukraine are separated from each other by the great belt of the Pripet Marshes, nearly 100 miles in breadth from north to south and about 300 miles in depth from west to east. Since this marsh was crossed by only a few roads built up on causeways and elsewhere was impassable to wheeled traffic, it formed a near-impenetrable barrier to any movement. The area to the north of the Pripet, between the frontier town of Brest-Litovsk and Memel on the Baltic, opened both into Belorussia, the direct route to Moscow, and into the occupied

Baltic States, the road to Leningrad. To the south of the Pripet, entry could be made into Galicia and the Ukraine.

Marcks's plan, and those plans which superseded it, intended that the main German thrust should be made in the center through Belorussia by von Bock's Army Group Center on to Minsk and Smolensk on the ancient Moscow highway, the same route that was used by Napoleon. South of the Pripet, Field-Marshal von Rundstedt's Army Group South was to attack both from occupied southern Poland and from Rumania into the Ukraine, while in the north Field-Marshal von Leeb's Army Group North, the smallest of the three army groups, was to drive from East Prussia north-eastwards on to Leningrad.

It was generally agreed that the immediate *operational* task was to seize rapidly the crossing places over the Dvina and upper Dnieper in the Baltic States and Belorussia, and over the lower Dnieper in the Ukraine, in order to destroy the enemy before he could withdraw eastwards into the interior. But Hitler could not make up his own mind as to what was to be done when the Dvina and Dnieper had been reached.

In the south, in the Ukraine, there was less of a problem because, as soon as the enemy had been destroyed west of the Dnieper, it was accepted that von Rundstedt would advance rapidly south-eastwards, seizing the Black Sea ports and moving into the Caucasus by way of Rostov-on-Don.

No agreement was reached, however, as to what was to happen to the north of the Pripet. Von Brauchitsch, Halder and von Bock proposed that on arriving at the crossing places over the upper Dnieper at Smolensk, Army Group Center, having rounded up the encircled Red Army formations west of the river, should advance directly on Moscow and beyond. Hitler himself was not convinced by their arguments.

Behind Hitler, in the shadows, stood Jodl, probably closer to the Führer than any other military officer except Schmundt, Hitler's military aide. A lean and saturnine general of artillery, Jodl briefed the Führer daily on all theaters of war and discussed at length plans and orders, so that he may unconsciously have served as Hitler's military tutor. Jodl was intelligent and able, ambitious and reserved and, although entirely under the spell of the Führer, whom he regarded as a military genius, he was not afraid in these early days to speak his mind, his Bavarian speech on occasions being blunt almost to the point of rudeness. The trouble with Jodl was that his ideas tended to be narrow and some of his views were wrong-headed, so that his influence on Hitler, such as it was, became malignant in that he fortified his master in his obstinacy.

Unknown to von Brauchitsch and Halder, Hitler had resorted to his customary practice of ordering the secretive Jodl who, as a member of the Armed Forces High Command (OKW), had at this time no responsibility at all for ground operations in the east, to prepare an independent appreciation and plan for the new war.[12] This plan was meant only for Hitler's eye and he subsequently used as his own many of the arguments contained in it, particularly where they differed from the German Army High Command (OKH) plan presented by Halder.

On the basis of Jodl's views the Führer began to voice doubts as to the necessity for an early advance eastwards beyond Smolensk. Moscow, he thought, "was of no great significance." The ports and naval bases in the Baltic had to be given priority. The seizing of Leningrad, too, and a junction with the Finns were of greater importance than just taking the Russian capital. The Führer became certain, on the basis of surmise rather than of intelligence, that the Red Army would give ground in the center, but hold fast on the outer wings, that is to say in the Baltic States and the Ukraine. It was absolutely imperative, the dictator said, to clear up the situation in von Leeb's area before taking up the advance to Moscow.

So Hitler decided that when von Bock arrived at Smolensk Army Group Center would have to dispatch about half its panzer and motorized formations to Leningrad and possibly much of the remainder to the Ukraine, in order to increase the momentum of the advance on the flanks.

This Jodl strategy, under the protective guide of *Führerstrategie,* was to find no favor with von Bock, who was sure that the early seizure of Moscow was essential to Germany's fortunes. The other main supporter of the Moscow school was Colonel-General Halder, the Chief of General Staff, a fifty-six-year-old artilleryman, an able, thorough, meticulous, cautious, obstinate Bavarian, who pressed his views on von Brauchitsch and, when the occasion allowed, on Hitler.

Halder believed that the Soviet determination to defend the capital would be such that a direct advance by von Bock from Smolensk to Moscow would draw on it the great bulk of remaining Red Army reserves, and that the destruction of these forces would tear a gaping hole in the Red Army defense line, a void which could not be closed. The loss of the capital, he argued, would be a great blow to Soviet morale and would deprive the Soviet Union of its seat of government, its main communication center and its large industrial complex. More important still was the fact that, as Moscow was the nodal point of all the railways in West Russia, its loss would break up the Soviet railnet. (This was only partly true.)

The arguments became heated and the Führer more caustic and derisive, but the sufferer was not Halder who, marshalling his arguments carefully and logically and being impervious to Hitler's choler, stood his ground stoutly; but the unfortunate von Brauchitsch, pressed by Halder to express himself more positively in the Führer's presence, became a ready target for Hitler's sneers.

The Führer remained obstinately indifferent to the arguments of von Bock and the OKH, and so it was left that the initial thrust should take Army Group Center down the Moscow road as far as Smolensk and the Dnieper. After that the Führer, who had already, in fact if not in name, taken over the command of the German Army in the field, reserved to himself the right to decide on the subsequent aims and strategy.

The German Army and Armed SS strength at this time numbered 208 field divisions, and of this total just over 150 divisions were committed to the war against the Soviet Union, only nineteen being panzer and fourteen of them motorized divisions. Of the balance, all but one, a cavalry division, were of marching infantry with horse-drawn guns and wagons.[13] The German Army in the East was to number 3,200,000 men, 500,000 horses and 3,550 tanks and have the support of about 2,000 combat aircraft.

Although Hitler boasted in 1940 that the German High Command organization was the envy of all and that the German Army was the most formidable fighting machine that the world had ever seen, in reality it was indeed questionable whether the Wehrmacht was at all ready for this new war. There were very few strategists in the OKW or OKH, and the new school of staff planners tended to be merely the Führer's executives. Hitler himself was no strategist.

There is little contemporary evidence, whatever may have been said after 1945, that any senior general, other than von Bock, raised doubts before Russia was invaded as to the political and strategic aims of the new war, although Halder certainly did so a month after the war began. Von Brauchitsch of course was not really in command and he tended to avoid both accepting responsibility and giving decisions in case his master should countermand them. Von Bock disagreed with the orders that he had been given by von Brauchitsch at the beginning of 1941 and could detect no overall master plan for the whole war; so he worried and fretted and badgered the OKH, complaining that he could get no real answer on matters of importance because the High Command busied itself only with trivialities.[14]

German intelligence on the Soviet Union was not good. In 1939 and 1940, during the short Russo-German honeymoon, Hitler had forbidden all activity against the USSR, and even before that time little German money or intelligence effort had been spent collecting information on the Soviet Union. General of Cavalry Köstring, the German Military Attaché in Moscow, in spite of a good knowledge of the Russian language and a long sojourn in the country, provided very little information of intelligence value because he, in company with the rest of the foreign diplomatic community, was allowed no access to the Soviet forces and peoples. General Thomas, of the Economics and Armaments Directorate *(Wi Rü Amt)* of the OKW, had produced a lengthy appreciation on the Soviet armament industry, a report which was so inaccurate as to be highly misleading, being based largely on estimate and out-of-date information. This appreciation cast serious doubts on the industrial and economic strength of the USSR and on the ability of the Soviet Union to maintain its armed forces in war.[15]

German operative and tactical intelligence, the responsibility of a General Staff branch of the OKH, was somewhat better, since a tolerably accurate enemy order of battle had been deduced for the main Red Army formations defending the western frontier of the USSR. Virtually no intelligence was available, however, on Soviet formations in the interior or on the Red Army reserves of troops and equipment.

Nor was the paucity of intelligence the only defect in the German High Command's preparations for war. Colonel-General Fromm's Replacement Army, which held all the reserves of men and equipment for the field force, had only 450,000 reinforcements for the whole of the German Army in all theaters, at that time no more being available. The reserves of petrol equalled three months' consumption rate and there was only enough diesel for one month. Rubber was in such short supply that no more tires could be provided for army wagons, and consideration was being given to replacing tires with steel-shod wheels. There was an acute shortage of all motor transport and much of that in use was of an unsuitable civilian pattern.[16]

The provision made for winter clothing for the troops was to prove entirely inadequate, supply being based on equipping only one-third of the divisions in the field, since it was intended that the Soviet Union should be overcome in a short summer campaign and the remaining two-thirds of the troops withdrawn from the USSR. Good maps of the Soviet Union were difficult to come by as these were treated as secret documents by the Russians.

In retrospect one may marvel at the foolhardiness with which the High Command and the German Army ventured so ill-prepared into such a vast and inhospitable land, placing their faith on the commitment of 3,500 tanks to reduce a continent in the space of a short hot summer, a puny force in comparison with the armored formations later to be raised by Germany's principal enemies. Yet hindsight does not capture the spirit of the times. No general, except von Bock, put forward any objections on the grounds that German resources were inadequate for the task. The German people, almost without exception, had an unshakable trust in the Führer and in his judgment. On the first day of the war the crowds turned out in their thousands to cheer the departing troops. As Lieutenant–General Rendulic later said, he himself, among his circle of acquaintances, never met anyone who did not believe that the Führer and the Government of the Reich knew what they were about and would take all the necessary steps to gain victory.[17]

CHAPTER TWO
THE WAR IS VIRTUALLY WON

JUST AFTER THREE o'clock, at dawn on the fine Sunday morning of 22 June 1941, German troops crossed the frontier from the Baltic coast, in the north, to the Carpathians near the Hungarian frontier, in the south. They gained tactical surprise nearly everywhere.

Von Bock's Army Group Center with a force of fifty divisions, nine of which were panzer and six motorized, supported by Field-Marshal Kesselring's 2 Air Fleet, had to advance rapidly on Smolensk in order to destroy the opposing enemy West Front (the Russian designation of an army group) which was centered on Belorussia.[1] Von Bock's plan was based on a deep double envelopment directed on Minsk, about 170 miles in the Red Army rear, to be made by two panzer groups, Colonel-General Hoth's from the south-east tip of East Prussia to the north of what was called the Bialystok salient, and Colonel-General Guderian's to the south of the salient from the area of Brest-Litovsk. A shorter double envelopment was to be made inside the armored pincers by Colonel-General Strauss's 9 Army in the north and Field-Marshal von Kluge's 4 Army in the south, encircling those Soviet troops forward in the Bialystok salient.

Only when the encircled Soviet formations had been destroyed was it planned to resume the advance for yet another 150 miles to the east as far as the Dnieper, Hoth and Guderian swinging out again in wide arcs, one to the north and one to the south, in order to meet once more, this time near Smolensk.

Von Bock and his two panzer group commanders had disagreed with the main operative objective given to them by the OKH, and considered that the first envelopment should have been directed on Smolensk and not Minsk. Long-drawn-out arguments had taken place in the period between March and June. Hitler was opposed to the deep

Smolensk envelopment because he considered, probably rightly, that
the marching infantry formations, which made up more than seventy-
five percent of the German forces, would be left too far behind and
would be unable to support the strung-out panzer and motorized
divisions in holding and destroying the encircled Soviet troops.

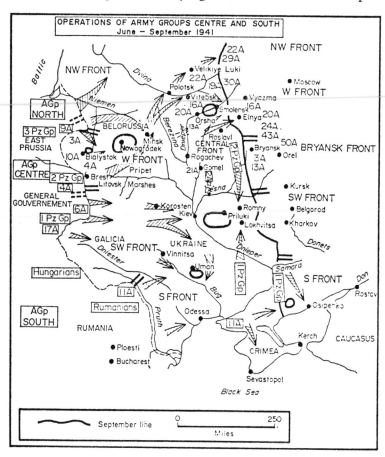

But no clear and binding decision had been given, even as an echo
of his master, by von Brauchitsch, who had become a shuttlecock
between the Führer and von Bock. So it came about that after the first
forty-eight hours of war von Bock, Hoth and Guderian were not
entirely sure whether to close on Minsk or whether they would be
permitted to go straight to the Dnieper.[2]

Personal diaries at this time reveal how effectively Hitler's *Basic Order No. 1* had come to be applied over the previous fifteen months, showing that German commanders were already displaying a remarkable ignorance as to developments in other theaters and sectors, sometimes even on their flanks; and they appear to have had but little understanding of the mechanics, the involved personal relationships and the source of the real power within the Army High Command (OKH). This not unnaturally resulted in confusion, and too often commanders were to lay the blame on their immediate seniors in the chain of command.[3]

The only senior staff officer within the Armed Forces High Command (OKW) who had any influence with the Führer, limited indeed though it was, was of course Jodl; but since Jodl had no responsibility for German Army matters on the Eastern Front, von Brauchitsch and Halder tended to consider him as an interloper, and they deliberately excluded him from Army planning. Within the OKH, the relationship between the Commander-in-Chief and the Chief of General Staff was cool.

Von Bock, who was regarded by the OKH as being difficult and uncooperative, was, notwithstanding, on moderately good terms with Halder; there was, however, some antipathy between him and Field-Marshal von Brauchitsch. Von Bock was the senior and the more experienced of the two and may possibly have considered that he had been superseded when Hitler had appointed von Brauchitsch to be Commander-in-Chief.

But it is more likely that von Bock's intolerance was aggravated by von Brauchitsch's apparent indecision, for the Commander of Army Group Center does not seem to have realized, at least until late in the summer, the extent to which the German Army Commander-in-Chief was overshadowed by Hitler. He wrongly believed that the Army plan for *Barbarossa* emanated from von Brauchitsch, not knowing that the Führer himself had laid down not only the general outline but also the execution. And so von Bock did not understand why von Brauchitsch could not be persuaded to alter (at von Bock's recommendation) *operational,* even tactical, details of the plan which had been imposed on Army Group Center, and he became increasingly impatient with what he regarded as the interference and the excessively close control exercised by the OKH.

Von Bock, overbearing with both superiors and subordinates, was not, however, inhibited from severely restricting the freedom of his own army commanders, even to the extent of meddling with matters which were scarcely his concern. His relationship with the level-headed Hoth was satisfactory but tension was to arise between von Bock and Strauss. He did not get on at all well with the energetic Field-Marshal von Kluge, so well esteemed by Hitler, and he had very little time for the arrogant, impetuous and undisciplined Guderian. Between Guderian and von Kluge there was bitter animosity and among many of the senior generals of Army Group Center there was a distinct lack of discipline and loyalty.

In spite of the many difficulties during the planning and preparatory phase, von Bock's success during the early stages of the overrunning of Belorussia was remarkable.

The Belorussians, or White Russians, are not Russians. They did of course form part of the early Kievan Russian Empire in the ninth century, but from the tenth to the eighteenth century they were governed by both Lithuanian and Pole. The people of Belorussia numbered less than ten million, of which nearly three million were Jews, and the White Russian was generally regarded by his Russian and Ukrainian cousin to be a rather low and mean-spirited fellow. The population was mainly rural and, even by the Russian standards of the time, was very poor and almost unbelievably primitive. The capital, Minsk, had about a quarter of a million inhabitants, but the other main cities, Gomel, Vitebsk, Mogilev, Bobruisk, Grodno and Brest-Litovsk (Brest of the Lithuanians), had populations of only forty to a hundred thousand. It had little industry, no mineral resources except peat, and the agricultural land was infertile.

To the German soldier, Belorussia was to conjure up a picture of the remains of primeval forests of oak, beech and lime (about one-third of the whole area was still wooded and the forests were thickest in the west near the old Polish frontier), vast potato fields covered with great rocks and boulders, pigs in profusion, innumerable dilapidated farmsteads and hamlets and broad lakes with high rounded banks. And to the south of Belorussia were the Pripet Marshes, slow meandering streams and creeks forming a great network of waterways; the swamps and surrounds were overgrown with dense rushes and an impenetrable tangle of aspen and alder. The humidity and mosquitoes added to the discomfort.

On the morning of 22 June the panzer corps passed through the great fifty-mile-deep belts of forests near the frontier and emerged into the more open country in the hinterland. Except at the frontier posts, where some of the NKVD border troops put up a most fanatical fight, the resistance of the Soviet West Front was in general neither determined nor protracted. Kesselring's 2 Air Fleet had almost undisputed command of the skies and the Red Air Force had shown that it was outmatched by Luftwaffe skill and equipment. Losses, particularly in aircraft destroyed on the ground, had been very heavy. The air situation, as had formerly been the case in Poland and in France, was decisive to the outcome of the land battle.

Much of the credit for the success was due to Kesselring, a former artillery officer transferred to the Luftwaffe, a born optimist whose ready grin earned him the nickname of "smiling Al." Kesselring was one of the few officers who could work with von Bock without friction, and to this more than anything else was probably due the excellent German Army and Luftwaffe cooperation.

The Soviet West Front, its control and communications organization gone, lay paralyzed and inert waiting to be hewn to pieces. Too rarely at this time did the Red Army troops in Belorussia show that heroism since attributed to them by communist propaganda; resistance was uneven; in places it was bitter, but for the most part the Soviet forces surrendered or ran off into the woods. Yet, only three days after the start of the war, the Führer, in a fit of nerves, bypassed von Brauchitsch and suggested to von Bock that the Minsk panzer envelopment should be abandoned in favor of a much shorter one; this proposal von Bock resisted with all the arguments at his command.[4]

Within a week of the start of the war Hoth and Guderian closed in on the important rail junction of Minsk, the sprawling capital of Belorussia on the Warsaw-Moscow highway, which stood in great fields of knee-high wheat and barley. When they joined forces near the city, the greater part of three Soviet armies, nearly the whole of West Front, had been surrounded. Although many of the encircled troops escaped eastwards using the cover of the woods and of darkness, by 3 July 290,000 prisoners, including several corps and divisional commanders, had gone into the prisoner of war cages. It was claimed that no less than 2,500 Soviet tanks were knocked out or captured.[5]

On this day Halder, the Chief of General Staff, wrote in his diary that it was probably not too much to say that the war against Russia, which he referred to as a campaign *(Feldzug)*, had been virtually won within fourteen days.[6]

On 26 June, by Hitler's express order and against von Bock's wishes, 2 and 3 Panzer Groups were removed from von Bock's direct control and put under von Kluge's command, ready for the second phase of the battle and the resumption of the eastwards march towards Smolensk and Moscow.[7] Guderian, not without malice, was subsequently to hint that the army group commander, tired of Führer control, was ridding himself of the direct responsibility for the coordination of the advance; yet it is probable that Guderian, who like von Bock was a difficult man with both superiors and subordinates, felt some pique in not being given the new command, for which his name had in fact been put forward but had been vetoed by Halder. So the new panzer command was given to the fifty-eight-year-old von Kluge, an able and active field commander, who was, however, an artillery officer without panzer experience.

Von Kluge was transferred, together with his 4 Army Headquarters, to take direct command over Hoth's and Guderian's panzer groups (each of two or three corps — the size of a small army) and von Kluge's new command was given the temporary and unofficial designation of 4 Panzer Army. Meanwhile, von Kluge's infantry corps were taken over by a new army headquarters activated from the reserve, Colonel-General *Freiherr* von Weichs's 2 Army.

The advance began towards Smolensk, but von Kluge's handling of armor found little favor with the hypercritical Guderian. Yet much the same view was taken by Hoth, a steadier and more objective character than Guderian, who was known affectionately to his staffs as "Papa Hoth"; Hoth, although by arm an infantry officer, was one of the most experienced tank generals of the time.[8]

One of the five panzer corps had been directed away from the main axis north-eastwards towards Polotsk and Velikiye Luki, once again at the order of the Führer, and the other four advanced in line on a very broad front without *Schwerpunkt* or reserve. Guderian, obsessed with his open southern flank, constantly extended to his right. Heavy summer rain began to fall, turning the roads and tracks into quagmires and bringing wheeled movement to a halt.

The success of the German infantry formations at this time was measured more by stamina and marching ability than by skill in fighting. In heat and dust, and sometimes knee deep in mud, they marched rapidly eastwards in the wake of the panzer corps; as is the case with dismounted infantry the world over, every yard of the advance was made by the men's own effort, most of their personal belongings being on their backs. Twenty to thirty miles were covered each day and every day, the men, unlike the horses which were resentful at the loss of the weekly rest day, were becoming harder and fitter as the weeks went by.[9] There was little or no time for bathing or washing, and there was little water to be had; clothing became filthy, and vermin, so dear to Mother Russia, had begun to appear. Yet morale had never been higher.

The tank troops, however, saw the war somewhat differently, for their lives and effectiveness were linked to their vehicles. When Schmundt, Hitler's military aide and his roving eyes and ears, appeared at 3 Panzer Group Headquarters near the city of Vitebsk on 13 July, Hoth told him that tank casualties had not been heavy and were in no way more severe than those suffered in France, but that the terrain and climate were proving far more wearing on vehicles and on men than had been expected. Mechanical casualties were high. The monotony of the landscape, the somber woods and the flatness of the plains had a very depressing effect on the German tank troops.[10] The bitterness and barbarity of the Red Army, too, had come as a shock; German prisoners in Soviet hands had been cruelly put to death. Because of the large numbers of armed Red Army men who had taken refuge in the woods, it was usually unsafe to leave the German bivouac areas.

Smolensk, at the head of the navigable Dnieper, although once ethnically White Russian, lay beyond the political borders of Belorussia in dairy farming country and fields of corn and flax, studded with woodlands and orchards. An ancient city with a kremlin and fortress walls, it had long been fought over by Russian and Pole, but, unlike Vitebsk which was already in flames, on this occasion it was to be spared; for Hoth and Guderian closed in, on 16 July, on Yartsevo, a cotton-milling town just to the north-east of Smolensk on the Smolensk-Moscow railway.

A huge pocket of Red Army troops stretching over seventy miles from Orsha to Smolensk was almost surrounded. The German panzer formations were too extended and the infantry divisions too far in the rear, however, to seal off the whole of the cauldron and many of the encircled troops escaped. On 25 July an angry and excited Hitler telephoned to von Bock demanding to know why the cauldron had not been closed and von Bock told the Führer "as much as it was good for him to know." Keitel arrived the next day to emphasize his master's displeasure. Meanwhile, the petulant Guderian, censured by von Bock, was demanding to be removed from his appointment.[11]

By the time that the marching infantry divisions began to arrive the end was not far off for the great seething mass of men and vehicles stretching as far as the eye could see along the Moscow highway. By 5 August all resistance inside the pocket had ceased and a further 300,000 prisoners and 3,000 tanks, intact or knocked out, fell into German hands.[12] Smolensk was about 400 miles as the crow files from Brest-Litovsk, Guderian's start line, and 200 miles from Moscow. Guderian and Hoth had arrived beyond Smolensk on 16 July, just over three weeks after the start of the war.

In the other two theaters German progress had, in the main, been very satisfactory. Field-Marshal von Leeb had attacked from East Prussia into the Baltic States, but, although he had seized the crossing places over the Dvina, he had been unable to prevent the Soviet North-West Front from withdrawing rapidly north-eastwards. Nor was von Leeb more successful in his efforts to envelop the enemy before he could withdraw into Russia, for the Soviet High Command showed little of the expected determination to hold on to the Baltic States. Soviet losses in equipment of all types were heavy, these including aircraft, tanks, vehicles, ships and naval vessels; but in personnel they were very light.

Comparatively few Red Army prisoners were taken by Army Group North. Towards the end of July, however, when von Leeb was nearing Leningrad and the German formations, strung out over a distance of 400 miles, were finding movement difficult in the close country, Red Army resistance began to stiffen most noticeably.

In the Ukraine the conditions of battle and terrain varied yet again. The Soviet South-West and South Fronts were jointly much stronger than the North-West Front in the Baltic States and the West Front in Belorussia, and the South-West Front in particular proved more alert and ready for action. Field-Marshal von Rundstedt made progress, however, to the south of the Pripet Marshes in spite of resistance which in places was fanatical, the Soviet troops making good use of the marshlands and the broken and wooded country in their defense.

On 30 June, 11 German Army in Rumania crossed the Pruth and, together with two Rumanian armies, began a steady advance through Bessarabia into the Ukraine. On 8 August came von Rundstedt's only notable success, the surrounding of about twenty divisions of South Front near Uman when 103,000 prisoners were taken, including two army and seven corps commanders.[13] Meanwhile, von Rundstedt was being heavily pressed by a buildup of Red Army troops on his far left flank, on the inter-army group boundary between himself and von Bock, along the southern skirts of the Pripet Marshes in the area to the north of Korosten and Kiev.

In spite of some failures, the German Army in the East had carried out the greater part of its mission. Army Group Center had crossed the Dnieper and destroyed West Front. Army Group North had passed over the Dvina and had cleared most of the Baltic States, advancing almost as far as Leningrad; it had not, however, taken the city, destroyed North-West Front or joined up with the Finns. Army Group South had probably had the least success since it had only just reached the area of the Dnieper and, in spite of the encirclement at Uman, had not destroyed the South-West and South Fronts which were still fighting strongly in fairly good order. The Führer had next to decide on the second phase of his strategy and the German Army in the East awaited his further orders.

Army Group Center Headquarters had established itself on the banks of the Berezina at Borisov, a town north-east of Minsk on the main trunk route, not far from the spot where Napoleon had crossed the river in 1812 on his way to Moscow. On 4 August, when Hitler visited Army Group Center to discuss strategic aims, von Bock was forced to the conclusion that the Führer himself just did not know what to do next. Von Bock had told him that Army Group Center could be in Moscow by the end of August, but Hitler, to von Bock's surprise and consternation, appeared to be little interested in a resumption of the advance eastwards.[14]

Hitler would talk continually around a difficult subject for weeks before he made up his mind, but as soon as he had taken a decision there was an end to the matter and none could shift him. Then would start another round of seemingly interminable arguments between himself, his staff and his commanders. In early July he had been stressing the economic importance of the area of the Baltic and the Ukraine and he had come to believe that the Crimea could be used as a Soviet aircraft carrier to bomb the German source of Rumanian oil at Ploesti; for this reason, he thought, the Crimea must be taken; the Crimea would be useful, too, as a stepping stone across the Straits of Kerch in the Caucasus. In fact, Hitler was determined to adhere to the Jodl strategy of the previous autumn.

In the second half of July, immediately after Hoth and Guderian had closed on Smolensk, the Führer confirmed his previous ideas and ordered the removal of Hoth's panzer troops to the area of Leningrad while Guderian's panzer group was to be switched southwards to destroy the flanking Red Army buildup in the area of Korosten and Kiev. Von Bock, he said, could advance the 200 miles to Moscow using only his infantry formation; Hoth would be returned to Army Group Center, after the taking of Leningrad, in order to help von Bock on *beyond* Moscow eastwards to the middle Volga.

So optimistic was the Führer in these early days that he was planning to recall Hoepner's panzer group (with von Leeb) back to Germany for garrison duties.[15]

At this point arose the violent argument as to whether or not Moscow should be taken before Leningrad and the Ukraine. This was to split the High Command and cause the rupture which eventually led to the dismissal of von Brauchitsch. Halder, and to a lesser extent von

Brauchitsch, had always considered that Moscow must be taken as a first priority, and had unsuccessfully pressed this course of action in the previous December. Hitler said he was convinced that Leningrad and the Ukraine were priorities and that Moscow was of no importance, being "merely a mark on a map."

For a whole month, until 24 August, the arguments continued, with Hitler on the one side and von Brauchitsch, Halder, von Bock, von Rundstedt, Guderian and Hoth on the other. Even Jodl had now changed his mind and considered that the main thrust should be continued on Moscow and he went so far as to undertake to use his influence to try and persuade the dictator to this end, dryly adding, however, that to make the Führer change his mind was going to be a very difficult task.[16] So it turned out.

Guderian protested to von Bock that his panzer group was tired and understrength and so near crippled by mechanical wear and tear that he doubted whether it could make the long march to the south and still remain effective; these were the arguments which von Bock and Halder wanted to hear. Guderian, who was on good terms with Hitler, was dispatched to the Führer's East Prussian General Headquarters in Rastenburg to press his views. But Guderian's efforts were hampered, so he subsequently said, by a tired and dispirited von Brauchitsch, who had just been bitterly reproached by the Führer for weakness, "being too much influenced by the views of the army group commanders."

Von Brauchitsch told Guderian, as soon as he arrived in East Prussia, that the Führer had already decided the matter and that "it was no use bleating against it." This cut much of the ground from under Guderian's feet, and yet he appears to have made only a feeble effort to dissuade Hitler, an attempt that was in the event singularly unsuccessful, because the panzer leader came away having been himself convinced by the wily and plausible Führer of the correctness of the dictator's views. Hitler's other supporters appear to have been those advisers without responsibility, Keitel and Schmundt.[17]

So it came about that when, in the height of summer, German troops were only 200 miles from Moscow, Hoth was sent 400 miles to the north while Guderian went the same distance to the south. As a concession, Hitler agreed that von Bock should rest his troops in the area of Smolensk until his panzer formations should be returned to him.

Stalin had always shown a close and personal interest in military affairs and, as Secretary-General of the Communist Party, had controlled the armed forces, according to Trotsky, "through the pliant Marshal Voroshilov." Voroshilov, until May 1940 the Soviet Minister for Defense, had in fact some organizing ability even though he was without real military experience or training. Following the Red Army defeats in the 1939-40 Finnish Winter War, Stalin removed Voroshilov from his appointment, replacing him by a professional soldier, Marshal Timoshenko, a forty-five-year-old cavalryman, formerly the Commander of Kiev Military district.

About three months later, in September of that year, there was a change of Chiefs of General Staff. The fifty-seven-year-old Marshal Shaposhnikov, who had been a regular officer of the Imperial Tsarist General Staff and was a colonel at the time of the First World War, being in indifferent health made way for a much younger man, the forty-three-year-old General Meretskov, an officer of a very different background.

For Meretskov, once a politically active Moscow factory worker, had entered the Red Army in 1918 as a political commissar and remained with the corps of commissars for twelve years. Advancement, this time as a military commander, had come rapidly following a short period of combat service in Spain and a year's tour of duty as Deputy Chief of General Staff. Shaposhnikov, an academician and author of a number of learned works, who was regarded widely as being the father of the General Staff, was re-employed as a Deputy Minister for Defense responsible for the fortifications in western Russia. The gentle and dignified Shaposhnikov was much valued by Stalin as a staff officer and planner; and the dictator was loath to lose him.

In December 1940 Timoshenko, who was an outstanding trainer of staffs and troops, held a series of presentations and lectures in Moscow, attended by all high-ranking Soviet officers in command and on the staff. This meeting was concluded by two elaborate war games covering a possible invasion of Belorussia and the Ukraine by German troops.

The task of invading the Ukraine was given to General Pavlov, the Commander of the West Front in Belorussia, while General Zhukov, the Commander of Kiev Military District, was responsible for its defense. For the invasion of Belorussia the two commanders exchanged their roles, Pavlov defending his own home ground of Belorussia, while Zhukov acted as the commander of the attacking German forces. The war games were conducted and umpired by Meretskov under Timoshenko's chairmanship. For this particular map exercise Zhukov was allowed sixty German divisions to overcome the resistance of Pavlov's force of fifty Red Army formations. The final summing up and *post-mortem* on the two games took place in the Kremlin in the presence of Stalin and the Politburo.

The recapitulation and assessment, like the war games they followed, were most confusing. Meretskov had had insufficient time to prepare his material and, under a barrage of searching questions from Stalin, became rattled and started to go to pieces. Stalin wanted to know which side had won and the reasons, and he was not deterred by Meretskov's long and involved explanations as to relative strengths. For, said Stalin, "statements that one Red Army division can rout a German division in an approach to contact is all very well for the propaganda clap-trap printed in field regulations, but here we want to know the truth."

Pavlov fared no better than Meretskov. Pavlov, a forty-seven-year-old, probably rather loud-mouthed and blustering cavalryman, who owed his position to his recent experience as a tank commander on the Ebro in Spain, tried in vain to laugh off some of Stalin's probes. Disconcerted, Pavlov then rounded with some heat on Zhukov, who had criticized the deployment of so many of Pavlov's formations forward in the Bialystok salient; Voroshilov had to put an end to their bickering by pointing out that the responsibility for the siting of defense lines, and for their development, rested with Moscow and Shaposhnikov, the Deputy Minister for Defense and Fortifications.

Worse was yet to come, for the *bête noire,* the *enfant terrible,* of the Soviet High Command, Marshal Kulik, then took the floor. A fifty-year-old artilleryman, a notorious ignoramus who headed the Main Artillery Administration where he was responsible for many aspects of weapon development, he spoke out in favor of the horse; he was against the use of massed tanks and against further mechanization; more money should be spent, he thought, on the development of horse-drawn artillery. These views caused a wag among the listeners to comment, *sotto voce,* "that every *kulik* [Russian for a snipe] prefers its own swamp."

Kulik's presentation was more than Stalin could stand and the meeting broke up in disorder. All of those present were disillusioned with Kulik's performance, and many were sorry for Meretskov and the General Staff. Shaposhnikov, the elder statesman of the General Staff, so our informant Kazakov tells us, took this fiasco very hard. As the crowd of high-ranking officers collected their papers and moved away, he remained seated, lost in gloom, glancing from time to time at the members of the Politburo. Only the sad expression in his big intelligent eyes and the faint twitching of his large elongated head showed the old man's emotion.

That day Stalin removed Meretskov from his position as Chief of General Staff, replacing him by the Commander of Kiev Military District, a very unwilling Zhukov. Zhukov, a forty-four-year-old cavalryman, had never served on the staff in his life.

The German invasion caught Stalin entirely by surprise because, although he had been well aware of German war preparations and the movement of troops into Rumania, East Prussia and the German-occupied *General Gouvernement* of Poland, neither he nor Lieutenant-General Golikov, the head of the intelligence directorate of the Soviet General Staff (the GRU) could bring themselves to believe that Hitler would embark on a war on two fronts. Instead Stalin viewed all intelligence suggesting the imminence of attack either as a British provocation or as a part of the nerve war which the communists knew so well, at the worst presaging new German political or economic demands.[18]

Although no steps had been taken until too late on the night of 21 June to bring the Soviet armed forces to a state of war readiness, the Red Army was in fact better fitted for war than was generally realized at that time in Germany or elsewhere. In September 1939 the age limit for conscription had been lowered by two years and, because of this, four annual classes, totalling over five million men, were with the colors in

1941. As already recounted, the strength of the field army was 303 divisions, of which seventy-five were in the process of being mobilized from cadre form.[19] The total tank holdings stood at the surprisingly high figure of 24,000 and the Red Air Force fighter strength was stated to be 7,000 first line aircraft.[20]

Except for the recently introduced T 34 and KV models the quality of the tanks was, admittedly, not high and could hardly be compared with the German Mark III main battle tank, but many of the older heavy Soviet models could not be penetrated by the standard 37 mm German anti-tank gun. Red Air Force aircraft in 1941 were very much inferior to those of the Luftwaffe. Other Soviet equipment, however, particularly artillery and small arms, was of excellent quality, often superior to the German, and had been produced and stockpiled in great quantities. Many of the weaknesses at the time of the 1939-40 Finnish Winter War had been rectified. Some of the senior officers who had survived the purge but who still languished in prison or in concentration camp, among them Rokossovsky, had been hurriedly rehabilitated and returned to duty.

There were 150 Red Army divisions on the western frontier between the Baltic and the Black Sea, with a further twenty divisions on the Finnish borders, and the field command was organized in very much the same fashion as that of the invading German troops.[21] Colonel-General F. I. Kuznetsov's North-West Front held the area of the Baltic States against von Leeb's Army Group North while General Pavlov's West Front was based on Belorussia opposite von Bock's Army Group Center. To the south of the Pripet Marshes the South-West Front, commanded by Zhukov's successor, Colonel-General Kirponos, defended Western Ukraine against von Rundstedt while General Tyulenev's South Front was in Bessarabia attempting to hold 11 German Army and the Rumanian forces.

Timoshenko, the Commander-in-Chief, together with Zhukov, the Chief of General Staff, was in Moscow. All these senior commanders, except for Kirponos, were cavalrymen, and all were in their forties.

When the invasion was launched on 22 June, Stalin, even in this thirteenth hour, tried to appease Germany in the vain hope that Hitler could be bought off. Then, according to the popular account circulated by his successors, he suffererd a severe bout of nervous hysteria which gave way to deep apathy. If this did in fact occur it must have been of relatively short duration because, by 26 or 27 June, Stalin was firmly back in the saddle. Beside himself with fury and worry, his first action was to remedy the truly disastrous situation of Pavlov's West Front in the only way he knew.

Pavlov, who had spent most of the First World War as a non-commissioned officer and a prisoner of war in Germany, although possibly not an outstanding commander, was an experienced cavalry and tank commander. He had a total of forty-four divisions, of which twelve were tank and six mechanized, facing von Bock's fifty divisions; he was, however, as had been noted at the time of the winter war game, badly deployed to meet an offensive since all his armies were forward in the Bialystok salient. In any case he was allowed no freedom of maneuver as all withdrawals had to be sanctioned by Moscow. The unfortunate Pavlov first became aware that his three armies had been surrounded from a radio conversation with Timoshenko, who had himself been informed of the encirclement by a monitor of the Berlin radio news.

Three of the four Marshals of the Soviet Union, Voroshilov, Shaposhnikov and Kulik, were ordered by Stalin to report to the West Front to find out what was going on. Lieutenant-General Eremenko, another cavalryman, who had just been flown from the Far East, reported to the West Front to take over command, this being the first intimation that the breakfasting Pavlov had that he was to be removed. The exhausted Pavlov's immediate reaction was one of resignation and relief at having shed his responsibilities, but within the hour he was arrested by the NKVD, together with Major-General Klimovskikh, his chief of staff, and his principal staff advisers. When Pavlov arrived in Moscow at the end of the month he had so changed in appearance that Zhukov could hardly recognize him.

Pavlov and several of his subordinates, including at least one army commander, were shot at Stalin's order, all of them being publicly condemned as traitors. Most military commanders trembled at the thought of another 1937 Purge, while many of the Red Army rank and file began to suspect their higher commanders of being in German pay.

In a matter of days Stalin had changed his mind once more. Eremenko, he thought, was hardly the man to save what was left of the West Front. Only Timoshenko could do that. So Timoshenko, the Bessarabian Ukrainian, whose reserved, polite and dignified exterior concealed the energetic and ruthless martinet underneath, was ordered to give up his appointments as Commander-in-Chief and Minister for Defense and take over the remnants of the West Front.

The functions of the Commander-in-Chief were assumed by two committees, the National Defense Committee, or GKO, consisting of certain members of the Politburo who dealt with the wider aspects of political, economic and military strategy, and the *Stavka* which was a subordinate, mainly military, committee, the principal members of which were Timoshenko, Voroshilov, the Commander of the Reserve Front Marshal Budenny, Shaposhnikov and Zhukov. Stalin was the chairman of both committees and was in effect Premier, Generalissimo and Commander-in-Chief.[22]

Most of the armies of Budenny's Reserve Front had been hastily moved westwards to defend the Moscow axis and came under the command of Timoshenko's West Front. Many of them were destroyed in the second of von Bock's great encirclements, that between Minsk and Smolensk. Budenny, a former non-commissioned officer of Tsarist cavalry and an old crony of Stalin's from the days of the Civil War, a marshal with little military education or experience, was sent to the Ukraine at the beginning of July to take over the new South-West Theater, formed from the combined South-West and South Fronts. Voroshilov, who was no more able than Budenny, assumed command of the new North-West Theater based on Leningrad, controlling the Leningrad, North-West and Karelian Fronts, while Timoshenko's command was upgraded from a front to a theater, although it consisted in fact of only the amalgamated West and Reserve Fronts.

There were other postings of senior staff officers. Shaposhnikov gave up his appointment of Deputy Minister for Defense (Fortifications) and was sent to buttress West Theater as Timoshenko's chief of staff, but since Shaposhnikov was not in good health, he had to to make way after a few weeks for Lieutenant-General Sokolovsky, a man of proven staff ability, who had formerly been a Deputy Chief of General Staff and Chief of Staff of Moscow Military District.

Now that Stalin had taken over Timoshenko's appointment, he was brought into direct and close contact with Zhukov. There is some evidence that the dictator was not too happy in these early days with his own choice of Chief of General Staff.

Zhukov was a man of the people. Like Stalin, he was the son of a poor cobbler, but unlike him he was a Russian (from the Kaluga *oblast*). As a youth he had been conscripted into the Tsarist dragoons and had served with distinction as a cavalry non-commissioned officer in the Ukraine and Bessarabia, twice being decorated for bravery.

After demobilization he rejoined the Red Army, still as a cavalry-man, being rapidly promoted from squadron to regimental commander in 7 Cavalry Division, the commander of which was Rokossovsky. By the mid-nineteen-twenties the Red Army had been reduced to 562,000 men, and the cavalry arm was a close and tightly knit circle. Everyone knew everyone else and the cavalrymen who escaped the Great Purge were to become the principal field commanders during the Second World War. Among the group of cavalry officers so close to Zhukov at this time were Budenny, Timoshenko, Tyulenev, Rokossovsky, Sobennikov, Eremenko, Bagramyan, Kostenko, Cherevichenko, Gorbatov, Muzychenko and Volsky. They were fellow students on the higher cavalry courses and followed each other in succession from appointment to appointment.

By 1931, at the age of thirty-five, Zhukov was commanding a division, and by 1937 a corps; two years later he was ordered to the Far East to command the forces engaged in border fighting against the Japanese and, in May 1940, was nominated to command Kiev Military District. At the time of this appointment he was interviewed, for the first time, by Stalin.

As a youth Zhukov had been a great reader, this in an age when a large proportion of the Russian peasantry was totally illiterate. His bookishness brought him to the attention of his sergeant-major, "old four and a half fingers," who tried in vain to browbeat him into becoming the squadron clerk. Yet Zhukov was, and remained, without the discipline of a higher academic education. Although he attended many long senior officers' courses, he was neither staff trained nor staff qualified. Much of his later knowledge, he claimed, was acquired by the wide reading of military history; and the instruction of his cavalry arm guided his inclinations towards campaigns based on movement and the study of war at *operational* level.

Stalin, probably for the first time, saw Zhukov for what he was, an outstanding field commander of cavalry and armor, but hardly a Chief of General Staff. It is possible that he began to compare Zhukov's qualities with those of the charming, pliant and clever Shaposhnikov, a man so liked and respected, even by the dictator, that everyone got on well with him.

Zhukov began to displease the dictator, who merely rode rough-shod over him. When Lieutenant-General Khrulev, the Quartermaster-General, was ordered by Stalin and Mikoyan to prepare a plan divorcing the ration and fuel supply and the medical services from the General Staff (which had previously complained that it was unable to cope with these problems), the paper was handed by Stalin to Zhukov for comment. Zhukov, suddenly objecting to the diminishing of his responsibility, began to splutter and protest. In silence Stalin took back the paper, reached for his pen and, with a hard and meaningful look in Zhukov's direction, signed it. Not another word was said.

The final break with Zhukov came only a few days later, at the end of July, when an angry Stalin, apparently displeased at Zhukov's suggestion that it might be necessary to evacuate Kiev, dismissed him, sending him first to command the Reserve Front and then, afterwards, to Leningrad, since the city appeared to be in danger of falling to von Leeb's forces.

Shaposhnikov returned once more to be Chief of General Staff, a post he held from the end of July 1941 to June 1942. For Shaposhnikov was to Stalin what Jodl was to Hitler.

Lieutenant-General Vatutin, the Deputy Chief of General Staff, shared Zhukov's temporary eclipse and was sent to North-West Front as Chief of Staff, the more important post of Deputy Chief of General Staff being given to Major-General Vasilevsky, the chief of the operations department, an officer who, in addition to becoming Chief of General Staff in 1942, was to undertake many command functions.

Stalin himself had little military experience. He had escaped being conscripted into the Tsarist Army in 1916 on the pretext that his arm was deformed and two toes grown together, and his only pretensions to military fame were based on his activities as a military commissar and political member of the military councils of the old revolutionary South and South-West Fronts, mainly at Tsaritsyn (Stalingrad), during the Civil War. There he had acted as Lenin's ears and eyes, the watchdog of the efficiency and political reliability of military commanders and staffs, and it was on the Volga that he had become acquainted with Voroshilov, Budenny, Timoshenko and Tyulenev.

Although he was to ascribe to himself the success of the Tsaritsyn operations in the accounts written after he had destroyed his rivals and taken over the USSR as its dictator, he appears to have shown no evidence of great military ability but rather an overbearing determination to assert his will.

Menace was never absent from Stalin's relationship and dealings with members of the Politburo and his military commanders and staffs, a number of whom had only just been rehabilitated from the terror and barbarity of the concentration camp. The evidence of Western observers at that time shows that Stalin's circle rarely dared to give an opinion before the dictator had spoken, and then it merely hastened to agree with him.

Soviet descriptions of the dictator, as he was during the war years, are often contradictory and sometimes exaggerated. Although much of the bitterly anti-Stalinist speeches made by Khrushchev in 1956 can be discounted together with parts of the more recent Zhukov account, an account which was probably written at the bidding of the post-Khrushchev rulers of the Soviet Union in an attempt to rehabilitate Stalin, nearly all of the descriptions make the same telling points.[23]

There can be no possible doubt that the overall direction of the war lay entirely in Stalin's hands. He alone was the Commander-in-Chief, and the General Staff and Ministry of Defense provided the organs through which Stalin prosecuted the military side of the war. The *Stavka* formed only an advisory council and its decisions, which in reality were Stalin's decisions, were executed through the General Staff.

Eventually a routine of work was evolved. Stalin rose shortly before noon to be briefed on battle developments during the past twelve hours, these reports having been telephoned to the Kremlin by the General Staff. At five in the afternoon he received a further telephone briefing. Late each night a General Staff delegation, headed by the Chief or Deputy Chief of General Staff, arrived at the Kremlin rooms which Stalin used as an office.

There, in the arched-roofed, light-oak-paneled gallery of the ancient fortress, under the massive oil portraits of the Tsarist generals Suvorov and Kutuzov (which, on the outbreak of war, Stalin had hung beside those of Marx and Lenin), the General Staff representatives, having brought their marked maps and more important documents with them, made their reports.

The listening Stalin would pace up and down the room. At a long table against the opposite wall members of the GKO would be sitting, and members of the *Stavka* and the heads of the arms and main directorates, Voronov, Yakovlev, Fedorenko and Novikov might be in attendance in case technical questions were raised concerning their own arm. These meetings often continued until three or four in the morning. Throughout the whole of his working day Stalin was in touch with the front headquarters in the field by telephone or shortwave radio, operated by his own adjoining signal center and secretariat under his personal secretary, Poskrebyshev.

Stalin demanded accurate, timely information and great exactitude in matters of detail. For the members of the General Staff in particular, working in close proximity to the dictator led to great mental and physical strain, for they were sometimes subjected to abuse and vilification and on occasion to summary punishment. Some broke down under the stress and never recovered. Yet all was forgiven Shaposhnikov, who, tactful and kindly, tried to shield his own subordinates and the staffs of the fronts in the field. Often he willingly accepted blame which was not his due. And this was known to Stalin.

Once, at the nightly briefing, it came to light that two of the fronts had not submitted to Moscow their evening battle situation reports, and that Shaposhnikov had himself drafted the record, based on his own knowledge, which he had read out to the dictator. Stalin was not satisfied and he probed until the truth came out. He asked angrily: "And have you punished those who apparently do not care to tell us about what is happening in their sectors?"

Voronov, who was present, has recounted that Shaposhnikov, not in the least put out, replied that he had reprimanded over the telephone both defaulting chiefs of staff, and, said Voronov, by the expression on his face and the tone of his voice, implied only too clearly that a verbal scolding by Shaposhnikov was the highest punishment which could be meted out in the Soviet Union.

Stalin reflected on this in silence; then said with a pained and gloomy smile, "For a military man such a reprimand is no punishment. The newest Party worker gets those every day."

From about the end of July 1941 the bombing raids on the capital began to disrupt the rhythm and routine of the work of government and so it was decided to take part of the *Belorusskaya* underground railway station into use as a General Headquarters. But this was not a success and the Command Center was moved once again to the *Kirovskaya* metro station in Kirov Street. This measure was, however, only a temporary one, and as soon as was practicable the offices were returned to the Kremlin and the General Staff buildings.[24]

Stalin's influence on military operations in these early days can probably be likened to that of the German dictator in the closing phases of the Second World War. In particular, Stalin's insistence on a rigid defense and on the holding of ground was almost disastrous. Yet Stalin already showed much common sense; he was energetic and down to earth and particularly well informed on the day-to-day state of the battle; his High Command was well organized and possessed many able officers. Stalin's word was law and his iron grip and brutal determination provided the driving force which kept the Soviet Union in the war.

In most respects Stalin's control over the Soviet armed forces followed the normal communist pattern, being based on that exercised by Lenin and by the revolutionary committees over the Red Army levies in the Civil War. On the outbreak of the Russo-German War, Stalin had displaced his own personal military and civilian political representatives to the armies.

The military representatives were of high rank and were well known to the dictator and included Voroshilov, Kulik and Shaposhnikov. Their attachments were usually of only a temporary nature, and they were moved from one crisis area to another. The civilian political representatives were usually deployed for the duration of the war and included members of the Politburo and Central Committee, Khrushchev, Zhdanov and Bulganin among them, and they dispatched the professional military commissars as the political members in most of the front and some of the army military councils. In this capacity they had the right of direct communication to Stalin and full powers of veto over the military commander, no order of consequence being valid unless bearing their counter-signature. At front level they often overshadowed the military commander.

In addition to this wartime system of personal military and political representatives with the higher formations, Stalin was well served by the normal armed forces political control structure, headed by the powerful Mekhlis, this commissar organization existing throughout all levels of command in the Red Army and Fleet, in all headquarters, staff branches, formations and units. The commissar was a soldier, as opposed to the political member of the military council, who could be a Stalin-appointed civilian.

The commissar's activities were devoted to the political education, awareness and reliability of officers and men of his formation or unit, but he often had experience or knowledge of command and undertook additional duties such as administration and welfare. The commissar was usually among the most knowledgeable officers of the Red Army and he reported regularly and privately on the political reliability of commanders through his own staff channels. Anything of real importance found its way to Stalin's ears through Mekhlis, the Commander-in-Chief. This channel of information was quite separate from that of the NKVD secret police within the Red Army, whose intelligence went to Stalin by way of Beria.

The whole of the command control and information system was in this way based on as many as five separate and totally independent channels all reporting on day-to-day activities as well as on personalities: two military, one political through the military councils (not below army), one commissar and one NKVD. Stalin was the terminal of each channel. It was for this reason that the dictator was so much better informed of current developments than his military commanders in the field.

Military commissars, too, originally had powers of veto over the orders of the commanders to whom they were accredited, but shortly before the war this power had been removed, the commissar being made subordinate to the military commander. The commissar's powers were restored once more to that of equality with the commander following the great defeats in the summer of 1941.

The Red Air Force did not exist as a separate armed service but formed part of the Red Army, the aviator wearing khaki army uniform with light blue arm of service gorget patches. Fighter and bomber regiments and divisions formed part of the Red Army order of battle in very much the same fashion as artillery formations and, with the exception of the small Long Range Air Force, were used only in tactical support of ground operations.

The Soviet Navy, although a separate arm of the service, was considered to be of very minor importance compared with that of the Red Army, for Stalin, like Hitler, had a continental cast of mind. Although the Navy was large in numbers of war vessels, it was in fact poorly trained and inadequately equipped. Most of the warships were obsolete. Opposed only by the lightest of German naval forces in the Baltic and the Black Sea, it nevertheless soon lost control of those waters to the Luftwaffe, and, had it not been for the intervention of the British Royal Navy in northern waters, would have lost the sea war in the Arctic Circle. But it is very doubtful whether Stalin had any interest in the naval war or in the Red Fleet, other than using it as a reserve of bayonets to provide marine infantry brigades for the land fighting.

History was soon to show that the Red Army had a number of higher commanders and staff officers of talent, yet the Soviet command and field organization in 1941 was unable to meet the stresses of total war. Red Army officers were already part of the privileged *élite* in Soviet society, their pay having been increased by as much as two to four hundred percent over the five years from 1934 to 1939, the greatest differential being that of the senior field and general officers.[25] Their effectiveness and training had not improved in the same ratio, however. Standards were uneven. The troops were often undisciplined and poorly trained and, because of the many nationalities which made up the Soviet Union, numbers were illiterate in the Russian language.

Soviet military theory and doctrine had originally been based on that of Germany, but from 1933 onwards, when Hitler had cut all military liaison between the *Reichswehr* and the Red Army, the Soviet High Command had been obliged, as far as it was able, to develop its own ideas. It had relied to some extent on the pattern of the French Army, this being reflected in the organization of the Red Army tank forces which were allocated piecemeal to infantry and cavalry divisions. No large Soviet tank formations existed in 1940 equivalent to the German panzer group or panzer corps.

The German victory in France caused the Soviet High Command speedily to revert from the French to the German model, and tank corps were rapidly thrown together, these being almost exact replicas of panzer corps, consisting of two tank divisions and one motorized division. The German invasion caught the Soviet tank forces still unprepared, with the new formations untrained and often incompletely equipped, and the great losses in tanks suffered during the summer of 1941 forced the abandonment of the use of any tank formation above that of a tank brigade, with a strength of about sixty tanks. Because of the poor state of field training, Soviet commanders at this time were unable to handle an armored formation of a larger size.

During that summer, too, the Soviet corps organization, that between the level of division and army, was done away with in order to save on overheads, particularly trained commanders and staff. Until the corps was reintroduced in 1943 an army, which was often reduced to the size of three or four divisions, became in fact the equivalent of a German corps. A similar reorganization took place in the Red Air Force, where the standard regiment was reduced from sixty to thirty aircraft.[26]

Meanwhile, at the end of July and the beginning of August, von Bock's Army Group Center was at Smolensk, apparently poised to make the final march on Moscow. Because the left flank of Timoshenko's West Front had been in the air and open to Guderian's probings in the south during the rapid German approach to the Dnieper, a new Central Front, consisting of only two armies, had been formed under F. I. Kuznetsov, this providing the link between Timoshenko and Budenny. Kuznetsov had been the unsuccessful commander in the Baltic States. He was no more successful here, for Guderian swept the Central Front away. In August the remnants were formed into a new Bryansk Front under Eremenko, having the same task as that of the disbanded Central Front, of preventing the German invader from outflanking Timo-shenko from the south and advancing north-east on Moscow.

On 28 July Zhukov, immediately before he had been relieved from his appointment as Chief of General Staff, was called to Stalin's office, Mekhlis, the Commissar-in-Chief and the head of the Main Political Administration, being present. The likely German intentions were dis-cussed, Zhukov insisting, so he has subsequently said, that von Bock would not continue his offensive towards Moscow "because he had suffered so many casualties." For this reason, said Zhukov, the German High Command would be obliged to turn south to the Ukraine.

It is doubtful whether Zhukov did in fact give his opinion at that time since his view fits too neatly into the later Soviet version of the battle. But if this was Zhukov's opinion it was hardly based on the facts of the situation, for the German casualty figures on 16 July *for the whole of the Eastern Theater* totalled only 102,000, just over three percent of the total field strength, and even by 2 August Army Group Center losses for all reasons, including sickness, had only risen to 74,000.[27] Hitler's decision to send Guderian to the south and Hoth to the north had of course been taken six months before the outbreak of war. At the time when Zhukov says that he gave this opinion to Stalin, hundreds of thousands of Red Army troops had been encircled between Minsk and Smolensk and were in the process of being destroyed.

During those fateful July days the Red Army in western Russia was in fact near disintegration. As an example, Major-General Gorbatov, the deputy commander of a rifle corps forming part of Lieutenant-General Konev's 19 Army, himself recently released from the concen-tration camp, has described how his troops arrived by train from the

Ukraine to stem the German advance towards Moscow. A fresh formation, which had never been in action before, it was dug in hurriedly as
it arrived; but no sooner had a few scattered shells fallen in the forward
defended localities than the leading infantry regiment deserted its
positions and, officers and commissars among them, streamed off the
field *en masse*.[28]

Rigorous measures were takan by Timoshenko to restore
discipline, including the setting up of catchment areas on the roads to
the rear where the retreating, and often leaderless and weaponless,
troops were reformed, re-equipped and sent back into the battle. There,
the retreating officers and commissars were singled out for trial by
flying courts martial and in many cases shot on the spot. Yet the great
retreats continued.

Nor did a number of the commissars, on whom the morale and
steadfastness of the troops much depended, distinguish themselves at
this time, and it went badly with many a soldier found retreating without papers, tunic or other means of identity, since he came under suspicion of being a commissar who had rid himself of the telltale stitched-
on sleeve badge in case he should be taken prisoner. For the commissars
well knew of Hitler's order requiring their execution without trial.

Since the old Reserve Front had been incorporated into the West
Front, Stalin had, on 14 July, authorized the formation of a new Reserve
Front under the temporary command of Lieutenant-General I. A.
Bogdanov, and two days later a new Moscow Front was brought into
being under Lieutenant-General Artemev, the Commander of Moscow
Military District.

In spite of what Zhukov has subsequently said, there seems little
doubt that, at the time, the Soviet High Command expected von Bock
to resume his attack eastward and it endeavored to hold at all costs the
area immediately east of Smolensk, together with the two corner-
stones, Velikiye Luki to the north and Gomel to the south. As soon as
it had become obvious that the German panzer troops had been temporarily taken into reserve, Timoshenko attempted to regain some
initiative and pressed his own infantry formations forward into limited
counter-attacks well supported by artillery and the newly introduced
Katyusha multiple rockets.

A static battle of attrition did not suit von Bock, for German successes since 1939 had been based on the correlation between fire and movement, the predominant factor, in which the Germans excelled, being movement. A war of movement involved few casualties and little ammunition, whereas the static battles of attrition always resulted in comparatively heavy losses of men and a great expenditure of the artillery and mortar ammunition needed to provide counter-bombardment and defensive fire. Von Bock had little ammunition available. The Army Group Center supply channel relied on the very limited third line motor transport resources of the OKH, since the Soviet railways could not be used until the rail track had been converted from the broad Russian to the standard Central European gauge.

The lack of artillery ammunition was to cause difficulties for the German defenders but this was not the only complaint which von Bock raised against the German High Command. In mid-summer 1941 the German troops had won their battles by concentrating their forces about the decisive points, so achieving the necessary local numerical superiority over a disorganized enemy, who was desperately trying to hold ground. In August 1941 the army group commanders were finding that the vastness of the Russian hinterland and the fact that its funnel shape resulted in the broadening of frontages the further east one marched, were giving rise to problems, since the Führer, requiring the whole area to be cleared of the enemy, insisted that advancing formations should keep in close touch with their flanking neighbors.

There were not enough troops to go round and in consequence formations became too widely dispersed, reserves could not be accumulated nor the momentum of the advance maintained. Moreover, because of the vagaries of the Führer's strategy, von Bock had lost four of his five panzer corps to Leningrad and the Ukraine, and three more infantry corps of von Weichs's 2 Army had been detached from the area south of Smolensk to accompany Guderian in his southward march toward Kiev.

Because of the wide frontages and the lack of troops von Bock's resistance to the concentrated Soviet counter-attacks about Smolensk and Elnya during late August and the beginning of September was somewhat weakened. He was not one to suffer quietly the removal of his formations and he did not fail to send a long string of complaints to the OKH both about, what he called, his own weakness and the growing enemy strength.[29] In order to save casualties it eventually became necessary to evacuate the small Elnya salient.

Yet, in truth, von Bock may have exaggerated and dramatized his difficulties, for elsewhere his troops held strongly enough. There was indeed some general surprise among German officers and men that the order had not been given to continue the march on Moscow, and a few of the infantry divisions had actually been detailed to provide working parties to assist in getting in the local harvest.[30]

Timoshenko's counter-attacks were later to be described as the Battle of Smolensk which, according to the Soviet official history, caused Hitler to alter his original plan and call off the attack against Moscow, Zhukov even going so far as to say that "according to the German generals" the Hitlerite forces lost 250,000 men in the battle.

Yet, in dismissing this view as a flight of fancy, it must be acknowledged that Timoshenko had so far restored the shattered morale of West Front that it was able to undertake the first offensive operations yet carried out against Army Group Center, even if these had only limited objectives. There is no doubt, too, that the attacks were pushed home with vigor. West Front was, however, in no condition to withstand a German thrust had one been intended, as the events of the next month were to show, for in a space of three days it was to fall apart under the German hammer blows and within a further week was to yield 600,000 prisoners. Nearly two years were to elapse before Red Army ground formations could hold their own against German troops and three years before the Red Air Force began to clear the skies of the Luftwaffe.

CHAPTER THREE
To Moscow

GUDERIAN RETURNED somewhat crestfallen from the Rastenburg meeting at which he had himself been persuaded that the Führer's decision to send armored formations to Leningrad and the Ukraine had been the correct one. This sudden change of face on the part of the panzer leader made Halder angry, to Guderian's surprise and hurt; von Bock recorded the details of the meeting in his diary on 24 August, commenting that he had little time for a man who was without loyalty and was too easily swayed. So in the last week of August Guderian, taking only two of his three panzer corps, in company with von Weichs's 2 Army, started on his long 400-mile march southward into the Ukraine, making slow progress because of the rain and the mud.

Guderian, eager to improve his fortunes and extend his operative command, persuaded Paulus, the Director of Military Operations *(Oberquartiermeister 1),* who happened to be visiting him at the time, that part of von Weichs's 2 Army should be put under 2 Panzer Group; but this proposal found no favor with Halder, and Guderian took the refusal as an expression of the general animosity which the OKH felt towards him. Guderian also asked for the release of his third panzer corps, but that request, too, was refused, since it was the only armored force retained by von Bock.

Guderian's stream of signals asking for reinforcements and information continued to incense the OKH, but Guderian still had no precise knowledge of his destination, whether it was to be Kharkov or Kiev, even as he struggled on to the south.[1] When, on 3 September, Guderian's OKH liaison officer attended a conference presided over by von Brauchitsch at Army Group Center Headquarters in Borisov, he represented Guderian's case too emphatically and was relieved of his duties. Even in victory the German High Command did not function smoothly.

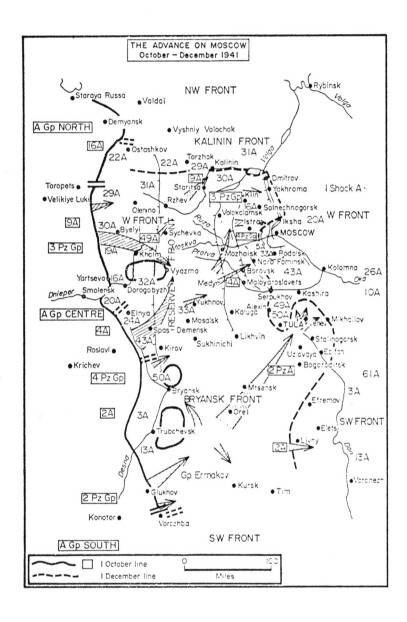

Guderian's movement southwards had been observed by Soviet reconnaissance but was still regarded by the Kremlin as an effort to outflank Timoshenko's West Front and the Reserve Front, both of which lay, one behind the other, covering the western approaches to the capital. Stalin could hardly be censured for failing to appreciate the seemingly illogical thought process by which Hitler had sent his main armored strength off at right angles to the obvious and shortest axis to Moscow.[2] The Bryansk Front was ordered at the end of August to launch an immediate offensive against Guderian's eastern flank.

The Commander of the Bryansk Front was the cavalry leader Eremenko who, in spite of his Ukrainian name, was of Russian peasant origin. He, too, had served in the Tsarist Army as a non-commissioned officer, was stern, determined, experienced, and had a particularly cool head when in a tight corner; he was not highly intelligent. Yet, although self-willed, he had the habit, too rare in many Soviet generals at that time, of readily hearing out his subordinates, even though, for the most part, he took no notice of their views.

Eremenko was not a sympathetic character and distrusted his subordinates and staff, this secrecy being taken to such lengths that, according to Sandalov, he would not tell even his chief of staff of his movements in case the units on his visiting list should be warned by telephone. For Eremenko preferred to arrive unannounced. He lived in mortal dread of Stalin, this fear showing itself in a boastful over-confidence when in the dictator's presence. He staked his reputation when he assured Stalin that he could hold and destroy Guderian, and his fellow generals, with whom he was not too popular, did not allow him to forget it.

Halder spent 7 and 8 September at Army Group South Head-quarters tying up the details of the joint Army Group South and Army Group Center plan to capture Kiev and destroy the great Soviet group-ings in the Dnieper-Desna bend on the inter-army group boundary. Guderian was to continue down his north-south axis while Colonel-General von Kleist's 1 Panzer Group (from Army Group South) marched directly north to meet him, the two panzer groups joining in the area of Romny and Lokhvitsa, about 140 miles to the east of Kiev and the Dnieper. These panzer thrusts were to cut off the whole of the

South-West Front of six Soviet armies in the great bend of the river, after which von Weichs's 2 Army and Field-Marshal von Reichenau's 6 Army were to destroy the encircled Soviet troops.

Eremenko's counter-offensive was a failure and in consequence Guderian and von Kleist made good progress towards meeting each other, in spite of the heavy rainstorms and the deep glutinous mud. On 11 September Gudenny, the Commander of South-West Theater, and Kirponos, the Commander of South-West Front, became aware of their danger and asked Shaposhnikov and Stalin for permission to evacuate Kiev and withdraw eastwards. Budenny, the former Tsarist cavalry non-commissioned officer whose military education did not extend far beyond his favorite catch-phrase of "sabre 'em down," so aggravated Stalin by this request that he lost his appointment, whereas Khrushchev, the political member of the theater military council, who during the war continually stressed how close he was to the dictator, was permitted to remain. Budenny was sent to the repository of the unwanted, the Reserve Front on the Moscow highway.

Since Moscow was no longer considered to be in immediate danger due to the change of direction of the thrusts of the German armor, Timoshenko was ordered, on 12 September, to give up the command of West Front to Konev, by then a colonel-general, and hurry south to take over the South-West Theater in the Ukraine. Meanwhile, Kirponos, who had already been given orders to prepare to evacuate Kiev, presumably by Budenny, had these orders countermanded and was told to stay on the Dnieper.

The last act of the tragedy was yet to be played out. Kirponos spoke on the telephone to Shaposhnikov representing the danger he was in, and Shaposhnikov, as usual, temporized. The military council of the South-West Front was in despair, knowing that the time was running out, but feared Stalin too much jointly to sign the urgent and resolute appeal drawn up by Tupikov, the Chief of Staff. Major-General Tupikov, once Soviet Military Attaché in Berlin and a very brave man, signed and dispatched it on his own responsibility; almost by return, Shaposhnikov, so Bagramyan says, called Tupikov a panic monger.

Timoshenko, Khrushchev and the military council of the South-West Theater knew that Tupikov was right but dared not intercede.

Instead they sent Major-General Bagramyan, the Theater Chief of Staff, with a verbal message suggesting to Kirponos that he take the law into his own hands; Kirponos was not to be drawn and referred the matter back to Shaposhnikov. Not until 17 September would Stalin agree to a withdrawal of the South-West Front, by which time it was more than twenty-four hours too late, since Guderian and von Kleist had already joined hands far to the east.[3]

The great Kiev cauldron, which was about 130 miles in width and in depth, was destroyed during the next ten days. About 450,000 prisoners were taken in the area of Kiev and in all 665,000 prisoners fell to both army groups during the operation.[4] The Soviet South-West Front, which had resisted von Rundstedt with such obstinacy and skill throughout the summer, had been totally destroyed, its commander Kirponos, together with his chief of staff, Tupikov, and the political member of the military council, Burmistenko, who was also a secretary to the Ukrainian Communist Party Central Committee, being killed, it is said, by a shell. The circumstances of their deaths are obscure.

For this great *operational* victory Hitler alone was responsible and many of his senior staff, General Wagner, the Quartermaster-General among them, were to marvel at the military genius of the Führer, who had crowned with success an undertaking against which he had been warned by nearly all his advisers.[5] He was to reap yet further success in the Ukraine, for von Kleist's 1 Panzer Group and von Manstein's 11 Army were, on 6 October, to surround and destroy two Soviet armies of the South Front in the area of Osipenko near the Black Sea coast, taking 106,000 prisoners. Von Manstein then turned back into the Crimea, occupying the peninsula, except for the fortress of Sevastopol, at the beginning of November with the capture of a further 100,000 Red Army men.

In the north in the area of Leningrad, however, Hitler was to have only minor success. In the first few weeks of the war the Finns had rapidly reoccupied the areas lost in the 1939-1940 Winter War, but they showed no inclination to advance on Leningrad or south of the River Svir. Hitler had come to the remarkable conclusion that he no longer wanted to occupy Leningrad but intended to raze it to the ground and obliterate it by shell, bomb and fire. For this reason von Leeb had been

ordered to give up any idea of a direct attack, in favor of an encirclement of the city to the east and an advance to the Svir. A panzer corps
and an air corps, removed from von Bock, were to assist him in
this operation.

By mid-September the remaining enemy pockets had been cleared
in Estonia and von Leeb reached the shore of Lake Ladoga near
Schlüsselburg, so cutting all road and rail communications between
Leningrad and the remainder of the Soviet Union. Meanwhile, a slow
but steady three-pronged advance was being made north-eastwards
towards the Svir and in the direction of Tikhvin and the Valdai Hills,
through heavily wooded swamps which made movement difficult.

When Hitler took the earlier decision to disperse his forces,
including the air and panzer formations so essential to German success,
over an area from the Baltic to the Black Sea a thousand miles in extent,
the reason he gave was that Leningrad, the Crimea, the Ukraine, the
Donets Basin and Caucasia all had priority over Moscow and the
destruction of the Red Army troops covering the capital.[6] Von Bock
had reached Smolensk on 17 July and cleared the great pocket by 6
August, but not until 23 August were the final orders issued for the next
phase of the campaign, the orders which were to shift the main striking
element of the German forces to the north and to the south.

On 5 September, only thirteen days after taking this weighty
decision, Hitler changed his mind and decided that, on the immediate
conclusion of the Kiev battle, an advance on Moscow had the over-
riding priority.

He made this decision at a time when the Kiev encirclement was
hardly under way and when the redeployed German troops had not yet
begun the fight for their distant objectives in the north and the south.
On 5 September Kiev, the Crimea and most of the East and Central
Ukraine were in Soviet hands and the Donets Basin and Caucasia were
not even remotely threatened by German troops. In the north von
Leeb's movement towards Tikhvin and the Valdai Hills had only just
started, and the transfer of the firepower of the air corps and panzer
troops from von Leeb to von Bock was to result in Army Group
North's advance coming to a halt in the face of stiffening Red Army
resistance.

The logic of Hitler's strategy in first turning away from Moscow is difficult to understand. Leningrad itself was of comparatively minor strategic importance and its encirclement and destruction were of no direct benefit to Germany's war aims, even though the Führer was to say that its capture might lead to the collapse of the whole Soviet régime.[7] Together with neighboring Kronstadt, it was of course a naval base, but this was without significance as the Baltic Red Banner Fleet had been bottled up in the Gulf of Finland by mine barrages and a great anti-submarine steel net strung from Estonia to Finland. In any case the Baltic Fleet was obsolete and outclassed, and lay stranded, largely uncrewed. In winter the Gulf of Finland froze over, imprisoning the Soviet war vessels where they were to lie a prey to the swift ski-mounted Finnish Army patrols which came racing over the ice.

There could be little advantage, either, in joining Army Group North with the Finns, who in any case were determined to wage war in their own way; for Helsinki was under heavy United States diplomatic pressure not to advance beyond their 1939 frontiers into the Soviet Union. The value of the Crimea could have been discounted since the Red Air Force long-range bombing strength was insignificant and its slow, heavy and cumbersome planes, operating without escort and flying in close formation, could be shot down by lone German fighters at will. The Donets Basin and the Caucasus would of course have been of great economic value but were too far afield to have been of use to Germany that winter.

The only gain in turning away from Moscow was the destruction of Kirponos's South-West Front, but this was done at an enormous cost in wear and tear in tanks, vehicles, men and above all in horses, which were dying through over-exertion at the rate of thousands a day. This cost could not be made good until the end of 1942. Equivalent, perhaps better, results might have been obtained by attacking and destroying Timoshenko's West Theater in front of Moscow.

As it was, Hitler was opposed to very deep *operational* panzer thrusts but preferred closer objectives, advancing uniformly by bounds across the map of Russia with a north-south line without salients or exposed flanks, and he over-exaggerated the importance of the Red Army concentrations at Velikiye Luki and Kiev near the army group boundaries, concentrations of troops which in any event were hardly mobile. So, as Halder said, he altered his strategy merely to counter the tactics of the enemy.

Whatever Hitler's reasons, the effect was that the impatient von Bock's Army Group Center, the only group which had up to then achieved any outstanding success, lay from July to October motionless and virtually passive only 200 miles from the capital.

In West and Central European Russia the winter snows do not melt until late March or April, the thaw giving rise to flooding and very bad going conditions. Spring comes suddenly and is very short, and the hot summer starts in late May. Rain falls regularly throughout the summer months, turning roads and tracks into quagmires, but the rainstorms are soon over and the tracks quickly dry out in the sweltering heat. The summer is already ended by the beginning of September, the autumn is very short and the weather finally breaks up in October, with alternating heavy rain, sleet, hard frosts, occasional snow and frequent thaws. This is the period of the *rasputitsa,* meaning the breaking up of the roads.

The countryside is often covered with great sheets of water over a foot deep as far as the eye can see. Hard roads begin to disintegrate and bridges are swept away or isolated in the floods; the tracks become canals of knee-keep, even waist-deep, slush and mud. The clouds are low and the skies leaden gray; and the constant rain has a most depressing effect on all but those of the most stolid temperament. Except on the railways all movement ceases and only the high-slung Russian *panje* carts, pulled by teams of small wiry native ponies, are capable of covering the ground.

The spells of hard frost and the approach of the colder weather harden the ground once more and traffic starts up again until the arrival of the heavy snows in December. Then movement off the main snow-cleared routes is very difficult except to tracked vehicles, sledges and ski troops. Water and mud, however, are far more effective obstacles to movement than snow.

During the hard winter the day temperature can drop to minus thirty degrees centigrade. In the hours of darkness it may be even colder. Only the warmly clad and well fed can stay out at night in the open without ill effects, and then only provided that the blood circulation can be maintained. Throughout the centuries the Russian peasant has become house-bound during the severest weather, his dwelling usually consisting of nothing more than a one- or two-roomed *izba,* a thatched wooden and plaster shack, built around a huge brick and mud stove on which the whole family slept. There they wintered it out, together with their livestock. German troops were to rely on these verminous little hovels to keep them alive in the coming months.

Hitler thought the war was almost over and he wanted to take Moscow as part of a major advance to reach the Archangel-middle Volga-Astrakhan line before the arrival of winter. Army Group South was to move into the Caucasus.

The resumption of the offensive was to become for Army Group Center a race against time, not merely to find winter quarters, but to arrive at such far-flung objectives as Yaroslavl, Gorki and Ryazan, some of which were 200 miles to the east of Moscow.[8] No winter equipment or winter clothing had as yet been provided for the troops. But the most serious problem by far, although this does not appear to have been appreciated at the time by the German High Command or by the senior field commanders, was going to be that of *operational* movement and logistics, that is to say, maintenance, supply and transport, during the late autumn rains and thaws. This factor was to be of the most crucial importance.

The first task was to concentrate in the general area of Smolensk the German troops earmarked for the offensive. Hoth's panzer troops moved back from von Leeb to von Bock, and Hoepner's 4 Panzer Group, formerly with Army Group North, followed. In all, von Leeb lost five panzer and two motorized divisions. His protests that their loss would not only halt his own advance but would leave him vulnerable to a Soviet counter-offensive were brushed aside with the retort that von Bock's eastward movement would weaken Soviet counter-pressures elsewhere. 8 Air Corps, commanded by von Richthofen, that had earlier been detached from Kesselring to the area of Leningrad, returned to its parent 2 Air Fleet in the center.

Guderian and von Weichs, 300 miles to the south, were much too far away to reach the vital Smolensk area in time for the new offensive, and so it was decided that they should attack in a north-easterly direction towards Moscow from the northern borders of the Ukraine.

In addition to the return of 2 Army and 2 Panzer Group from the Ukraine to Russia (they had never been part of Army Group South), von Rundstedt was obliged to transfer to von Bock nine divisions, of which two were panzer and two motorized, and he was to regret the loss of these forces when he himself came to be thrown out of the doorway to the Caucasus later in the year. Since the only railway lines which had been retracked to the Central European gauge were those which ran from west to east, all the infantry divisions transferred from the Ukraine to Smolensk went by the march route on their feet.

By thinning out Army Groups North and South the strength of von Bock's Army Group Center had been raised to seventy divisions, of which fourteen were panzer and eight were motorized infantry.[9] Air support was to be provided by Kesselring with two air corps comprising about 1,000 aircraft of the 2,400 then available in the East.

The Soviet strength covering the approach to Moscow was estimated by German intelligence at the end of September to be as high as eighty infantry divisions, eleven tank brigades and nine cavalry divisions, in the event a reasonably accurate assessment, and the total Red Air Force on the whole of the Russo-German front was put at only 1,100 aircraft. The Army Group Center frontages extended over 400 miles and von Bock held less than two divisions as army group reserve. The OKH held no reserves at all.

The new offensive, which was later known by the name of *Typhoon,* was based on the outline of Hitler's Directive 35 of 6 September, the main planning being done between the OKH and von Bock's headquarters, all orders being subjected to the Führer's scrutiny and veto. The deployment of the six armies of the enemy West Front and two of the three of the Bryansk Front to the immediate south, all of which were in contact, was known to German intelligence, but, as was normally the case, there was no information at all on Red Army formations to the rear. The hurriedly constructed lines of defenses right back to the capital, however, were easily identifiable from the air.

Von Bock's immediate task, before moving eastwards on his way to the Archangel-middle Volga line, was to destroy Konev's West Front, and this was to be done by the practiced and well-rehearsed double panzer envelopment.[10] The left pincer, made up of Strauss's 9 Army and Hoth's 3 Panzer Group, was to circle out from the area of Smolensk and, breaking through the enemy defenses, advance rapidly in a great arc which was to close on the railway junction and city of Vyazma, just over a hundred miles in the Red Army rear. The right pincer, of von Kluge's 4 Army and Hoepner's 4 Panzer Group, was to move from the area south of Smolensk and, first circling southwards, come in upon Vyazma from the south.

As usual the penetration was to be the responsibility of the infantry armies and the task of rapid envelopment that of the panzer groups. Within limits the plan was a repetition of the June encirclement at Minsk.

At the same time it was intended that, in the south, Guderian and von Weichs should envelop and destroy Eremenko's Bryansk Front.

The operation for the destruction of the West and the Bryansk Fronts was well conceived and planned. But, as Hitler saw the situation, it was only the preliminary to the main aim, the advance to the final occupation line. The Führer's views were becoming increasingly bizarre, and his earlier statement that "the city of Moscow had no significance" began to take on a more vivid meaning. For, apparently believing that when the West and Bryansk Fronts had been destroyed there would be no worthwhile enemy forces left in Old Russia, he had decided that he would not occupy Moscow at all but would merely ring it with his troops and, in a fate it was to share with Leningrad, destroy it by bombing and artillery fire. None of the civilian population was to be let out and any enemy offers to surrender the city were to be rejected.[11]

In this way Hitler showed how little Moscow mattered to him as a historical and cultural center, and the value he placed on the lives of its inhabitants. Yet it is almost beyond credibility that Hitler, as statesman or as soldier, should have wantonly destroyed Moscow as a seat of government and an industrial complex, and disregarded its value as a communication and rail center. Common sense should have told

him that in it were the only available winter quarters for a large proportion of his troops.

Since the Führer was determined to advance beyond Moscow,
he intended that Guderian's 2 Panzer Group, which after 6 October
was to be redesignated as 2 Panzer Army, should outflank Moscow
from the south in the direction of Mtsensk and Tufa while von Weichs's
2 Army should, after the destruction of the Bryansk Front, cross
the panzer group axis and move due east from Orel towards the
Don and the great industrial center of Voronezh, 200 miles to
the south of Moscow. Von Kluge's 4 Army and Hoepner's 4 Panzer
Group were to bypass Moscow immediately to the north and south
of the city, while Strauss's 9 Army and Hoth's 3 Panzer Group were
to turn north-east from Vyazma towards Kalinin and the Valdai
Hills, about 150 miles north of the capital, as part of the advance
towards Yaroslavl.

At the beginning of October von Bock recorded his disagreement
with this wide dispersal of his forces.[12]

The many German assessments of the fighting value of the Soviet Fleet
and the Red Air Force at this time are in general accord. The Red Fleet
was an almost negligible factor since it was poorly trained and inadequately equipped and its higher command tended to lack enterprise.
The Red Air Force, although large in numbers, was equipped with aircraft mainly obsolete and of very crude design.

The standard fighters were the I 15 or I 153 biplane with a maximum speed of only 230 mph, and the I 16 low-winged single-radial-
engined monoplane known as the *Rata,* which, although very
maneuverable, had a maximum airspeed of only 285 mph. Neither of
these fighters was a match for the German Me 109 and they were
actually outpaced by the Luftwaffe's medium bombers. The TB 1 and
TB 2 heavy bombers had top speeds of about 130 mph, while the fast
medium bombers, the SB 1 and SB 2, could not fly faster than 260
mph. Although 1,700 modern fighters had been brought into use by
June 1941, mainly Yak 1, Lagg 3 and Mig 3, all of these were inferior
to the Me 109; only eighteen air regiments had been re-equipped with
them and most of these were destroyed in the summer fighting.

The new *Stormovik* Il 2 single-engined ground attack fighter with an armored rear was already in service in limited numbers, and although this plane was admirable as a tactical support aircraft, in some respects being superior to the German equivalent, the *Stuka* Ju 87, with a top speed of 280 mph it hardly ranked as a fighter. The Pe 2 twin-engined fighter bomber, a copy of the German Me 110, with a speed of 340 mph, was occasionally to be seen.

In the summer and autumn of 1941 these more modern aircraft were only rarely met and the Red Air Force continued to rely on the I 15, the *Rata* and the ubiquitous two-seater biplane first designed in 1927 and known as the Po 2 or U 2. There were large numbers of these about and they were to fly throughout the whole war as reconnaissance and intercommunication aircraft and as light bombers. They had an airspeed of only 100 mph.

At the beginning of the war the auxiliary equipment in Soviet aircraft was of very inferior design. Little radio was used, there was no intercommunication equipment inside the aircraft, and no radar or modern direction and locating aids were in service, pilots flying at treetop height by map and their own keen eyesight. The repair and maintenance system was primitive.

Red Air Force pilots in these early days of the war were no match in leadership or flying skills for the well-trained, superbly equipped and battle-experienced Luftwaffe. Soviet fighter pilots in particular lacked spirit and dash and would often avoid engagements, turning away even from unescorted Ju 52 transports (all of which carried defensive armament) when these were flying in close formation. Red Air Force bomber pilots on the other hand showed determination and courage and, because they were unescorted or unsupported by Soviet fighters, suffered heavily in consequence. The U 2 pilots were renowned for great ingenuity and skill.

All aviators and ground crews had great endurance and hardiness, being particularly clever at improvisation, and they flew in all weather, however low the cloud and however restricted the visibility.

The vastness of the theater of war and hinterland and the fact that the Red Air Force decentralized its resources to ground formations as low as that of army, the air forces being actually under the command of the army general rather than in support, saved the Red Air Force from being completely destroyed by the German air arm. For this latter reason, too, the Luftwaffe's mastery was never total and the Red Air Force always had something in the air.

On the other hand, except for the very early German successes in Belorussia in June and July, because frontages had become so vast and because both German and Soviet air resources were so limited, air intervention by itself was never decisive to the outcome of the land battle in the Russian theater. Not until the Red Army re-entered Central Europe in 1944, when frontages were once more restricted and the Luftwaffe very weak, did the Red Air Force play a major part in the land fighting.

Although there is general agreement on the fighting value of the Soviet sailor and airman at this time, contemporary German opinions on the Red Army soldier vary widely. It is known that tens, even hundreds, of thousands gave themselves up with hardly a fight and that many took to their heels. Before the end of 1941 Army Group Center alone was to take over 1,900,000 prisoners.[13] Yet in some sectors Red Army troops would fight with the greatest obstinacy, at times their resistance being fanatical, and there was no clear pattern for the very wide dissimilarity.

The Red Army was of course multi-national and polyglot and so its characteristics and efficiency were not uniform. Some soldiers, still smarting from the more recent communist repressions, listened too readily to the German loudspeakers; others, no less gullible, were incited by their commissars to race-hatred and barbarism. Yet these were not the only explanations. Some formations or units would suddenly surrender *en masse* after resisting obstinately for a day; others, after starting badly and losing heavily in line-crossers, would quickly regain their resolution and fight to the very end.

Terrain seemed to affect the Red Army behavior. In mountain waste or in broken and close country, forest or marsh, on conditions favoring the defense and where he was not threatened by German armor, the Soviet soldier generally fought better than in the open.

The resistance varied, too, by theaters. Russian formations in the far north were inferior to the Finns, but they were equal to German troops. Soviet resistance to Army Group North near Leningrad and in the wooded swamps to the north of Lake Ilmen was uniformly bitter. But in the Ukraine and in the area of Smolensk, the fighting value of the Red Army might be high or negligible. For when 52 German Infantry Division was ordered, on 16 August, to take a limited objective near the Belorussian railway town of Rogachev, just a hundred miles to the south-west of Smolensk, many of the defenders fled in terror and, for the lightest of casualties, the German division took, within twenty-four hours, 15,000 prisoners, 1,000 horses, 40 heavy guns and much other equipment.[14]

The influence of the commissar was not particularly strong at this period in spite of the fact that his power had been restored to that of parity with the military commander, so that no orders could be issued without his counter-signature. The authority of the commissar was to become stronger, however, as the months of war went by, and Red Army prisoners in German hands were to recount how their own troops had been shot down in battle by commissars for reluctance to move when under fire.

Sometimes an inexperienced, stupid or headstrong commissar was a hindrance and an obstruction, yet the threat of the commissar's pistol and his incessant propaganda did galvanize the lethargic and passive soldiery into activity and often achieved a surprising degree of efficiency. And Stalin's criminal law, which held hostage the relatives of soldiers taken prisoner, presumably prevented some troops from deserting. Yet the influence of the commissar cannot be judged as entirely political or necessarily obstructive, for often he worked hand in glove with the military commander and sometimes he was an experienced soldier with many years of service behind him.

Comparatively few commissars appear to have been taken prisoner; some took their own lives, some fled; some, throwing away papers and tunic, denied their true identity and passed themselves off as soldiers, running the gauntlet of the SS *Einsatzkommandos* who attended at the prisoner of war cages and who offered the Red Army prisoners rewards for the denunciation of Jews and commissars among their number. For in those early days a commissar prisoner often met his death with a pistol bullet in the back of his neck.

Moscow had suffered its first air attack on 22 July and further attacks followed on subsequent nights. A small percentage of the population was evacuated and, as already recounted, part of the Soviet High Command was temporarily transferred to the Moscow underground railway stations. The German bombing attacks, made by about 200 aircraft, appear to have been ordered on political and emotional grounds rather than for reasons of war.

The Wehrmacht was only 200 miles away and the Kremlin lived in daily expectation and fear of the final thrust on the capital. Frantic efforts had been made to build two great earthwork systems west of Moscow using a large civilian labor force, most of whom were women, the defenses being based on linear anti-tank ditches fifteen to twenty feet deep, ditches which were, in the event, of only minor value. For as soon as enemy infantry and engineers reached the obstacle at one or two points, the ditch was easily bridged or filled in, enabling hundreds of tanks to penetrate at each crossing place. So the enormous effort required to dig the hundreds of miles of tank traps was largely wasted.

The great belts of anti-tank ditches were thickened up by minefields, barricades and strong points, the forward of these defensive systems, known as the Vyazma line, running from an area about thirty miles east of Ostashkov near the Valdai Hills in the north, to the region west of Vyazma and then to beyond Kirov in the south, being in all about 200 miles in length. The rearward Mozhaisk line was about eighty miles to the west of Moscow and ran from Volokolamsk to Likhvin and was about 160 miles in extent. A further four semi-circular defense lines ringed Moscow from the west.

The defense of the approaches to Moscow had been entrusted to West Theater, commanded by Timoshenko until 12 September, when he had been sent off to the Ukraine. The West Theater stretched from its boundary with Lieutenant-General Kurochkin's North-West Front at Ostashkov in the north, to Vorozhba at the junction with the South-West Front in the south, and was made up of three separate fronts.

Of these the principal was West Front, commanded by Konev, deployed sixty miles to the west of Vyazma and stretching from the Ostashkov Lakes to the town of Elnya, about forty miles south-east of Smolensk. Konev's West Front consisted of six Soviet armies all deployed in line from north to south, and all in contact with the enemy.

The Reserve Front, temporarily once again under the command of Budenny who had just arrived from the Ukraine, consisted of a further six armies in line from north to south and echeloned in depth behind Konev's West Front. The Reserve Front was roughly on the Vyazma line, from the source of the Volga near Ostashkov in the north to Elnya in the south. Budenny's troops were not in contact with the enemy except on the extreme left, where Lieutenant-General Rakutin's 24 and Major-General Sobennikov's 43 Armies formed the link between the West and the Bryansk Fronts.

To the south of Sobennikov's 43 Army of the Reserve Front, beyond the Roslavl-Kirov railway line, ran Eremenko's Bryansk Front, consisting of Major-General Petrov's 50 Army, Major-General Kreizer's 3 Army and Major-General Gorodnyansky's 13 Army, with the Ermakov Group of cavalry, tanks and infantry covering the southern flank and maintaining contact with the most northerly formation of the South-West Front.

West Theater numbered eighty-three infantry divisions each of an establishment of about 10,000 men, nine cavalry divisions which numbered no more than about 3,000 men each, and thirteen tank brigades — in all 1,200,000 men, 770 tanks and 360 aircraft, this amounting, according to the Soviet account, to forty percent of the field holdings of infantry formations and about thirty-five percent of the available tanks and aircraft.[15] The tank brigades, of fifty or sixty tanks each, had been allocated to the infantry armies.

When, in the second week in September, Timoshenko had given up the command of West Theater, Stalin had brought the three fronts directly under his own control.

Stalin was unaware, until the end of Septemer, that a gigantic German thrust was about to be launched on his center in the direction of Moscow. He was in any event being oppressed by bad news from all other fronts and he could scarcely credit that the Wehrmacht was capable of undertaking yet another, almost simultaneous, major offensive.

Zhukov was in Leningrad, having been made responsible for the defense of that city against the furious German attacks which took von Leeb to the shores of Lake Ladoga. The destruction of Kirponos's South-West Front in the great Kiev cauldron was not completed until 26 September and Timoshenko had recoiled eastwards closely pressed by the German pursuit, forming as he did so another South-West Front out of the South-West Theater Headquarters and such remnants of the field forces as could be collected.

Further to the south events had not stood still. Since 24 September General von Manstein's 11 Army had been making determined attacks down the Perekop Isthmus to get into the Crimea, and Stalin had no great faith in the ability of the local military commander, F. I. Kuznetsov, to hold him, for Kuznetsov had already failed twice in his earlier appointments. Von Rundstedt had turned von Kleist's I Panzer Group (after 6 October redesignated as I Panzer Army) southwards across the River Samara in what was obviously to be an attempt to envelop Lieutenant-General Ryabyshev's South Front.

There were indeed diversions enough to distract the attention of Stalin and Shaposhnikov away from the area of Smolensk.

The German High Command achieved *operational* and tactical surprise for the simple reason that it was impossible for the Soviet leadership and the General Staff, even if they had been endowed with great clarity of vision and excellent intelligence, which they were not, to understand the thought processes of the Führer's brain or to have read a strategic pattern into the German operations. Of the inconsistencies of Hitler's military *Flittergelehrsamkeit* and the vagaries of his *Flederwisch* logic Stalin's *Stavka* had no understanding, and for this they could hardly be blamed. For when Halder, the Chief of General Staff, heard some of the detail of the Führer's plan, including the outward thrust to the Valdai Hills, he could only shrug and note in his diary that the operational intention was to him entirely unclear.

As the Moscow offensive was about to start, Hitler issued an order of the day in which he promised his troops that "in this last decisive battle of the year the enemy would be destroyed together with the instigator of the whole war, England. For, as soon as the enemy was destroyed, England would lose its last ally on the Continent." He went on to liken the Soviet Union to a danger to Europe no less frightful than that of the Huns and Mongols.

The next day, on 3 October, the Führer made the announcement that "not before then was he permitted to tell the German people that the foe was already broken and would never rise again."

CHAPTER FOUR

THE RASPUTITSA

———————◆———————

WHEN HITLER TURNED the German Army towards Russia, Fromm's Replacement Army held about 450,000 reinforcements, petrol for three months and diesel for one. By the end of August the casualties, which, although only fractional of those suffered by the Red Army, had not been light, totaled 440,000, of which 94,000 had been killed.[1] Only 217,000 reinforcements had been allotted as replacements, but many of these were still on the long march route to the field divisions and had not arrived at their destinations. Halder's proposal that twelve infantry divisions should be broken up to find reinforcements had been vetoed by the Führer, for whom large numbers of divisions in the field always exercised a fascination.

Except in the Baltic area, where coastal shipping could be used, the German transport situation over the whole of Russia and the Ukraine was extremely precarious. Since very little Soviet railway rolling stock had been captured, the railnet could not be taken into use; the retracking of the system was a slow process. Much of the ancillary equipment of the Soviet State railway, including the telephone system, had been looted by the local population and by Axis troops. Even when retracked the railway had only a limited capacity, since it consisted in places of only a single line and could not operate efficiently until all sidings, turn-tables and repair sheds had been converted.

The German motor transport organization was overburdened and about thirty percent short of establishment, and at the end of August the tank formations had been reduced by casualties and breakdown to less than fifty percent of their proper war strength. There was great difficulty in obtaining new vehicle assemblies to make good the losses caused by long mileages, heat and dust.[2]

These deficiencies, serious though they were quoted in round totals, did not accurately portray the situation on the ground. Shortages in men are borne mainly by the infantry companies of the field divisions, for it is there that most casualties occur. Deficiencies in tanks or vehicles shown on the tally boards in higher headquarters do not reflect the actual tank fighting strength or the numbers of vehicles roadworthy.

According to Guderian, Munzel's 6 Panzer Regiment, which had an establishment of about 150 armored vehicles, was, on 14 September, reduced to a fighting strength of ten tanks. Motorized infantry companies were down to fifty men each and there was a notable lack of combat training and toughness among the few replacements. There was no winter clothing or technical winter equipment of any type and Guderian was complaining of an acute shortage of boots, socks and shirts.[3]

The marching infantry fared even worse. 98 Franconian-Sudeten Infantry Division, one of those on the long 400-mile march from Kiev to the area west of Moscow, was 3,800 men understrength on 27 September when the first reinforcements began to arrive, and these were so few in number that they were noted as a drop in the ocean.

The modern general service wagons with rubber tires and ball-bearing-mounted wheels had long since broken up under the strain of the appalling tracks, and had been replaced by locally impressed and apparently indestructible Russian farm *panje* carts. Good-quality army horses foundered daily through over-exertion and lack of fodder, but the scrubby Russian ponies, although too light for heavy draught work, lived on, eating birch twigs and the thatched roofs of houses. Equipment, including ammunition, had to be abandoned for lack of transport to carry it.

Gradually the most simple necessities of life disappeared, razor blades, soap, toothpaste, shoe-repairing materials, needles and thread. Even in September there was incessant rain and a cold north-east wind, and every night brought with it the scramble for shelter, squalid and bug-ridden though this usually was; when this could not be found the troops plumbed the very depths of wretchedness. The rain, cold and lack of rest increased sickness which in normal circumstances would have warranted admission to hospital; but the sick had to march with the column over distances of up to twenty-five miles a day, since there was no transport to carry them and they could not be left behind in the wild bandit-infested forests. The regulation boots were starting to fall to pieces. All ranks were filthy and bearded, with dirty, rotting and verminous underclothing. Typhus was shortly to follow.[4]

By 26 September the German losses had risen to 534,000 which, although only fifteen percent of the total manpower on the Eastern Front, probably represented over thirty percent of the infantry strength.[5] There were two reasons for the more rapidly increasing casualty rate. Much of the fighting between Leningrad and Smolensk had become static position warfare, the brunt of which had been borne by infantry formations unsupported by tanks. Even when these infantry divisions were taken out of the line, there was no rest for them, for their relief and refit period had become synonymous with combing the wooded rear areas, not for partisans, who were still rare at this time, but for armed stragglers and infiltrators, some of whom were actually connected by telephone to the Red Army positions.[6] In clearing forest and marsh all the advantages lay with the hidden Russian, and the operations were often costly in German casualties.

These field deficiencies were only a part of the Quartermaster-General's problems, for on 9 October Wagner outlined to Halder the seriousness of the position. The rationing of troops and prisoners of war had become an almost insoluble difficulty. Experience at Kiev had shown that the equivalent manpower of a German division was needed for every 20,000 prisoners, for guarding, sorting, transporting and administration, and although an enormous quantity of good quality war booty had been left on the field of battle it was impossible to find German labor to supervise its collection and storage. There was insufficient petrol to cover the needs of the formations in the field and stocks of rubber would be exhausted by the following March.[7] The only good item of news was that the German tank fighting strength had risen by the end of September to seventy percent of establishment.

Wagner did in fact overcome many of his difficulties, although perhaps not in the way which he would have wished. The invention of *buna* ended the need for rubber and the increased production of synthetic petrols helped to ease the motor fuel position. But for the most part the fuel situation improved because of Germany's rapidly sinking tank and motor strengths during the winter of 1941 and because many of the vehicles were long immobilized by the weather. The ration position was partially solved by the very high mortality rate among Soviet prisoners of war, who died in their tens of thousands of typhus, malnutrition and ill-usage. Unlike the Red Army the German Army had no organized booty service and only began to make use of captured equipment at a much later stage of the war.

On 26 September von Bock had issued the Army Group Center directive for the offensive which was based on the Führer's more recent ideas, since it concentrated entirely on the destruction of the West and the Bryansk Fronts and the subsequent advance to the line of the middle Volga. Moscow was only mentioned as a possible Luftwaffe bombing target.

Meanwhile, the region between Smolensk and Roslavl, partly open flax, rye, oats and potato-growing country, with some mixed forests, had become a gigantic concentration area for tanks, vehicles and infantry arriving in dust covered columns from as far afield as the area of Leningrad and Lake Ilmen, from Minsk and from the Reich. One panzer division railed from France actually detrained complete with tropical equipment. Trees and telegraph poles at every road junction were covered with a rash of formation sign posts and indicator boards, and it took hours to sort out the great traffic jams caused by the joining and crossing of supply routes. The air umbrella provided by Kesselring's fighter divisions made Soviet air reconnaissance impossible.[8]

The country to the south of Smolensk in the Bryansk *oblast,* bordering on the Ukraine, where Guderian and von Weichs were concentrating, was more heavily wooded than in the Smolensk-Roslavl area. Even here, however, much of the land was open and cultivated.

Guderian's 2 Panzer Group on the extreme right consisted of three panzer and two infantry corps, in all fifteen and a half divisions, of which five were panzer and four motorized infantry.[9]

On the morning of 28 September, in a heavy ground mist which was to herald a fine sunny autumn day, Guderian attacked along the Army Group Center southern boundary, a boundary which coincided with the junction point at Vorozhba between Eremenko's Bryansk Front and Timoshenko's South-West Front. Boundaries and junction points were often weak links in the enemy defense but this occasion proved an exception. Kempf's 48 Panzer Corps, the formation which made the initial thrust, soon found that it had lit upon a hornets' nest and it was counter-attacked in strength and held by Soviet tanks and infantry.

The next day Guderian decided to move the axis of his attack a little farther to the north nearer Glukhov, where he hoped resistance would be lighter. The redeployment of the assaulting formations took time and was disturbing to the state of mind of the attacking troops. It proved impossible to disengage two of the divisions of Kempf's corps, both of which were hotly engaged by the enemy, one of the divisions having lost numbers of men and vehicles when it had been overrun by Soviet tanks. There was nothing for it but to make the attack along the new axis using only two of the three panzer corps. The offensive was to be resumed on 30 September.[10]

As fortune would have it the new axis crossed an area only lightly defended and Geyr von Schweppenburg's 24 and Lemelsen's 47 Panzer Corps soon made the open country in the Red Army rear.[11] Ermakov, who commanded in this sector, had obviously been surprised at this new thrust, for his resistance lacked cohesion, and the fighting, although no less fierce, became sporadic, the action of scattered groups and formations in withdrawal.

Yet the day was a tense one. As the German troops poured through the gaps there were frequently counter-attacks by T 34 and KV tanks which were particularly nerve-racking to the German infantry since the 37-mm anti-tank gun had become, in their own words, little better than a museum piece. The German infantry corps, protecting the flanks of the panzer breakthrough, were marching hard in the wake of the tanks, great columns of men and horses cloaked with the all-pervading dust, each division stretching out as far as the eye could see, great winding snakes twenty miles long.

Enemy dead and dying lay in heaps where they had been caught in the machine-gun fire of the German tanks, which by then were many miles ahead. Abandoned equipment was everywhere, including

American quarter-ton jeeps, never before seen by German troops. In two days the panzer forces advanced eighty miles, German casualties being very light. The fine weather held.

The rapid advance continued across the heavily wooded black earth steppe to the rail, road and industrial center of Orel on the Oka. This city, once, in Tsarist times, a place of exile for revolutionaries, lay well to the east of the Bryansk Front and about 130 miles from the German start line.

There were reports from 4 Panzer Division of having overrun a women's rifle battalion in the area, and so unexpected was the arrival of 24 Panzer Corps that the people were in the streets, the shops were open and the trams were running. The dismantling of the factories was still in progress and mountainous heaps of machinery lay awaiting rail movement to the east.

The panzer troops fed off the country but Geyr von Schweppenburg was unable to advance up the Mtsensk road towards Tula until fuel had been airlanded at Orel airfield by the Luftwaffe. Meanwhile, Lemelsen's 47 Panzer Corps, in accordance with its earlier orders, had turned north-westwards away from the main panzer axis and on 6 October, in a *coup de main* raid, entered Bryansk, the site of Eremenko's front headquarters.

The ancient city, founded in the twelfth century, stood at the bridge on the high western bank of the Desna, but the new industrial suburbs and railway junction had extended the built-up area far to the east. Although it had a population of only 80,000, it was of considerable importance as a transport center and river port. On Lemelsen's arrival the city was full of Soviet troops and supply installations.[12]

Guderian's future success was to become dependent on a number of factors which he himself, had he known of them, would probably have judged as irrelevant, even though his own right flank was involved. In the Ukraine, von Rundstedt had been ordered to march on the Caucasus through Rostov, this movement in a south-easterly direction drawing von Kleist's 1 Panzer Army, together with its flanking 17 and 6 Armies, away from the inter-army group boundary between von Rundstedt and von Bock. Guderian himself, commanding the most southerly formation of Army Group Center, had an axis which went north-eastwards towards Tula, and so an ever-increasing gap appeared between 2 Panzer Army and von Reichenau's 6 Army in the area of Kursk.

Guderian was now plagued by a stream of long and diverse orders which, he rightly sensed, originated not from von Bock but from the German High Command in Rastenburg, these, in Guderian's view, showing a lack of understanding of the position on the ground. He was instructed to destroy Eremenko's Bryansk Front, which was by then a hundred miles behind him to his west, seize the city of Kursk, which was a hundred miles to his south, and take Tula, which was a hundred miles to the north-east. All orders were to be executed immediately. When Guderian asked for priorities to be allotted to his three separate missions he received no reply.[13] So he was forced against his inclination to disperse his forces; one panzer corps had already been deflected to Bryansk and a second was diverted to Kursk. Only 24 Panzer Corps remained on the Tula axis just short of Mtsensk.

In the Kremlin the position on this south flank looked very serious for, by the third day of the offensive, Guderian's army had already covered 150 miles, or half the distance to Moscow, and was much nearer the capital than any other German troops. In fact the southern Soviet flank appeared to be wide open. Lieutenant-General Zakharkin's 49 Army holding the southern extremity of the Mozhaisk line, just to the west of Tula, was ordered by Moscow to go forward to meet the panzer thrust and, driving Guderian back westwards, retake Orel. Events, however, outran these orders.

The night before, on 1 October, when the danger of Guderian's thrust had first been recognized, Stalin sent for Major-General Lelyushenko, a general of tank troops who had had some battle experience earlier in the year when he had commanded a mechanized corps against von Manstein's panzer troops in Latvia. Lelyushenko was awaiting a new field command and had already been appointed as commander of 1 Special Guards Rifle Corps, but since this had not yet been formed he was in fact a commander without troops; in consequence he was one of the few men available and in some part qualified for the task of holding Guderian's panzer thrust.

The rough-and-ready way in which the defense was hurriedly organized was in some respects typical of the Soviet High Command methods at that time. Having had the battle situation explained to him by Shaposhnikov, Lelyushenko was ordered by Stalin to undertake the defense of Mtsensk and was dispatched post-haste on his mammoth task. A motorcycle regiment, the only available troops in Moscow Military District, was sent after him and thereafter Shaposhnikov was to route and redirect to Lelyushenko, by road and rail, formations, units and detachments.

As he passed through the great industrial center of Tula, Lelyushenko, according to his own account, collected all the guns from the artillery school and, as they lacked tractors, had them hitched to Tula municipal buses.[14] The ccortège moved off south-westwards. Any units met on the way were directed towards Mtsensk.

Katukov's 1 Tank Brigade, recently from the Leningrad area, which happened to be on rail flats between Kalinin and Moscow, was ordered on to Mtsensk railway station by Fedorenko of the Main Tank Directorate of the Soviet High Command. Katukov, who four years later was to fight his way into Berlin in command of 1 Guards Tank Army, unloaded his tanks, mostly KVs and T 34s, and leaving the sidings and stockyards behind him, clattered through the small rural town of Mtsensk, in peacetime a fruit and meat canning center. Just south of the town, on the night of 6 October, Katukov ran headlong into Geyr von Schweppenburg's 24 Panzer Corps which, still awaiting fuel, was leaguered up.[15] The Germans were the more surprised and in the heavy fighting which followed Guderian lost numbers of his tanks and received a temporary but significant check.

On 7 October the German situation in this area took a turn for the worse when the first sleet and snow fell; this did not settle but roads and tracks rapidly became churned up into seas of mud, breaking up the only good route from Orel to Mtsensk on which all wheeled traffic depended. The bridges had already been blown and the verges mined by the withdrawing Soviet troops, and 2 Panzer Army was forced to begin the laborious and deadly slow task of constructing corduroy roads of tree trunks laid side by side for miles on end.

Wheeled motor vehicles could not move and the trickle of petrol and diesel supply suddenly ceased; tracked vehicles eventually became stranded for lack of fuel. For the time being Lelyushenko, whose command had grown from nothing into two guards rifle divisions, two tank brigades, part of an airborne corps and a tactical support air group, aided by the weather had accomplished his mission.[16]

Over a hundred miles to the west Eremenko had not had the same good luck. He had tried to close the breach made by Guderian to his immediate south, but the counter-attcking troops of Gorodnyansky's 13 Army had been driven off northwards by the marching German infantry which protected the flanks of the panzer army. On 2 October von Weichs's 2 Army made a frontal attack from the west on all the three armies of Eremenko's Bryansk Front.

Von Weichs, a sixty-year-old cavalryman and panzer leader, had no tank formations, and his own infantry were tired and understrength. Without rehearsal or rest they were led by night from their defensive positions to the forming-up places for the assault.

The attack began under cover of darkness, the weather being cool and dry but the cloud low. Some early gains were made but the Soviet enemy reorganized quickly and his resistance stiffened. Red Army artillery defensive fire became intense and some German units were driven back over their start lines by tank counter-attacks.

With its casualties mounting steadily 2 Army made only slow progress towards the River Desna, but did at least pin the bulk of Eremenko's troops. The Soviet defense began to collapse, however, from 6 October, when Bryansk fell to Lemelsen's panzer corps, on which day von Weichs had already covered twenty-five miles of his eastwards march. Shortly afterwards, Gorodnyansky's 13 and Kreizer's 3 Armies were encircled between von Weichs and Lemelsen, and Petrov's 50 Army to the north of Bryanks, although not encircled, was being cut up between 2 Army and 4 Army further to the north.

As a fighting formation the Bryansk Front had ceased to exist.

On 3 October Eremenko lost radio contact with 50 Army and three days later could himself no longer communicate with Moscow. On 8 October the front commander, on his own responsibility, ordered a general withdrawal to be made by filtrating out of the great pocket under cover of darkness. Many troops succeeded in escaping in this way, but they left their equipment and at least 50,000 of their number behind; Petrov, the Commander of 50 Army, was among the dead.[17] Von Weichs's task of holding and breaking up the encircled troops was made more difficult by the very low cloud, which hampered air reconnaissance, by the partially wooded country and by the torrential rains which were just arriving in the area.

1 German Cavalry Division near Trubchevsk, one of the formations covering Guderian's left flank, had been detailed to operate closely with von Weichs's 2 Army and break up the enemy cauldron. Heavy rain and sleet began to fall on the night of 9 October and the leaden and heavily weighted clouds opened in a deluge; swamps appeared everywhere and torrents of water poured across the wooded tracks so that conditions, in the words of their historian, became catastrophic. Motor vehicles had to be abandoned and the horses were up to their girths in slime. The lightest cart needed a great team of draught animals and the supply and transport system broke down.

The caped East Prussian cavalrymen, wet through to the skin, watched without surprise as a corps headquarters tried to shelter itself in a verminous one-room house together with the pigs and poultry. The area in which they were operating was one of thick and tangled primeval forest and marsh, the clearing of which was both a time-consuming and a dangerous business, and, although prisoners said that the Headquarters of Kreizer's 3 Soviet Army was near at hand, the cavalrymen were unable to find it.[18]

The main German offensive in the north along the Smolensk-Moscow axis, which was aimed at enveloping the Soviet defenders to the west of Vyazma, did not begin until 2 October, two days later than Guderian's attack. It was to have much greater success.

To the right of the Smolensk-Vyazma highway von Kluge's 4 Army had the task of pinning the enemy to its front, while Hoepner's 4 Panzer Group, which was under von Kluge's command, breached with three panzer corps the two left flanking armies of Budenny's Reserve Front.

Using infantry divisions allocated to him for the purpose, Hoepner closed up to the Desba and in fine, clear weather attacked at first light on 2 October. The attack was unexpected by the Russians, and before noon Hoepner had his tanks over the river; by evening he was twenty miles behind the Soviet positions. On his right flank, Red Army troops in the area of Sobennikov's 43 Army surrendered in droves or, throwing away their weapons, made off to the rear. Guns and tanks were abandoned everywhere.

On the left, where the going conditions were more difficult for German armor, the defense of Rakutin's 24 Army was stiffer, but, even there, after forty-eight hours no further organized resistance was met. Yukhnov, a small saw-milling town on the Ugra about a hundred miles behind the enemy lines, was taken on 5 October by General Stumme's 40 Panzer Corps and not until the Mozhaisk line was reached, about twenty miles farther to the east and about sixty-five miles from the center of Moscow, was there any sign of enemy activity. On Stumme's left General von Vietinghoff's 46 Panzer Corps turned north towards Vyazma while General Kuntzen's 57 Panzer Corps protected the south flank.

The weather continued fine and clear and the countryside was bathed in the warm autumn sunlight. German success had been overwhelming in spite of a severe shortage of artillery ammunition, which had curtailed the preparatory bombardment and restricted the covering fire program.

To the north of the Smolensk-Vyazma axis the attack fell squarely on four armies of Konev's West Front. Strauss's 9 Army made the initial breakthrough but the northern envelopment on Vyazma was the task of Hoth's 3 Panzer Group.

Hoth had a mission hardly less onerous than that of Guderian in the south since he had a twofold commitment, to close in on Vyazma and join there the corps of Hoepner's panzer group so holding the encircled enemy between Yartsevo and Vyazma until the arrival of Strauss's and von Kluge's infantry corps, and at the same time to make a rapid advance north-eastwards on Kalinin and distant Rybinsk in support of the left flank of von Leeb's Army Group North. Kalinin was 100 and Rybinsk 180 miles north of Moscow.

Unlike Guderian and Hoepner, Hoth had two, not three, panzer corps, and these were not his own; both had been transferred to him from Hoepner's 4 Panzer Group near Leningrad. Hoth's original panzer formations remained scattered between the Baltic and the borders of the Ukraine. Corps had been redistributed to panzer groups and divisions to corps, leaving none with the formations they started with, so that, as Hoth was to comment, it was difficult to make head or tail of what was going on.[19] The two panzer corps had, however, only three panzer and two motorized divisions between them, and one of the corps, Reinhardt's 41 Panzer on the left, instead of being concentrated and keeping close contact with its partner, General Schaal's 56 Panzer, was directed on a divergent axis north-eastwards towards Rzhev and the upper Volga on the road to Kalinin.

Strauss's offensive started with a short artillery preparation and the blare of propaganda loudspeakers inviting the Red Army defenders to cross to the safety of the German prisoner of war cages. Resistance was much weaker than had been expected and at first it was thought that the enemy had withdrawn. The line was soon breached and, *to the Germans' surprise,* since they themselves had given no thought to the hard weather ahead, it was noted that the Russians had already begun to prepare their positions with overhead cover and stoves for the onset of winter. Many Red Army formations could be seen in the far distance leaving the field of battle, marching off in long columns, abandoning much of their equipment and making no attempt to throw out rearguards. The remainder of the Soviet formations still in the line were pinned frontally by Strauss's attacks, but one of the German infantry divisions marching north-east to cover Hoth's left flank suffered heavy casualties.

General Reinhardt, hearkening back to the halcyon days of the 1940 campaign in France when panzer divisions had two panzer regiments each, fought his panzer corps in two separate elements, one panzer and one motorized infantry, by forming the two panzer regiments of his two panzer divisions into one panzer brigade of two regiments. As resistance to the north of Reinhardt's sector, near Byelyi, showed signs of stiffening, Hoth directed Reinhardt to move his axis farther to the south to bypass the area and add impetus to Schaal's attacks in the early stages of the breakout. Reinhardt's panzer brigade began to move rapidly eastwards against scattered opposition to Kholm-on-Dnieper, where two bridges were seized intact on 3 October.

In the bright, clear skies the Luftwaffe reconnaissance and close support were excellent, and yet Hoth was to complain on 4 October of heavy Red Air Force activity.[20] Near Kholm the brigade was counter-attacked in strength by a Soviet tank division from the Far East, on the old style establishment and completely equipped with new American tanks. The tank formation, which had never been under fire before, was almost destroyed and lost sixty-five tanks in a few hours.

On 5 October 3 Panzer Group was in difficulty with its fuel supply and asked for an airlift, but this shortage of fuel did not prevent a panzer division of Schaal's force from cutting the Moscow highway near Vyazma and, two days later, joining with von Vietinghoff from the south. The armored pincers of Hoth's and Hoepner's panzer groups had accomplished their mission and four Soviet armies, two of the West and two of the Reserve Fronts, together with many other troops, in all nearly three-quarters of a million men, had been surrounded.

The capture of Vyazma itself was of considerable importance. For although this ancient city on the Vyazma River, dating from the eleventh century, had a population of only 30,000, employed for the most part in rural industries, tanning, flax milling and oil pressing, it formed in fact the hub of five main trunk railway lines, radiating in all directions, and was on the main enemy north–south lateral rail link.

Konev, the forty-four-year-old Commander of West Front, was of peasant Russian origin, a non-commissioned officer of the Tsarist Army who entered the Red Army as a political commissar, which he remained until 1927. He then transferred to command appointments, graduating from the Frunze Military Academy in 1934. Simple in his tastes, a thoughtful man, he read much and drank little, but, like most Russian commanders at that time, was harsh and exacting towards his subordinates but subservient to his superiors. He was a favorite of Stalin's.

Konev was subsequently criticized by Zhukov for failing to prepare his defenses near Smolensk and for a faulty deployment of his troops. Konev defended himself by attributing the German success to the massive air support by the Luftwaffe and the overwhelming strength of the concentrations of enemy tanks, in what was in fact the last of the great German *blitzkrieg* offensives of the Second World War.

As the Germans had deduced, the offensive had caught the Soviet West and Reserve Fronts entirely unawares.[21] At the beginning of October Soviet plans for limited attacks had been dropped and all troops went over to the defensive. Six armies of Konev's West Front and two of Budenny's Reserve Front were forward in the line, while a further four armies of the Reserve Front manned the Vyazma defenses about fifty miles to the rear. Except for the tank brigades, few of the troops were mobile and the Soviet defensive strategy was based on the obstinate holding of ground. Only at the very last moment was an attempt made to form a front reserve under Lieutenant-General Boldin, a deputy front commander, by withdrawing a number of divisions from the forward areas, possibly those same marching columns seen by Hoth retiring eastwards without deploying rearguards.[22]

By 2 October Strauss and Hoth had already penetrated between Lieutenant-General Lukin's 19 and Major-General Khomenko's 30 Armies. To meet this threat a very complicated Soviet regrouping took place within West Front in which Lieutenant-General Ershakov's 20 Army was ordered to take over the divisions of Major-General Rokossovsky's 16 Army; Rokossovsky's headquarters was pulled out to take command of all other troops in the area of Vyazma, while Khomenko's 30 Army was relieved by Major-General Dolmatov's 31 Army; other army headquarters were withdrawn, leaving their divisions *in situ*. It is not known exactly when this regrouping took place but there is more than a suspicion that it was aimed at the rescue of the higher commanders and staffs.

At about this time the Soviet field signals communications broke down.

Between 2 and 4 October the attention of Stalin and the Soviet High Command appears to have been still riveted on the danger from Guderian's breakthrough to Orel in the south. Lelyushenko was already in Mtsensk, and Artemev, the Commander of Moscow Military District, had been sent to Tula to organize the defenses there. It was known that the Bryansk Front was hard-pressed both frontally and

from the southern flank, but it was not realized that Eremenko's formations were encircled and on the point of breaking up.

On 4 October the Soviet monitoring service brought in reports
of the Berlin radio speech made the previous day by Hitler, the text of
which was similar to that of the order of the day already issued to
German troops, in which the Führer had announced the opening of the
general offensive which would finally destroy the Red Army. The
report of the speech mystified the Soviet High Command, since there
had been no news from Konev or Budenny of any heavy German
attack. This, however, was not surprising since telephonic communications with the West and Reserve Fronts had been broken, a fairly
reliable indication of a sharp reverse.

Early the next morning, on 5 October, some stragglers of the
administrative services of Budenny's Reserve Front arrived at Maloyaroslavets, these men reporting that the enemy had broken and encircled
parts of 24 and 43 Armies three days before; this information was
discredited and the men were arrested as panic spreaders.

Aircraft of a fighter regiment belonging to Moscow District were,
however, sent forward to reconnoiter the battle area. On their return,
at about midday, the pilots reported that great columns of German
tanks and motorized infantry were moving eastwards from Spas
Demensk to Yukhnov deep in the Soviet rear. Telegin, the political
member of the military council of Moscow District, telephoned the
information to Shaposhnikov who refused to credit it. A second and
then a third fighter reconnaissance flight were sent out to verify the
reports before the puzzled and doubting Shaposhnikov went to inform
Stalin. Within minutes Stalin was back on the telephone to hear in
Telegin's own words the latest intelligence. Only then was the situation
accepted.[23]

Later that day, line communication was temporarily re-established
to the Reserve Front. Budenny was missing, but Major-General
Anisov, the chief of staff, reported for the first time that the front was
under heavy attack and that the position was very serious. He was told
to withdraw to a new line about twenty miles east of Vyazma.

On 5 October, when Zhukov happened to be in the communications center at the Headquarters of Leningrad Front, he received a

message to telephone Stalin; he was told by the dictator to come to Moscow as the situation there was "somewhat complicated." He arrived in the capital two days later, and was taken by Stalin's bodyguard to the dictator's sickbed, for Stalin had influenza. Stalin wanted a clear picture of the battle situation and directed Zhukov to go to Mozhaisk himself and find out what had happened.

After collecting a battle map from the strained and exhausted Shaposhnikov, Zhukov motored westwards, trying to study his maps by the light of a pocket torch, stopping the car from time to time to walk about in case he should fall asleep. He found the Headquarters of West Front without much difficulty and was ushered in to the military council, Konev, Sokolovsky, Bulganin and Malandin, all sitting around a table in the candlelight looking pale and worn-out. Having heard the battle picture as it was known to them, Zhukov recounted it to Stalin by telephone, and suggested that all available reserves should be sent to thicken up the Mozhaisk line, eighty miles west of Moscow. He then set off in the direction of Maloyaroslavets to look for the Headquarters of Reserve Front, since no news had been heard of Budenny for several days.[24]

Leaving Konev at 2:30 in the morning, Zhukov went on southwards until, near a little settlement called Obsinskoye by the River Protva, he came upon two Red Army signallers laying telephone cable. The presence of signallers at work was always a guide to the location of higher headquarters, since only these were served with early line connections. But, when asked for the destination of the cable, the soldier, not recognizing Zhukov, at first replied in the surly and secretive fashion so common to Russian troops that "the cable would go where it had been ordered to go."

The detachment proved, however, to be part of the Reserve Front Headquarters which had just left the location two hours before. Zhukov found the headquarters but not Budenny, who was presumed to be somewhere in the area of Sobennikov's 43 Army, the same formation which had taken the brunt of Hoepner's attack. Anisov, the chief of staff, and Army Commissar Mekhlis, detached to the Reserve Front as Stalin's personal representative and observer, could give no concrete information as to the situation. Budenny, they feared, was lost.

Zhukov left them poring over their maps, with Mekhlis making the necessary arrangements to net, re-arm and re-form the fleeing stragglers. No man could do it better. A Jew, once a clerk and formerly Stalin's secretary, who had no compunction in advising the dictator to have formation commanders shot, Mekhlis was feared and disliked by his Red Army colleagues. He would allow no one even to see his signals which he himself laboriously and carefully drafted. So determined was he to keep Red Army commanders at their distance that he declined any social contact, even the drinking of tea with them.[25]

Maloyaroslavets, only sixty miles from Moscow, although it had an ancient charter as a city, numbered in 1941 only 10,000 inhabitants and was in fact a provincial railway town set in great fields of cherry orchards. It must have brought back memories to Zhukov, for it was there, twenty-five years before, that conscript Zhukov had first reported for military service. There recruit Zhukov, as he was being marched away from the town, had asked a cavalry non-commissioned officer for their destination, to be gruffly told, once more, that "they were marching whither they had been ordered to march."

Maloyaroslavets was dead, amost completely deserted except for two army cars which stood before the Central Administrative Building. Waking the driver of one, Zhukov found that the vehicle belonged to Budenny, who was inside the building setting up his maps.

Zhukov was of course well known to Budenny, particularly as he had once served on Budenny's staff when the latter was Inspector-General of Cavalry. Even in the present difficult circumstances the swaggering, empty-headed Budenny remained cheerful, replying in his peculiarly high-pitched voice that he knew little, not even the whereabouts of his own front headquarters; he said that Rakutin's 24 and Vishnevsky's 32 Armies were cut off and that he himself had narrowly escaped capture. He did not know who held Yukhnov (in fact Hoepner had taken it three days before) and when he had driven through Medyn, the tiny city was as silent as the grave. As far as he was aware, the only Soviet force known to him to be covering the great gap "consisted of three policemen."

Zhukov left the building and drove southwards along the Mozhaisk defended zone towards Kaluga, keeping a careful look-out since enemy panzer troops were known to be in the area carrying on a running fight with men of Sobennikov's 43 Army who were fleeing eastwards. He came upon, hidden up in the woods, a whole Red Army tank brigade which for two days had done nothing, in spite of the sounds of battle all around it, since it had been given no orders. Such lack of initiative was common during those days, and Zhukov instructed its commander, who, in spite of his lack of enterprise, was apparently a man of some worth, to put out reconnaissance vehicles to get information about the local situation and to send a liaison officer to front headquarters to ask for orders.

While still *en route* for Kaluga, Zhukov received the dispatch telling him that he had been nominated to the command of West Front by a GKO order of 10 October. When he reached his new headquarters, he found another Stalin-appointed fact-finding commission, made up of Molotov, Malenkov and Voroshilov, busy in West Front collecting information to be taken direct to the dictator.

And so the able and ruthless Zhukov took over the field command which was to bring him such fame.

In the field reorganization which followed, Konev was appointed as the Commander of the Kalinin Front, a new front raised to cover the great gap in the north between the North-West Front and Moscow caused by the destruction of the armies of West Front. Budenny's Reserve Front was to be incorporated into the West Front and all available forces concentrated on the holding of the Mozhaisk line.

Colonel S. I. Bogdanov, like Katukov later in the war to become famous as a colonel-general commanding the tank army which was to take him into Berlin, was given the task of preparing the Mozhaisk defenses for the arrival of the new troops. So few of these were available that, at the best, only the main routes eastwards could be covered.

There was no hope of extricating the Soviet troops entrapped in the Vyazma pocket. No reserves were available to relieve them and in any case all troops arriving to the west of Moscow were needed to man and develop the Mozhaisk line. It proved impossible to establish even radio contact with Lukin, the senior general inside the cauldron.

As soon as the infantry divisions of Strauss's 9 Army and von Kluge's 4 Army arrived in the area west of Vyazma, they began to break up the encircled enemy; communications and control inside the pocket had broken down and resistance was entirely uncoordinated. The battle lasted hardly a week and ended with the destruction of forty-five divisions and the loss of 673,000 prisoners. It is claimed that 1,200 tanks and 4,000 guns were taken inside the pocket. These figures are supported by contemporary German documentary evidence.[26]

On 7 October the OKH had issued another directive for the continuation of the offensive but this merely confirmed what had been said before: 9 Army and 3 Panzer Group were to take no part in the eastwards advance beyond Moscow, but were to continue to strike northwards and north-eastwards away from the capital. Far from being concentrated about the decisive point, the German armies were being dissipated over the breadth of Russia. Commenting on the directive, Reinhardt, who had replaced Hoth as Commander of 3 Panzer Group, suggested that his axis should be altered to due east towards the city of Klin, but this proposal was rejected by the OKH.

Since the good weather held in the north, 3 Panzer Group and 9 Army continued to have some success. 56 Panzer Corps was still engaged in holding the Vyazma cauldron, but on 8 October 41 Panzer Corps, under its new commander Model, together with 6 Corps of 9 Army, turned north-east. On 10 October the railway town of Sychevka was occupied although, during the fighting, part of 1 Panzer Division had been surrounded for some time by a Red Army counter-attack.

Numerous Soviet prisoners were taken and the routes were blocked by mile upon mile of abandoned trucks and guns. An airfield was seized on which *Ratas* were still landing. The Luftwaffe support and cooperation were excellent, von Richthofen, the Commander of 8 Air Corps, himself calling on many of the forward headquarters during the course of the battle in his Fieseler *Storch* light aircraft.

Because of the shortage, the remaining motor fuel was pooled in order to make a motorized infantry battalion, supported by a tank company and artillery battery, fully mobile. This motorized battalion group was detailed to make the thrust on the great city and industrial area of Kalinin, fifty miles to the north, and it made excellent progress during 12 October, the demoralized and panic-stricken Soviet enemy running away, leaving trenches and equipment at the sight of the armored personnel carriers. German tanks in the van nosed and pushed aside into the ditches the abandoned vehicles and guns which blocked the roads. Friend and foe rushed headlong through the dusk towards Kalinin which, after dark, could be clearly pinpointed a few miles to the north by the beams of its searchlights. The small German force's advance into Kalinin was delayed until the following morning; meanwhile Ju 52 transport aircraft brought urgently needed fuel supplies into a nearby airfield.

On the morning of 13 October the German infantry made towards the great railway bridge over the Volga just outside Kalinin; as they neared it the Red Army guard and demolition party took to their heels. Tanks and personnel carriers then crossed over the Volga and successfully established a bridgehead to the north of the river.

Kalinin, named in 1931 after the Tiflis locksmith who, at the start of the war, was the figurehead President of the Soviet Union, stood on the site of the ancient city and powerful principality of Tver, once a rival to Moscow, gaining much of its revenue in olden days by controlling the land porterage of Caspian and Baltic merchandise between the upper Volga and the River Volkhov. Originally founded on a twelfth-century fortress, it was burned down and rebuilt in the eighteenth century with wide and straight boulevards and streets crossing each other at right angles in a gridiron pattern.

In 1941 it remained the major river port on the upper Volga, the capital of the *oblast,* and a great industrial city with a population of nearly a quarter of a million. It was unprepared for defense and the handful of German motorized troops, sweeping through the broad avenues, captured it in a day. The distance from Vyazma to Kalinin was the same as that from Vyazma to Moscow.

Model was then ordered to prepare a further advance northwards from Kalinin, and Schaal's 56 Panzer Corps, still delayed in the area of Vyazma by mopping-up operations and the shortage of fuel, was to join him as soon as it could move.

By then, however, the weather had broken over much of the area and it continued to rain incessantly for days on end; slowly the German offensive came to rest in the mud. Infantry, advancing at a snail's pace, began to overtake the stranded panzer and motorized formations.[27]

In the south Guderian had hardly advanced a step since 7 October. On the far right flank of 2 Panzer Army, Kempf's 48 Panzer Corps, without a drop of vehicle fuel, lay in the mud to the south of Orel on its eastward route to Livny. The vehicles on which it depended for supply, for the most part two-wheeled-drive civilian wagons, were sunk up to their axles on the waterlogged roads. Geyr von Schweppenburg's 24 Panzer Corps, even when it had pooled all its fuel reserves, still could not take Mtsensk.

The supply and transport position in the rear of 2 Panzer Army was made the more precarious by the hordes of Red Army soldiery moving eastwards, stragglers from the Bryansk and West Fronts, and by the formed units and part formations which attempted to fight their way out towards the Mozhaisk line and freedom.

There was confusion everywhere. The woods were places to avoid, but many a pitched and bloody battle was forced on the slowly advancing German infantry who, goaded forward by the higher command, were at this time anxious to bypass resistance. At night the roar of engines and the clatter of Soviet tank tracks showed that the enemy at least still had fuel. The rapidly sinking German vehicle strength due to the severe going conditions, breakdown, lack of fuel and enemy action, robbed German formations of their mobility so that they became strung out over hundreds of miles and almost inextricably mixed with each other. The whole area from Trubchevsk to Bryansk was a rapidly changing battlefield with fierce independent engagements being fought back to a depth of 150 miles.

In the middle of this chaos three heavy Soviet bombers put down on an airfield occupied by 29 Motorized Infantry Division, having come to pick up Eremenko and the staff of the Bryansk Front.

Although Hitler was demanding movement north-east on the great industrial city of Tula, he was still obsessed with the gap on the right between Army Groups South and Center. As Kempf's 48 Panzer Corps could not move towards Elets and Voronezh, von Vietinghoff's 47 Panzer Corps was sent over from Guderian's left flank to the right, to join it. This transfer took time and much effort and it was obvious that, if one panzer corps could not be maintained with fuel in that sector, two were hardly likely to fare better.

Von Weichs's 2 Army was directed to join the two panzer corps after it had completed the liquidation of the encircled troops near Bryansk. 48 Panzer Corps was eventually transferred to von Weichs's command.

Meanwhile Guderian, by then reduced to two panzer corps, still sat on the Tula road just outside Mtsensk having established his own command post with Geyr von Schweppenburg's 24 Panzer Corps. Finally, after two days of heavy fighting in the extensive minefields, Mtsensk was taken on 24 October at the cost of considerable casualties in tanks. The slow advance by 24 Panzer Corps was then resumed towards Tula, mile upon mile of log corduroy road still being laid down behind it.

Yet at this stage Hitler had begun to lose interest in Tula and was giving serious consideration to abandoning the north-east axis in favor of a new one from Mtsensk to Voronezh, which was about 150 miles to the south, and he was only deterred from doing so by the absence of roads in that direction.

Guderian had reduced 24 Panzer Corps to the size of a panzer brigade by discarding all vehicles which could not be fueled; this brigade, under Eberbach, the regimental colonel, struggled on against mud and mines but comparatively light enemy resistance, arriving on 28 October at a point a few miles to the south of Tula; it had taken four days to cover fifty miles, remarkably fast going even for tracked vehicles considering the state of the ground. There Guderian was to learn of Hitler's latest instructions "for fast moving units to secure the Oka bridges east of Serpukhov."[28] These bridges lay yet another sixty miles to the north.

An attack into Tula in an attempt to seize the city by a *coup de main*, in the same way that Kalinin had been taken by Model, failed in the face of the determined resistance of a reformed 50 Army under Major-General Ermakov. German tank casualties were again heavy.[29]

At Geyr von Schweppenburg's urging all attempts at further movement were broken off until the frosts should set in, since it was possible to gain ground only very slowly and that at a great cost in wear and tear on vehicles and equipment. Some of the panzer detachments had only been kept on the move by fuel air-landed or air-dropped

by the Luftwaffe; the air transport allocated for this task had been
woefully small.

Von Weichs's 2 Army was still clearing up the area of the encircled
Bryansk Front near the Desna and had been left far behind the spearhead of the advance and out of touch with the main enemy. In the
second week in October, the clearing operations having been
completed, its three infantry corps began their long march eastwards
through the streaming rain and mud. The men were exhausted after the
break-in battles and mopping-up operations near Bryansk, but there
was no question of giving them even a few days' rest. Pursuit eastwards
was the order of the day. Tired and verminous and soaked to the skin,
boots and socks never dry, the infantry trudged slowly southeast from
Bryansk along the Orel highway.

Infantry was the only arm capable of moving by its own efforts,
even though this movement was hardly eight miles a day. With its few
possessions on its back it moved itself, fed itself and quartered itself by
living off the land, improved its own tracks and built its own light
bridges. Not only did it march, but it found the willing hands which
pulled the horses out of mud-filled shell holes and gullies, and provided
the heaving backs which got the ditched wagon wheels turning again;
yet without the horse the infantry itself would have been lost.

Most roads and tracks had disappeared and those remaining were
so few in number that several divisions were allocated to a single route,
this congestion slowing down the rate of march. No wheeled motor
vehicles accompanied the columns. Although the progress of the dismounted men was painfully slow, that of the horses in harness was even
slower. In the end the infantry companies were ordered on ahead and
they left behind them the vehicle-loaded stores, heavy radio and
ammunition and the horse-drawn anti-tank guns and artillery. Fleeter
of foot, they began to overtake other units and formations, no further
effort being made to keep to a march table, so that regiments and divisions became mixed and broken up.

The hamlets through which the columns passed were crammed
with German troops; too often the towns and bigger villages had been
destroyed in the fighting or gutted by the local inhabitants, who looted
all materials and fixtures which could possibly be carried off. For the

most part the troops remained out at night in the rain and the cold; sleep was out of the question. Although movement was not delayed by the enemy or by mines, it took von Weichs's marching infantry formations fourteen days to cover 125 miles. Even then, most of the equipment had been left behind.

By 26 October, when the van of 2 Army had reached the area between Mtsensk and Kursk, it was directed to thrust on Efremov, Elets and the area north of Voronezh. Von Weichs, having crossed Guderian's lines of communication from left to right, was moving away from him and could no longer cover the 2 Panzer Army right flank.

Immediately to the north of von Weichs's 2 Army, 52 German Infantry Division moved near the inter-army boundary towards Kaluga on the far southern flank of von Kluge's 4 Army. The formation had started from Sukhinichi, leaving the forest belt behind it, when, on 13 October, the rains began in earnest. The general service army carts were ditched because they were slung too low, and Russian farm vehicles were seized from the fields. The loads which could not be carried forward were abandoned and the remaining horses pooled in order to provide spare teams. Only two light guns in each battery were taken on, together with their limbers, each piece being dragged forward by ten horses, while the unharnessed animals brought up the rear.

Within two days the horses, up to the knees and sometimes the girths in mud, had lost their shoes, but in the soft going could manage without them. The infantrymen, whose calf boots were frequently sucked from their legs as they waded on, knee deep in water, were not so fortunate. Their boots were already in pieces. After the first day's march the horse-drawn guns and baggage, light though it was, could not keep up with the men, and the troops went rationless except for the tea and potatoes looted from the farms. No longer could they rely on the support of the gun and mortar in clearing up enemy resistance.[30]

Unwittingly, they longed for the coming of the front and the winter.

About 150 miles to the north, on the left flank of 4 Army sector, the fine weather in the first week in October had been followed, not by heavy rains, but by cold and frost. Some snow, the first of the year, fell on 7 October. Part of von Kluge's troops, together with Kuntzen's 57 Panzer Corps of Hoepner's 4 Panzer Group, started to close up towards the Mozhaisk line, preparatory to breaching it. Medyn, a small rural city in dairy farming country, had been taken on 11 October. Except on the frozen and slippery slopes, hard and cold weather made all movement relatively easy.

From the night of 7 October new Soviet formations were observed by Luftwaffe reconnaissance, moving westwards down the Mozhaisk highway to the new defense line only fifteen miles east of Medyn. This Mozhaisk defensive zone was truly formidable, having been organized in some depth both in front of, and behind, the system of great anti-tank ditches. Great skills and ingenuity had been shown in camouflaging minefields, obstacles and defenses; pill-boxes and tank turrets mounted in concrete were concealed by sheds, farm carts and piles of logs. The positions were well wired and in places provided with electrically detonated flame-throwers.

Kuntzen's 57 Panzer Corps was hurrying its preparations to breach the line while the cold weather lasted, when suddenly, on 13 October, it was violently counter-attacked by the Soviet 43 Army from the area of Borovsk, tanks and artillery being used in strength. The infantry 37-mm anti-tank guns were rolled flat by the oncoming KV and T 34 tanks, and the position was only restored by Luftwaffe intervention, by the *Stuka* dive-bombers and by the 88-mm flak guns.

Two days later 19 Panzer and 3 Motorized Divisions themselves went over to the attack. For the first few hours Soviet resistance was desperate, but the defensive zone was breached, not by the firepower or tanks but by dismounted infantry infiltrating through into the depth of the positions. When the defenders came under attack from the rear they lost their heads and fled and, in doing so, suffered heavy casualties. German tanks with infantry mounted on them emerged from the main defenses and rolled rapidly eastwards, covering forty miles by nightfall. Maloyaroslavets and Borovsk and the bridge over the River Protva were taken. In these rear areas the panzer corps passed thousands of Russian civilians, mostly women, still at work on the field defenses.

The next day, on 17 October, 43 Soviet Army, commanded by Major-General Golubev, a survivor of the Bialystok salient, who was a giant of a man with a forceful personality but limited intelligence, counter-attacked once more, this time on Borovsk. But the attack was less successful than that of a few days before, being uncoordinated and lacking fire support; it eventually broke down under the weight of German artillery fire and air attack.

The mobile element of 57 Panzer Corps, still consisting of a panzer and a motorized division, resumed its advance towards the River Nara only forty-five miles south-west of Moscow. But on 20 October the hard cold spell of weather gave way to thaw, the quickly melting layer of snow became deep slush, and movement slowly came to a halt. In spite of the open flanks and poor going, 57 Panzer Corps reached the Nara on 24 October and won a bridgehead on the further bank near Naro Fominsk. There it was joined by 15, 98 and 258 Infantry Divisions.

The enemy at first met in this sector was of low morale; many line crossers came into the German positions each day. Abandoned enemy equipment was plentiful and Soviet anti-tank guns were turned round to protect the position. On 25 October the Soviet enemy counter-attacked once more and overran a great store of spirits and alcohol; from that time onwards many of their number ceased to take any further interest in the fighting. Nearly 2,000 prisoners, many of them drunk or insensible, were rounded up on 28 October.

For the time being there could be no further German movement forward of the Nara as the supply position of von Kluge's 4 Army, like that of its neighbors, was rapidly deteriorating. An attempt by the army engineers to take into use the Soviet railway, as yet unconverted to Central European gauge, using horses to tow goods trucks, was of very little help.

The *rasputitsa* had reached its zenith. On von Kluge's left the main Moscow highway had become a closely packed graveyard for Russian vehicles and could not be used until the debris had been cleared. There was no fuel and no rations. 292 Infantry Division reported that a team of sixteen horses was unable to move a single howitzer of the divisional artillery.[31] The air stank of the putrifying carcases of dead horses. Motor vehicles could only move about a mile a day unless they were tracked, and a supply transport column took six weeks to cover 120 miles. When the Moscow highway was eventually taken back into use its surface soon began to break up, becoming so unroadworthy that between Gzhatsk and Mozhaisk over 2,000 German motor lorries stood for a week, unable to move forwards or backwards. Whole infantry divisions were allocated to traffic control, road repair and road clearing, rescuing vehicles and getting them on the move again.

Even when the railway gauge conversion was completed between Roslavl and Gzhatsk at the end of October, the capacity of the line was still low; even so, there was not enough road transport to clear the supplies as they arrived at the railhead.

33 Infantry Division to the north of the motorway was on the right flank of 5 Corps, which was itself the right-hand corps of 9 Army; the rain and thaw on 19 October had brought this division to a standstill. The infantry companies, although down to a strength of little more than thirty men each, trudged on to the east through knee-deep mud. Motor vehicles, wireless stations, heavy artillery and baggage were left behind between Klushino and Sereda. Some light guns were kept on the move, each piece and limber being dragged laboriously forward by no fewer than twenty-four horses. Surgeons with the field surgical teams were loaded into *panje* carts and sent forward with the infantry, and an effort was made to bridge the thirty-mile supply gap between the forward troops and the new railhead about to open at Gzhatsk, using pack animals and carts.

On 20 October the infantry were over the River Ruza against the lightest of resistance (that of Rokossovsky's 16 Army), the enemy being short of field guns but not of mortar and medium artillery ammunition. Between 24 and 26 October it appeared as if the whole Soviet defense was about to disintegrate and the ancient little fortress town of Volokolamsk was taken the next day. Four days later 35 Infantry Division, although it had just been reduced from three to two infantry regiments and was so very much understrength, had taken 1,800 prisoners and covered sixteen miles of the most difficult waterlogged country in five days. No further progress could be made until guns, ammunition and supplies could be brought up, and on 31 October a fortnight's pause was ordered.[32]

German movement for the first time during the course of the Second World War had been brought to a standstill, and, according to contemporary German accounts, it was halted during the second and third weeks in October by rain and mud. Soviet historians, on the other hand, scoffing at what they describe as German excuses, maintain that von Bock was halted by the valor and skill of the Red Army.

For the first two days of the German October offensive, the Soviet stand was, for the most part, determined and tough and was to show once more that given a spade and sufficient time for preparation, the Red Army soldier in defense was difficult to dislodge. But the Bryansk and West Fronts had been surprised and, once the defenses had been penetrated, the Soviet resistance rapidly collapsed. It was to stiffen again on the Nara and outside Tula.

There is, in fact, little doubt that the German advance, which at first promised to be as rapid and spectacular as any of those of the late summer, abruptly petered out because of the weather and state of the ground. In the first fortnight of the *Typhoon* offensive Army Group Center destroyed at least 700,000 of the Soviet defenders at little cost to itself and with another three weeks of dry and clear weather would have been in Moscow. No Russian could have stopped it.

German successes up to this time over the Polish, French, British and Soviet Armies had been brought about by the much superior mobility and firepower made possible by the massing of tanks and concentrations of tactical air forces, by good communications and by bold leadership. The key, however, was mobility. Once this mobility was removed, firepower was also lost and the German concept of *blitzkrieg operations* foundered.

The almost unbelievably disruptive *rasputitsa* in Russia halted the wheels and destroyed the horses. When the wheels stopped the tracks came to rest. The low cloud and poor visibility made difficult any form of sustained air offensive, or air transport support. In any case there was a shortage of all types of aircraft. Only the German infantry could get forward, and this without ammunition, equipment, food, clothing, warmth, shelter and medical care. Suddenly, almost overnight, the

Germans were to depend for success in their thrust on Moscow on the efforts of a number of unsupported, tired and understrength spearhead infantry battalions, while the rest of the great Wehrmacht fighting machine, the German Army and Luftwaffe, immobilized and grounded, stood powerless and idle.

CHAPTER FIVE

PANIC IN THE CAPITAL

O N 6 A N D 7 O C T O B E R, Stalin was frantically combing out reserves to fill the great vacuum left by the disintegration of the armies of the West and the Reserve Fronts. Troops had recently arrived from the Far East Maritime Territories and others were still *en route* on the Trans-Siberian Railway; in addition, Lieutenant-General Kurochkin's North-West and Marshal Timoshenko's South-West Fronts had been ordered to send a number of formations to the Moscow area.

By the second week in October fourteen rifle divisions, sixteen tank brigades and forty artillery regiments had been rushed forward to cover the main approaches on the Mozhaisk line under four reformed army headquarters which had suffered so severely in the recent fighting: Rokossovsky's 16 Army, which had earlier left all its divisions in the Vyazma cauldron, a new 5 Army under Lelyushenko, 43 Army under Golubev, and Zakharkin's 49 Army on the southern extremity of the defense line.[1] Zhukov had established his West Front Headquarters at Vlasikha, about fifteen miles due west of Moscow near the railway town of Perkhushkovo, where he had good direct signal communication with Stalin and the air and ground armies.

The Soviet population and the outside world were given little information as to what was really happening on the main battle fronts and the Kremlin bulletins were, to say the least, highly misleading. Most civilian radio sets had been called in by the militia at the start of the war and people relied for news on the press and street loudspeaker. In spite of the censorship it could not be disguised that the war was going very badly, and the Soviet population, no less than the Red Army, were very conscious of the German superiority in war.[2] The long string of failures left the people puzzled and distressed.

The High Command's and the Propaganda Department's claims of German losses and Soviet successes were hardly to be believed, for Stalin was to broadcast estimates of 4,500,000 German casualties in the first four months of the fighting, as against a Soviet loss of 350,000 dead and 378,000 missing.[3] Although *Pravda* on 7 October reported that "after a glorious and heroic struggle our troops have been forced to give up the city of Vyazma," the ignominious end of the larger part of the West and Reserve Fronts could not be concealed from the Muscovites, however skillfully the news was presented.

Towards the end of the second week in October a great panic spread through the capital and many of its inhabitants appear to have believed that the Soviet State was in the process of breaking up. Every night the German bombers were over the city.

The GKO, and this meant Stalin, ordered the evacuation of the diplomatic corps and many of the government ministries to far-away Kuybyshev in the interior; much of the industry was to be moved farther east. A large number of officials and their families, with or without permission, joined in the flight. Looting became widespread, the British Embassy being pillaged, and the police disappeared from the Moscow streets.[4]

Several months before, Stalin had taken the precaution of appointing Lieutenant-General Artemev, the Commander-in-Chief of the NKVD military forces, to the command of the Moscow Military District, it being a fairly common practice to replace Red Army commanders by NKVD men in sensitive posts which required unimpeachable loyalty and utter ruthlessness. Artemev, who was only forty-three at the time, had been a Red Army commissar in his youth before transfer in the late twenties to the NKVD border guards.

On the morning of 19 October Artemev received a summons to make a personal report to Stalin on the situation in the capital. His shadow, Divisional Commissar Telegin, who was a Red Army commissar and the political member of the Moscow District Military Council, was to accompany him.

The GKO was already in session, Pronin, the Chairman of the Moscow Soviet and Shcherbakov, the head of the Moscow party organization and a Secretary of the Central Committee, being present.

According to Pronin, Stalin had asked the GKO whether the government should stay in Moscow but the dictator answered his own question when he said that it should; this being the case there was little discussion and no argument.

When Artemev and Telegin were summoned they could feel the tension in the air and it was obvious that Stalin was angry. The members of the GKO sat at the long table fearful, subdued and silent. Stalin paced up and down irritably. He gave the newcomers no greeting but snapped at Artemev to report; asked for suggestions, Artemev recommended that a state of siege be proclaimed in the capital and to this Stalin agreed.

When Malenkov, a member of the Politburo, started to read a long and wordy draft of a proposed proclamation Stalin became impatient, ripped the papers out of his hands and began to dictate his own orders to Shcherbakov. Having read and agreed on his draft, the notes were then given to Poskrebyshev, Stalin's secretary, for issue to the press and posting around the city the next day. Among other things the state of emergency provided for a curfew and authorized the shooting on the spot of offenders against the proclamation. Artemev was given other special powers to deal with the situation.[5]

Order was soon restored. Looters, rumor mongers, and panic spreaders, real or suspected, were handed over to the military field courts-martial; some offenders were shot. Artemev was made nominally responsible to Zhukov for the security of the capital (although it is doubtful whether this meant anything at all since Artemev got his orders from Stalin), the area sixty miles to the west of the Kremlin outside the city boundaries being Zhukov's sole responsibility.

Moscow, the capital of both the Russian Republic and of the Soviet Union, standing on the low rolling hills on both sides of the meandering Moskva River, had grown up around the Kremlin, the ancient fortress on the northern left bank, bounded on three sides by its old triangular crenellated wall. The city had extended concentrically from the twelfth century onwards, each ring of outer walls of the expanding city eventually being replaced by circular boulevards or ring roads. The other main streets ran out in a radical pattern from the center so that the street plan looked like a spider's web.

In 1935 a vast reconstruction project had begun, excavating the underground metro railway, widening the streets and building arterial ring roads around the city. The population in 1941 was just over four million and the metropolis was the transportation hub of the West Russian rail and road net.

In 1937 the Moskva-Volga canal had been completed, largely by forced labor, and ran due southwards from Ivankovo at the east end of the great Volga reservoir about sixty miles north of the capital, past Dmitrov and Iksha, climbing the marshy Klin-Dmitrov ridge by a pumping system and a number of locks each of which formed a series of reservoirs. From the Khimki reservoir in the north-west city suburbs the canal descended again by means of further locks to the Moskva River west of Moscow. This canal, which was eighty miles long, had turned Moscow into a major inland port through which arrived oil from the Caucasus and coal from the Donets. The canal was to be an important feature in the defense of Moscow.

Hasty measures were taken inside the city to evacuate industry and expand the fire-fighting service and civil defense organization. Over 100,000 male inhabitants began part-time military training in addition to their normal daily work. Following the pattern of besieged Leningrad, twelve home guard divisions had been raised and these were incorporated into the military district; three were dispatched to the front where they were to go into action alongside the regular units.

On 12 October a secondary defense line had been decided on behind the Mozhaisk zone and three concentric fortified lines were developed ringing the capital from the west, the outer ring having north and south extensions along the Moskva River and the Moskva-Volga canal. Barricades were raised in the suburbs and the outskirts of the built-up areas.

During the second half of October Moscow was defended by three separate fronts: Konev's Kalinin Front in the north, Zhukov's West Front immediately west of Moscow and the remants of Eremenko's Bryansk Front to the south.

Konev's Kalinin Front stretched from the Ostashkov Lakes to the area south of Kalinin and was made up of Vostrukhov's 22 Army, 29 Army commanded by Maslennikov who, like Artemev, was an NKVD

General serving with the Red Army, Dolmatov's 31 and Khomenko's 30 Armies (three of them surviving armies of the right flank of Konev's former West Front), together with an operational group under Vatutin, the Chief of Staff of the North-West Front.

Zhukov's West Front stood on the Mozhaisk line and the Nara and had five armies in contact with the enemy, from north to south, Rokossovsky's 16, Lelyushenko's 5, Golubev's 43 and Zekharkin's 49 Armies. The fifth army, a new 33 Army under Lieutenant-General Efremov, had been raised in mid-October to cover the area on the Nara threatened by the advance of Kuntzen's 57 Panzer Corps. A new 26 Army under Major-General Kurkin, formed from Lelyushenko's earlier command of 1 Guards Rifle Corps and later to become famous as 2 Shock Army, stood in reserve.

Eremenko and the shattered divisions of the Bryansk Front were making their long and perilous march, some in formations and some as stragglers, due eastwards to Tula, Efremov and Elets.

Tula *oblast* lies about 120 miles to the south of Moscow and is part of the Central Russian upland, being drained by the great Oka River (a tributary of the Volga) to the north-east and the upper Don to the south-east. The *oblast* is partly forested but the woods decrease towards the south-east so that the countryside, which is slightly hilly, takes on the appearance of open downland, covered with wheat, potatoes, flax and sugar beet. The rivers and streams, here as elsewhere, have cut deep gullies and ravines into the soft soil. The area is rich in minerals, lignite and iron being mined in large quantities.

The city of Tula, which in the early sixteenth century was a forti-fied outpost to protect Moscow from the incursions of the Tartars, became an iron-working center at which Peter the Great, in 1712, built the first Russian armament center. Standing on the Upa, a tributary of the Oka, on a five-way rail center, by 1941 it had become a huge indus-trial complex with a population of over a quarter of a million, a center for the chemical, iron, steel, transportation and armament industries, its nearby deposits of lignite being converted both to fuel and gas.

When Guderian neared Tula towards the end of October there were only the remnants of three divisions of 50 Army in the area and these were said to have had a strength of less than 1,500 men each, as few as four guns remaining to one of the divisional artillery regiments. But in the control and administrative arrangements so peculiar to the Soviet Union the responsibility for reforming 50 Army was to rest not only on the GKO, *Stavka* and General Staff organization, but, more particularly, on the local Tula Party cadres.

As was the common practice, the city of Tula provided representatives to attend the 50 Army military council and take note and action on the formation's needs. Much was made good from local resources, including stores, clothing and, most important of all, recruits to swell the depleted ranks, these being inducted not through the military recruiting organization but simply detailed off by Party representatives from field and factory floor.

Tula city and district had regional defense committees commanding their own home guard levies and a great pool of labor organized, and sometimes armed, as workers' regiments. A military officer, Major-General V. S. Popov, later to serve with distinction as the Commander of 10 and 70 Armies, had been delegated to coordinate the static defenses and in this capacity was nominated to be a deputy commander to Ermakov's 50 Army.

The anti-aircraft artillery defenses were given alternative anti-tank tasks and these saved the city, for when Guderian's *Brigade Eberbach* attempted to take Tula by a *coup de main*, just as it had taken Orel before, it ran headlong into a Soviet 85-mm anti-aircraft regiment deployed in a ground role and lost over twenty tanks in almost as many minutes.

Towards the end of October it became obvious in Moscow that von Bock's thrust had lost its momentum and that the German troops were poorly equipped and supplied. Moscow, temporarily but much relieved, went about its business once more and Stalin started to draw formations out of the line for re-equipping and retraining. By 15 November a further 100,000 men, 300 tanks and 2,000 guns were routed to West Front. During that month Eremenko's Bryansk Front was broken up and its formations shared between the West Front and the South-West Front.

At the end of October the German troops on the Nara, on the approaches to Moscow, were in the most miserable condition. Only part of von Kluge's thirty-six divisions were in contact with the enemy, for, although the infantrymen themselves had closed up, all the heavier equipment was still stranded miles to the rear.

98 Franconian Sudeten Division, after its long 500-mile march from the Ukraine, had joined 4 Army just after the Vyazma battle and had fought its way forward from Maloyaroslavets, a point only sixty miles from Moscow, taking over the pursuit in the late October muddy period when 17 Panzer Division came to a halt near the Protva. There was heavy low cloud with continual rain and snow showers but, since the motorized formations had been left behind, the infantry enjoyed the nightly warmth of the miserable little hovels, while the panzer troops, stuck in the mud, wintered it out. It was weeks before some of these detachments got moving again and meanwhile, in danger of starving, they had their nightly fire fights with the many Red Army stragglers and the occasional partisans. Supply columns could only move if they had been lucky enough to get hold of captured Soviet tractors. The Red Army rearguards fought with skill and left numerous stay-behind parties in the scrub and forest. Resistance stiffened each day.

It is impossible to generalize on the fighting value of the Red Army in front of Moscow at this time. Except for their officers and cadres, many of the divisions were made up of peasants and factory workers hurriedly put into uniform; some of the conscripts were convicted criminals and political prisoners who had been pleased to exchange one garb for another. Many divisions had very limited fighting value at this time and some were no more than an undisciplined rabble.

And yet, other divisions arriving before Moscow were hardened veterans from the flanking fronts, or regular formations which had been in existence in the interior or in the Far East for many years. Some of them were first class troops. These divisions, although inferior to German mobile formations in fluid operations, were well trained in the more static type of fighting to which they had been committed on the Nara. So it came about that, whereas the panzer troops of 57 Panzer Corps were rounding up drunk and insensible Red Army prisoners of 43 Army in hundreds, their nearby neighbors in 98 Infantry Division were fighting one of the deadliest battles of their lives against the *élite* troops of 5 Soviet Airborne Corps.

It was 98 Infantry Division's grim fortune to be committed to hold the Nara bridgehead not far from the great monument of Tarutino on the Napoleonic battlefield of Borodino. On 25 October, at 8 A.M., the division was to take up the advance in order to clear a gap for 19 Panzer Division, which had just closed up, to penetrate to the Moscow highway.

The rifle companies of 289 Regiment, barely stronger than platoons, seized an undulating feature known as the Chernishnaya Height, but an immediate enemy counter-attack threw it off again. This would have been unheard of in the early days when German infantry could not be pried loose of their objective. 290 Infantry Regiment took up the attack supported by armored assault guns, but became separated from their armor and in their turn were driven off by hurrahing Bolsheviks.

The enemy began to probe in his turn, his thrusts being pushed home with such vigor and in such strength that intense rates of fire were called for to beat him off; the German troops became anxious as their ammunition stocks rapidly dwindled. The 98 Division itself resumed the attack once more and had to fight for every yard, slowly edging its way towards the Moscow highway. This it reached by dusk.

The increasing boldness of the enemy led 98 Division to believe that it was facing new and fresh formations, and the coming of darkness was awaited with trepidation. The night passed quietly, however. But 26 October was a day which all were to remember.

Daylight came with the usual heavy cloud and pouring rain. Then began a great Soviet artillery bombardment. German losses through enemy mortar and rocket fire were heavy and fighters and bombers dropped continually out of the clouds, bombing and machine-gunning the near-defenseless troops who were still not properly dug in. The divisional artillery, deficient in guns and ammunition, had to change position repeatedly because of the terrific weight of the enemy's counter-bombardment fire.

At eight o'clock in the morning a line of T 34 tanks, a type never met by 98 Division, came rumbling into the attack, closely followed by Red Army infantrymen. The Soviet artillery continued to pound the German positions, making it difficult to hear or see what was going on. Finally, as the tanks closed in on the village called Gorki, the defending infantry of a battalion of 282 Regiment leaped out of their weapon pits in panic and ran, leaving their wounded behind. This no unit would do unless *in extremis,* since German troops falling into Red Army hands were often brutally murdered.

A second German battalion was overrun by the oncoming T 34 tanks, the 37-mm anti-tank guns being flattened under the broad tank tracks, to the terror of the gun crews who kept them firing until the last moment. The tanks then clattered through the village crushing the houses like matchboard so that the living and the dead found a common grave under the rubble. Nor were the defenders able, as was so often possible on the Eastern Front, to separate Soviet tanks and accompanying infantry, as the parachute regiment, well trained and ably led, kept close behind the T 34s and used its great superiority in automatic weapons with devastating effect.

98 Division made good its losses by hurriedly reinforcing its battalions with engineers, signallers and clerks; the divisional anti-tank battalion was converted to infantry. But the position was not stabilized until the panzer regiment of 19 Panzer Division arrived in the area. 98 Division, as one of its officers noted in his diary at the time, had been burned to a cinder.

At daybreak on 27 October the Bolsheviks returned to the attack and, after an enormous expenditure of artillery, mortar and rocket ammunition, launched tank and infantry attacks against the German defenders, whose infantry companies, led by second lieutenants or sergeants, sometimes numbered no more than twenty men. The attack penetrated along the regimental boundary between 289 and 290 Regiments and something like panic broke out again. A calm and unruffled regimental colonel appeared on the scene and the men returned to their positions. The German failure lay in the lack of good anti-tank guns but, when a few 88-mm flak guns were brought forward, these, handled boldly and coolly by their crews, soon began to pick off the T 34s. The German infantry breathed again. Even a few Luftwaffe fighters appeared overhead.

Undaunted by its losses, the enemy 5 Airborne Corps of 43 Army renewed the attack at midday. Once more the tanks broke into the forward infantry positions and milled about trying to grind in with their tracks the German infantrymen who were cowering in their weapon pits. This time the tanks had outrun the Red Army infantry and they caused few losses to the German defenders. Meanwhile, several of their number were hit by long range flak fire and blew up or burst into flames; the remainder then withdrew, to the great relief of the sheltering German infantry.

The third attack was the heaviest of the day and was launched just before dark, by tanks and infantry in line. This time the German defenses were well coordinated and the attack was driven off by artillery, flak and tank gun fire, with heavy losses to the attackers, before it could reach the forward defended localities. The effect of this co-ordinated fire was shattering; tanks were left burning and the enemy dead lay in heaps where the machine-guns had torn great holes in the advancing ranks. Yet that day the division itself lost 50 dead and 175 wounded, equivalent to the loss of a battalion. By 28 October it was obvious that the Soviet counter-attacks had spent themselves.

The divisional supply arrangements, meager though they were, were dislocated even further by the violence of the Soviet artillery harassing fire and the air attacks in the rear areas, these making the German ammunition re-supply difficult and sometimes impossible. On 30 October, after a few hours pause, the heavy rain began again and continued without stop for the next three days and nights, filling all the weapon pits with water. Some days the troops went rationless. One officer was to comment that the troops held grimly on to life only forty-five miles from Moscow, and was to wonder whether other formations were in such a wretched state as they. The positions lacked depth and had no reserves; so few men remained in the ranks that, come what may, forest fighting was to be avoided at almost all costs.[6]

Soviet prisoners were in incomparably better condition and better equipped than the German troops, who, bearded and filthy—it was months since they had last bathed or changed their clothes—lay cramped and stiff and tormented by lice in their narrow water-filled weapon pits; any daylight movement brought down heavy enemy artillery fire. Their feet were so cold and numbed that they lost all feeling. Yet it was the losses, not the danger and hardship, which caused the lowering of morale. And, as soon as the fighting stopped the sickness rate rose. For in the thick of battle the *Landser* had no time to think of his ills and a sense of duty and comradeship kept him in the ranks long after he should have left.

On 2 November a regimental commander reported that his troops had no further fighting value, and that day two regiments of the division were withdrawn from the line. The division was temporarily reorganized on a six batallion basis, and 13 and 14 Companies of each regiment, the artillery and anti-tank companies, became infantry platoons.

On 5 November the army commander, Field-Marshal von Kluge, visited the division in order to find out for himself its fitness for battle; he was forced to agree that it needed re-equipping, reinforcing and a minimum of four weeks rest before it would be really fit for offensive operations once more. But since the condition of the formation was in fact no worse than that of many other divisions, and because reinforcements and new equipment were not available anyway, there was little to be done. Meanwhile the regiments enjoyed their well-earned but uneasy few days' rest, the last rest which they were to have for the winter.[7]

The attempt by 3 Panzer Group to penetrate north of Kalinin had failed and on 28 October Hitler decided to support it more closely by bringing 9 Army further to the right. Instead of moving northwards towards Valdai, Strauss was to take the north-eastwards axis parallel to that of 3 Panzer Group on Rybinsk and Yaroslavl. These two objectives lay about 170 miles to the north-east of Moscow.

That same month the Führer removed from Army Group Center Kesselring's 2 Air Fleet Headquarters and a number of air formations, all of which he sent to Sicily. At the same time a German infantry corps and the East Prussian cavalry division were withdrawn from von Bock and returned to Western Europe. Yet in a German High Command paper prepared on 6 November, which if anything understated the seriousness of the position of the troops on the Eastern Front, the 101 infantry divisions in the East (outside Finland) were reckoned to have a fighting effectiveness no greater than that of sixty-five divisions at near-establishment strength. The seventeen panzer divisions had been reduced to the effectiveness of six. The force in Russia, which numbered 136 divisions according to the order of battle, had a fighting strength equivalent to only 83 divisions.[8]

Soviet resistance had been uneven, but in front of Tula and on the Nara, where new formations were arriving, it had been most determined and tough. To the north of Moscow it had been insignificant particularly in the area of Volokolamsk, the Caucasian cavalry there giving themselves up in large numbers. The Red Army suffered, of course, the same problems of movement as did the Germans but, whereas von Bock was at the end of a thousand-mile-long line of communication with a railway which had a potential of only sixteen trains a day against a maintenance requirement of thirty-one, with only part of his available strength in contact, the Red Army had fallen back to within forty miles of its main bases, sustained by the great reserves of Muscovite manpower. Any conditions which inhibit movement must favor the defense.

It would be entirely wrong to attribute the German failure solely to the weather or misfortune; the main failure was that of misjudgment and mistiming. The offensive had been mounted too late in the year, at a season when the weather was due to break up. A secondary cause was the lack of understanding of the effects on mobile operations of the weather and the ground, and the third was the ever-present problem of inadequacy of resources. Too much had been asked of German troops, and strengths had been allowed to drop too low.

Meanwhile in the Soviet hinterland nine new armies had been raised during October and November, these being deployed on a line Lake Onega, Yaroslavl, Gorki, Saratov, Stalingrad and Astrakhan. Two complete armies and parts of another three were to reach the Moscow area towards the end of November.[9] Many of the divisions in these armies were raised from newly inducted recruits, but some were well trained and equipped and had been withdrawn from the military districts in Central Russia and Siberia. In order to move and concentrate these troops behind the West Front the whole of the Moscow railway complex was put entirely under military control. According to the Soviet account, large numbers of military trains ran from Tomsk,

Omsk, Sverdlovsk and Kuybyshev, without stopping to change locomotives or crews, covering between 500 and 600 miles a day.[10]

In October and early November the *rasputitsa* had brought all Red
Army wheeled motor vehicles to a halt, and Khrulev, the Quartermaster-General, could only do what the Germans had already done,
replace motor vehicles first by horses and carts, and later by horse-
drawn sleigh trains. This caused some caustic comment from commanders and men. When Khrulev asked Stalin for permission to form
seventy-six horse transport battalions, each of 250 wagons, the dictator
asked sarcastically "why, in an age of technology, the Soviet Union
must resort to oats, wagon drivers and sleighs." But he agreed to
Khrulev's proposal, nevertheless.

The problems caused by the shortage of transport, the weather and
the ground were readily recognized by the Soviet High Command and
seven days' rations, six refills of vehicle fuels and three first lines of
ammunition were dumped with the forward troops.

Defenses were restored and thickened up and Moscow awaited the
second stage of the German offensive which it knew must follow at the
end of the *rasputitsa*.

CHAPTER SIX
RETREAT TO THE EAST

O N 4 N O V E M B E R Halder, the Chief of General Staff, soberly noted that the German casualty figure, rising more steeply, stood at 686,000 men, of whom 145,000 were dead and 29,000 missing. Of the remainder, the wounded, about two-thirds could expect eventually to return to duty.[1]

Halder had been in hospital, in nearby Lötzen, having injured himself a month previously in a fall from a horse, but on 4 November he returned to his office and his diary. The meticulous and careful Halder recorded the details of all business, visits and telephone calls, together with his impressions and thoughts, in his own secret notebook which he wrote up daily in a form of shorthand (Gabelsberger Schrift) and kept secure in his safe. This must have put him in a very strong position in his day-to-day dealings with the Führer and his colleagues, for unlike them he never relied on the uncertainties of memory.

Halder, as was his custom, noted down the overall situation on the Eastern Front. Von Rundstedt's Army Group South had lost contact with the enemy and most of it was stuck in the mud, except for von Kleist's 1 Panzer Army which was about to renew its thrust along the Black Sea coast towards Rostov. In the distant north, von Leeb was making his way slowly to the bauxite-producing area of Tikhvin and towards the Finns on the Svir. In Army Group Center there was no great change except that Guderian had lost all contact with the enemy on his right flank to the south-east of Tula.

The whole situation, Halder commented, had been governed by the supply situation, the lack of capacity of the railway and the road transport service. There was no point, he thought, in just pressing forward blindly, and any subsequent advance must be made step by step after building up a solid foundation; failure to do this might result in a dangerous reverse. He was puzzled at the vacuum which had appeared in front of the boundary between Army Groups Center and South and wondered whether it might indicate an enemy withdrawal to the east of the Don. He had noted, too, the press reports which spoke of the movement of the Soviet government out of Moscow to Kazan [sic].

Halder wracked his brain for a solution to the problem of how to regain mobility in the east and speedily occupy "those areas which were being evacuated by the enemy." Pursuit *kommandos,* even armored trains, came to his mind.

That same day von Brauchitsch returned from a visit to the headquarters of Army Group South at Poltava, where he had been pressed by von Rundstedt to give up all attempts to reach, that year, the lower Don and its tributary, the Donets. In reply von Brauchitsch had merely echoed Hitler's view and had said, somewhat breezily, that the difficulties in the supply situation were well understood but that it was necessary for Army Group South to take Voronezh, Maikop and Stalingrad as quickly as possible. Since two of these objectives were still more than 300 miles away von Rundstedt voiced his doubts so firmly that von Brauchitsch returned to Rastenburg convinced that the Commander of Army Group South was tired and unwell.[2]

The reports from von Leeb's Army Group North matched those from Army Group South. The supply system had failed. If the troops had not managed to live off the country by looting potatoes and killing horses, they would have starved.

The next day General of Panzer Troops Kuntzen, the Commander of 57 Corps from Army Group Center, the same corps which a week before had so successfully breached the Mozhaisk defensive zone and driven through to the Nara, made a routine call on Halder. The Chief of General Staff was unfavorably impressed by Kuntzen's somber and gloomy *(düster)* outlook and he came to the conclusion that Kuntzen was overtired. Yet the problems were clear for all to see and, during these first few days of November, they all reflected the origins of the coming crisis.

Von Bock telephoned, complaining bitterly about the lack of Luftwaffe air support, a shortage caused by the removal of Kesselring's 2 Air Fleet Headquarters and 2 Air Corps to Sicily and by the withdrawal of other air formations for rest and refit. The Red Air Force, on the other hand, he said, had become both strong and aggressive. Following this telephone call, Paulus, the Director of Operations, who, until a few days before, had been engaged in drawing up plans which would have taken the German Army into Iran, was ordered by Halder to transfer his attention to the more immediate problem of tactical air support in front of Moscow. But he could get little satisfaction from Colonel-General Jeschonnek, the Chief of Air Staff, concerning air transport, air reconnaissance or anti-aircraft defense. So von Bock went without.

Even though a number of infantry divisions had been reduced from nine to six battalions, there were insufficient reinforcements to bring this reduced number of battalions up to war establishment unless twenty divisions were disbanded.

Although the OKH remained uninformed on the likely enemy intentions, an underlying theme of optimism was apparent; the General Staff was obviously expecting, and looking for, a Red Army withdrawal in depth over most of the Eastern Front; for the German High Command was inclined to take its cue from the Führer's thoughts rather than from the appreciation of its own intelligence staffs. There was no apparent sign of an enemy in front of von Reichenau's 6 Army or Hoth's 17 Army, and little in front of von Weichs's 2 Army, but these German armies were still stuck in the mud and could not move forward even to reconnoiter. The situation on Guderian's eastern flank continued to be puzzling. And as for what was happening deep in the enemy rear, German intelligence itself was very much in the dark and could produce little to confound the views of the theorists.

On 9 November Kinzel's Foreign Armies East department received through radio intercept intelligence that there were five Soviet armies in the Caucasus; this the perplexed Halder simply could not credit. The doubting Chief of General Staff became prey to the most improbable surmise, wondering whether these were British divisions moving in from the Middle East and serving as part of Red Army higher formations.[3]

Winter clothing and equipment had been ordered for only a third of the troops on the Eastern Front and this had not reached the field formations because of the breakdown in transport. Halder was forced to accept that the clothing would not arrive at Army Group South until January, and that von Bock's Army Group Center would not get it until the beginning of February.

On the morning of 10 November, von Brauchitsch was suddenly struck down by a serious heart attack. Halder was left on his own and had to decide on the advice which he should offer to the Führer, should such advice be asked for.

Long meetings followed between Halder and his advisers, each of them having long telephone consultations with their opposite numbers at the army groups. Finally Halder came to a number of important conclusions. Although Army Group South might be in a position to resume the attack by the beginning of December, there could be no question of an offensive towards the Maikop oilfields in the Caucasus until the beginning of January. Von Bock's Army Group Center, he thought, could not possibly resume the attack before the end of November or the beginning of December because of its precarious supply situation.

Having cleared his own mind, Halder, on 11 November, discussed the situation with von Bock and von Greiffenberg, the Chief of Staff of Army Group Center. Differences of opinion immediately arose on three counts: the timing of a possible resumption of the offensive, its objectives, and the employment of Guderian's 2 Panzer Army.

Halder insisted that too early an offensive, before adequate preparations had been made, could be dangerous, but even he, the cautious Bavarian, still had his eye firmly fixed on the distant *operational* objectives two hundred miles to the enemy rear.

Von Bock, on the other hand, was quite sure that even the line Ryazan–Vladimir–Kalyasin was no longer attainable and he was doubtful even, in view of the condition of his troops, whether a much closer line could be reached. He had given his army group the provisional objective of the line River Moskva and the Volga canal, this taking in the Russian capital and its suburbs. Army Group Center was not yet in condition, he told Halder, to attempt even this limited mission until more ammunition arrived with the field formations, for it had proved impossible to stockpile any reserves by rationing the artillery, since there was, in any event, little enough to beat off the many Soviet probes.

Yet, as against this, von Bock could not agree with Halder's view that no advance should be made until the forward troops had been re-supplied and refitted to a satisfactory condition. There was a very grave danger, the army group commander said, that the oncoming of winter would find Army Group Center in its present exposed position and that heavy snow might put an end to all movement. The advance must be resumed as soon as the ground hardened and some ammunition could be got up. It was important, too, emphasized von Bock, to stick to close tactical objectives; artistic and fanciful deep envelopments were already out of the question.[4]

Von Bock remained convinced that Moscow, and only Moscow, must be taken. Hitler, on the other hand, was entirely dissatisfied with von Bock's views, which he regarded as unjustifiably pessimistic, and he made plain his lack of confidence in the Army Group Commander when he ordered a subordinate officer, von Kluge, who was no friend of von Bock's, to visit Rastenburg to report on conditions. On his return from East Prussia on 30 October von Kluge gave to his army group commander the details of the meeting he had had with the Führer, telling him that the dictator was disturbed that Moscow had not already fallen and simply could not credit the written reports of von Bock's staff. Not without reason Hitler considered it amazing that the difficulty of climate and movement should not have been foreseen.

Von Bock's only solace was to censure Hitler (in the privacy of his own diary), blaming the Führer's decision of the previous August when he had turned away from Moscow into the Ukraine, for, said von Bock, "stuck in the mud as he now was, the capital might as well be 600 kilometers away."[5]

As far as is known, there was only one firm and confident voice which spoke out, on 26 October, against resuming the attack and in favor of an immediate withdrawal 150 miles to the rear. Surprisingly enough, it was Hoepner's. Yet that dashing cavalryman and distinguished panzer leader had a reputation, even among his daring fellows, for *élan* not far removed from recklessness.

The position to the south between Tula and Voronezh was both confusing and disquieting, for Guderian had suddenly been attacked in great force from the east flank and was fighting to hold his ground.

Yet to his south von Weichs and von Reichenau were still out of contact with the enemy.

How Guderian's force could be used as part of the new German offensive was uncertain. Although it was meant to be a fast-moving wing which would envelop Moscow from the south and the rear, 2 Panzer Army had little armor and had already assumed the characteristics of an infantry army, having taken permanently under its command a number of infantry corps. And, if it was to make the rapid advance required of it in the November offensive, it would first have to disengage and shake off its attackers; Army Group Center doubted whether Guderian could do this. Halder consoled himself with the thought that the eastward thrusts of von Kluge's 4 Army from the Nara, in the center, would not depend on the success of Guderian's 2 Panzer Army; but in this view he was, in all probability, wrong.

At eight o'clock on the night of 11 November, Halder, having visited the sick von Brauchitsch to give him an outline of events, left by special train from the nearby East Prussian railway station of Angerburg for a conference at Orsha, near Smolensk, accompanied by Wagner, Buhle, von Grolman and Gehlen (both of the operations department). Halder intended to meet the formation chiefs of staff in order to get a clearer picture of the position on the ground, but there was in fact no question of varying the scope and aims of the coming operation, since Hitler had already laid these down.

The meeting, which lasted all day, was presided over by Halder and was attended by von Bock and the chiefs of staff of the army groups and of all armies except 1 Panzer Army.

According to the General Staff appreciation which was issued to those present, the arrival of the cold weather would allow the German troops to go forward rapidly once more and secure positions from which the war could be waged with success during the winter and coming spring. The enemy, it said, no longer had sufficient troops to form a continuous front from the Black Sea to Lake Ladoga, and it appeared likely that the Russian would defend only the area of Moscow and the Caucasus, although he might of course try to hold the line of the Don simply as a lateral communication between these two vital areas. The Soviet Union, so the OKH believed, might possibly be able to raise and equip a further fifty divisions.

The operational objectives dictated *(diktiert)* by Hitler, according to this General Staff appreciation, were set out as a maximum and a minimum line, the maximum stretching as far east as Maikop, Stalingrad, Gorki and Vologda, about 250 miles east of Moscow, and the minimum from the lower Don to Tambov and Rybinsk, about a hundred miles beyond the capital. The overrunning of these areas would, it was thought, remove from the Soviet Union its last remaining armament and industrial area capable of providing the equipment needed to put new formations into the field. The OKH realized, the document stressed, the burden which these demands would make on the troops, but all the risks had been carefully weighed; it had been thought preferable to attack the severely weakened enemy now rather than await the coming of the New Year when the foe would be re-organized, rested and re-equipped. To attack him then would bring much heavier German casualties.

At its face value the General Staff appreciation seemed to have logic on its side. Moscow was the nodal point of the railway net and its loss would be a severe blow to the Soviet Union, which would undoubtedly regard the region as of the greatest importance. Yet, as against this, the seizing of the capital alone would not in fact have completely dislocated the railway system, as lateral lines remained which would connect north and south; it was for this reason that the Führer had placed such stress on advancing beyond the capital and seizing the great triangle Moscow-Vologda-Saratov, since this would mean a complete loss of the rail connections between the main theaters of operations, the Urals, the Caucasus and the incoming Anglo-Saxon aid. The weakness of Hitler's strategy was that it was not related to the conditions on the ground.

Wagner, the Quartermaster-General, and Eckstein, the *O Qu* representatives with Army Group Center, had to admit that there could be no guarantee of supply and maintenance. This, not unnaturally, was ill received by the listeners. Some of those present protested that they doubted that the far-flung objectives were in the least attainable, von Liebenstein, the Chief of Staff of 2 Panzer Army, pointing out that the month was not May and 2 Panzer Army was not in France. He himself thought that the tanks could not roll the few miles to Venev. Von Bock still wanted to get to Moscow as quickly as possible but did not think that he would get beyond it, and he won over the prudent Halder to his view that the offensive must be resumed without further delay as soon as the ground had hardened and sufficient gun ammunition could be got up.[6]

The fighting ability of the Russians was still underestimated; and the further removed from the battle front, the more sanguine did German opinions become. No General Staff consideration appears to have been given to the possibility of a disengagement by Army Group Center and a general withdrawal.

The document presented by Halder was in fact a *Führerbefehl* rather than a General Staff appreciation and in it Hitler was insisting on reaching the same objectives which he had descrribed to the OKH some months before. He had changed none of his views. Halder and the General Staff merely had the task of presenting Hitler's requirements in a logical and rational light. At the end of this conference Halder, von Bock and von Greiffenberg said that they were in favor of an immediate resumption of the offensive and Halder summed up the view of both the German High Command and Army Group Center when he said that the resumption of the offensive was a better solution than spending the winter on the open wastes *(die Überwinterung in der Einöde).*

Yet on the German side, for the first time during the whole war, a feeling of approaching crisis was to be noted, even at army group level, since it was obvious that the Red Army, in spite of its very heavy losses, still had a very good railway net, an efficient supply system and plentiful reinforcements and resources. Nor were the intelligence experts inside the OKH itself unaware of the growing danger, for they had gained no credit for their estimates of the enemy. They had become very cautious. Kinzel, the head of the Foreign Armies East intelligence directorate, which specialized on the Red Army, had had good reason to alter some of the opinions which he had expressed a year before on the strength and effectiveness of the Soviet armed forces.

On 4 November Kinzel put out an intelligence appreciation disagreeing with the view once held in Thomas's *Rüstungsamt* that the

Soviet economy would not be in a position to produce new equipment for its forces before the summer of 1942, and he gave as his belief that by May the Red Army would be able to re-equip thirty cavalry and 150 rifle divisions "together with a number of new tank formations using United States or English equipment."

Before the end of the year Kinzel was to issue a rewrite of the German Army Handbook on the Soviet Armed Forces which bore little relationship in its assessment to that put out a year before. The Red Army, it said, had been made into a fighting force serviceable to a degree which would not have been thought possible before the war. What was most astonishing was not its numerical strength but rather the great stocks of available weapons, equipment, clothing, tanks and guns, stocks far exceeding those previously held anywhere else in the world. German intelligence was frankly surprised how quickly the Soviet High Command recognized and remedied its own weaknesses, and the handbook admitted that it had hitherto underestimated Soviet organizational powers and the ability of the government, the High Command and the troops in the field to overcome their difficulties by improvisation.[7]

General Georg Thomas of the OKW *Wi Rü Amt,* too, had completely changed his views, for in a report dated 2 October he said that even if the Gorki industrial center and the Baku oilfields were lost to the USSR the Soviet position would not be disastrous. Only when the Urals were taken, he thought, would the Soviet Union begin to break up.[8]

These second thoughts and doubts were shared by Fromm, the Commander of the Replacement Army, who, although not a strong character, was a highly intelligent man whose appointment gave him some insight into German losses and needs. During November he was tentatively and timidly to suggest to von Brauchitsch that the time had come to make peace proposals to Moscow. The reaction of the High Command was one of scorn.[9]

Hitler appears to have had no doubt as to the future success of the resumption of the offensive and, in order to ensure the cooperation of the half-hearted, he expressly forbade the preparation of any rearward defensive positions for use in case of failure. Von Brauchitsch, who had left his sickbed, had become infected with the impatience of the Führer, and began to goad the field commanders forward. Even Halder shared von Bock's conviction that the Russian was weaker than the German and that success was a matter of willpower and the throwing in of the last reserves.

Yet Halder did not leave the Führer in ignorance of the difficulties at the front. On 19 November he told a long tale of gloom. The railway situation was catastrophic, particularly as the sudden spell of cold weather had put the German locomotives out of action. Of the half million motor trucks on which the German Army relied, thirty percent were beyond repair and a further forty percent awaited overhaul. Only thirty percent were still on the road. Army Group South was said to be at a standstill because of the weather and the failure of supplies, and, as Halder moved from theater to theater and sector to sector round the Eastern Front, the same telling words "failure of supplies" and "insufficient strength" were repeated.[10]

The new offensive was subsequently to become known in Germany as a retreat to the east *(Flucht nach vorn)*.

Hitler's former ideas of directing 9 Army and 3 Panzer Group northeastwards on Rybinsk had changed again in favor of an advance eastwards to the Moskva–Volga canal about thirty miles to the north of Moscow, in order to protect the left of von Kluge's 4 Army. To the south of the capital Guderian's 2 Panzer Army, after seizing the great industrial area of Tula, was to take Kolomna on the Oka Rier with its great railway factories before striking northwards and encircling Moscow from the east. Von Kluge's 4 Army, together with Hoepner's 4 Panzer Group, was to advance east from the Nara, skirting Moscow from the north.

2 Army on the extreme right had to cover the far southern flank and move on the industrial cities of Livny and Elets, so that it really took no part in the actual Moscow operations.

Although the temperature had dropped to zero at the beginning of November, hardening the ground and enabling the wheels to move once more, it was expected that the formations would take a fortnight to close up. Strauss, Reinhardt and Hoepner on the northern wing were to be ready to attack on 15 November; 2 Panzer Army forming the southern wing was to take up the offensive two days later. It was hoped that these German attacks on the two flanks would take some of the growing Red Army pressure off von Kluge's 4 Army in the center and so enable him to go over to the attack as the third phase of the operation, *for which no date had been set.*

Von Weichs was ill and his place as Commander of 2 Army had been taken temporarily by General Rudolf Schmidt, formerly the commander of 39 Panzer Corps. Schmidt's new command consisted of two infantry and one panzer corps, and he started eastwards from the area of Orel and Kursk in order to close up towards the upper Don, behind which, it was wrongly believed, the enemy had retired.

There was of course a shortage of petrol, all types of ammunition and anti-tank weapons. But even the common necessities of life were missing, without which a soldier rapidly became almost totally ineffective. Spades, picks, entrenching tools, saws, vehicle and mechanics kits, technical equipment and mobile machinery were beyond repair or had been lost. Nothing was being replaced. Guns, radio and vehicles stood derelict awaiting spare parts. The miserable troops were still in their threadbare and filthy summer uniforms which gave no protection from the icy and biting winds. There had of course been no issue of winter equipment, underclothes, boots, gloves or other clothing, nor were there any white camouflage smocks.

As Rudolf Schmidt's men started their march eastwards in a temperature of minus 20 degrees centigrade, the heavy snow storms and driving wind soon filled hollows and ditches. Great waist-high drifts blocked all tracks. Motor vehicles could only be kept going with spades and chains and the utmost care and cosseting by their anxious drivers; there was no anti-freeze coolant and the radiators froze while the trucks were on the move. Horses fell in drifts, never to rise again. Each frozen stream and river became a formidable obstacle, since vehicles and guns had to be lowered on ropes over the deep and overhanging cliff-like banks and pulled up again on the other side.

On Rudolf Schmidt's northern flank Guderian's 2 Panzer Army was in no way better equipped for its task than 2 Army. The same clothing shortages existed and these were of course common over the whole of the Eastern Front. Many of the troops had robbed the well-clad Russian dead or prisoners of their clothing and sported fur caps, quilted jackets and felt boots, so that it was difficult to distinguish friend from foe. Tanks were unable to climb the frozen slippery slopes or cross the ice-covered rivers, since no calks had been provided for the tracks. The tracks of the German tanks were so narrow, and the nominal ground pressure ratio was so high, that their tactical mobility in soft snow was much inferior to that of the broad-tracked T 34. Optical instruments became useless unless they gave off a bloom in the extreme cold.

The three panzer diisions of Geyr von Schweppenburg's 24 Panzer Corps had a fighting strength of fifty tanks against a war establishment figure of about 500. Fuel was in very tight supply and on 17 November the army commander described the general supply situation as appalling. Frost-bite was increasing the sick rate by leaps and bounds and, because of the exposed condition under which they lived and fought, this took a heavier toll among the infantry than any other arm.[11]

The sliding parts of machine-guns jammed through freezing since there were no low temperature lubricants and graphites. Artillery failed as the oils in the buffer systems froze, and only the mortar could be relied upon in an emergency. In a phenomenon unknown to German artillerymen, the intense cold affected the ranging of the guns, causing shorts which fell among their own troops.

Before the offensive could be launched, the vehicles, which were scattered over a very wide area, had to be freed from the axle-deep mud which had frozen into a solid, iron-hard rock. They had to be chipped out laboriously by hand. Pickaxes and spades broke up. Many vehicles were damaged irreparably in the attempts to tow them free. The muddied roads and tracks had frozen into hard-set corrugated ruts and these broke up axles and vehicle suspensions.

10 Motorized Division, which was part of Guderian's 2 Panzer Army, had been moving slowly north-eastwards from the area of Orel. Like every other formation it had become strung out during the *rasputitsa* and had left its stranded motor vehicles behind. The motorized infantry replaced lorry by *panje* wagon and moved on foot. After the arrival of the frosts the motor vehicles were collected up and brought

forward, but so few of them were fit for further use that four of the six motorized battalions were ordered to give up their remaining motor transport to make two battalions mobile. The dismounted infantry battalions remained as infantry of the line equipped with horse-drawn transport. Because there were no spares, workshops stood idle, and when a truck broke down it was usually abandoned; many vehicles had no spare wheels as these had been pooled and there were no replacement tires.

With the coming of the snow there was a scramble by the divisional quartermaster *(1b)* staffs to scour the countryside in search of *troika* sledges on which anti-tank and light field guns could be mounted. [12]

On the 4 Army front due west of Moscow two of the regiments of 98 Infantry Division were enjoying their short rest after Field-Marshal von Kluge's decision to withdraw them from the line. On the Nara the Bolshevist had gone over to the defensive and momentarily all was quiet. Red Air Force planes dropped leaflets to their own kinsmen behind the German lines telling them to leave their townships and villages and make for the woods after gutting or burning all shelter; there were no suggestions as to how the Russian population was to survive exposed to the bitter weather. Propaganda sheets in German were showered over the fighting area urging German troops to desert, guaranteeing good treatment and an early return to Germany after the war. Very few — if any — troops did so, for, as their divisional commander commented, they had already seen enough of the Soviet paradise. In any case all feared captivity more than death.

On 6 November the cold weather arrived in the 98 Infantry Division sector, with a strong biting east wind which coated all the birches with a heavy hoar frost. Just a few pairs of winter gloves and thick overcoats had been issued, but these were only for motor vehicle drivers. The *panje* drivers were expected to keep themselves warm by walking. Meanwhile the troops prepared themselves for winter as best they might, by painfully digging down into the ground below the frost line and building underground bunkers with improvised stoves.

The sickness rate rose very sharply with cases of exhaustion, scarlet fever and diphtheria; the more dreaded spotted fever or typhus began to appear. Heavier caliber Soviet medium artillery was active in a harassing role and this disturbed rest and sleep.

On 10 November the last of the regiments of 98 Division came out of the line into the rest area.

Two days later there was some snow borne in with the driving wind; that night the heavy rumble and growl of Soviet artillery could be heard all along the front. Their neighbor on the right, 34 Infantry Division, was under attack and a message was received by 98 Division towards morning to stand by, as corps reserve, ready to move at half an hour's notice.

Regiment by regiment, they moved out of the home which they had tried to make comfortable over the last few days and went back to the line. The last to go was 282 Regiment, which had had exactly thirty-six hours rest. The easterly wind cut like a knife. The rutted tracks were frozen and hard and the heavily laden men stumbled and staggered over the sharp edges and ridges, blaspheming and cursing as they went. By 3:30 P.M. it was already dusk and the front had not yet been reached. After dark further progress became impossible and, where no shelter was to be had, the men spent the night in the open huddled in tiny groups. Sleep was impossible. The thunder of artillery was all around them and the flashes of gunfire and the red glow of burning villages could be seen to the east and south-east. At the first sign of day the regiment collected itself together and was off again to an open and exposed area, where it had to dig new positions in the iron-hard ground.[13]

6 Rhine-Westphalian Division, yet further to the north, was the left flank of Strauss's 9 Army and lay about a hundred miles north-west of Moscow. Its casualties from the beginning of the war to 1 November, about 3,000 men, had been light. Like all other divisions, the arrival of the cold weather found it stretched out to the rear for a hundred miles or more, and during October the supply system had failed entirely. The first and second line gun ammunition had been almost shot off and there was no barbed wire to be had.

There were no rations but, more fortunate than many, 6 Division had managed to live off the land. Local Russian horses were slaughtered and for nearly six weeks the troops ate little but horsemeat. In some areas they were lucky enough to collect potatoes and thaw them out;

they even made bread, the men threshing the rye themselves, and everywhere formations and units raised their own foraging commandos, looting horses, food and fodder. Even in the rear areas this took tactical skill and guile and was not without danger from partisans and Red Army infiltrators.

A horsed artillery foraging commando, on a visit to a collective farm in a quiet sector removed from the fighting, came up to it from a covered and hidden approach, first keeping the buildings under observation for signs of Russian males. Only women were to be seen about their farmyard chores. Suddenly, to the surprise of the hidden onlookers, several Soviet *BA Broniford* armored cars came bumping along the track up to the farm buildings. An officer, leaning out of the turret of the first vehicle, began a long and animated conversation with a woman at an upper window.

Since the armored car crews showed no inclination to dismount and the eloquent pair no sign of breaking off their talk, the German patrol commander brought matters to a head by ordering a sharpshooting rifleman to open fire. The first round was a hit, for the officer fell slumped over the turret. Unseen hands dragged him down out of sight, the cupola hatch was slammed shut and the cars made off at high speed.

With the coming of the cold weather, supply and movement in 6 Infantry Division were gradually resumed. Relay teams of horses brought *panje* supplies up from Sychevka to Ulitino, until fifteen tons a day were being delivered against a minimum requirement of thirty. By mid-November the stock of artillery ammunition was partially replenished, but all incoming vehicle fuel was needed to tank up the isolated and stranded vehicles miles to the rear. All the artillery could not be made mobile because of the shortage of horses, a shortage which was not helped by the bad going conditions, since as many as fourteen horses were needed to move a single gun. The grumbling artillerymen compared their equipment, often in graphic terms, unfavorably with that of the Red Army, which used quite a number of gun-towing tractors in addition to horses.

There was some good news, however, for ten percent of the divisional winter clothing had actually arrived at Smolensk railway station at the beginning of November, and a detachment had been sent back by road to fetch it.

Lack of a proper diet, irregular meals and the eating of hard frozen foods caused vomiting and stomach ailments. The wounded in this division, as in most others, suffered untold agonies, being evacuated across the frozen, broken and rutted tracks in *panje* wagons filled with straw, with straw-built roofs to keep off the frost. Casualties due to the cold were increasing rapidly. No soldier could be left alone in the open without a second man to watch him for the first signs of freezing, and the wounded often died where they fell, not from their wounds, but from the shock and frost-bite due to the loss of blood.[14]

Rarely can troops have been less ready for an offensive.

CHAPTER SEVEN
THE FINAL PUSH

O N 6 N O V E M B E R, on the eve of the 24th Anniversary of the October Revolution, Stalin made a speech to the Moscow Party leaders in the *Mayakovskaya* metro station.

In this, he speculated on the causes of the German failure to reach the line of the Urals in a summer campaign. It had been, he said, Hitler's hope to attack the USSR as part of an anti-communist coalition which would include the United States and Great Britain; yet not only had the German dictator misjudged the political situation, but he had arrayed against him these two powers. Hitler had made another error, too, when he had imagined that the Soviet Union would fall apart, nationality against nationality, peasant against worker. And (here Stalin went straight to the heart of the matter) Hitler had completely failed to overcome the problem of space and movement inside the Soviet Union.

Stalin then praised the achievements of the Soviet armed forces in somewhat extravagant terms, explaining away the great Soviet defeats of the preceding summer by blaming Britain and America (which was not at the time even at war with Germany) for failing to establish a Second Front in Europe. He claimed, what was of course entirely un-true, that the key to the Germans' success to date over the Red Army lay in their great preponderance in numbers of tanks and aircraft.

On the following day, 7 November, the traditional Moscow parade was held in Red Square by Stalin's order, much against the wishes of his military commanders. This parade was normally re-hearsed for two months, but in view of the seriousness of the times no arrangements had been made and no troops were available. German air raids, too, were becoming increasingly frequent, sometimes during the day, and the holding of the parade was not without its risks.

Stalin, however, had his way and Artemev, the Commander of Moscow Military District, was ordered to lead the parade which was to be reviewed by Budenny. Some tanks and infantry from reinforcement formations were collected together and given three days' drill outside the suburbs of Moscow, but, as no artillery could be withdrawn from the area of operations, Colonel-General Yakovlev, heading the Main Artillery Administration, had a number of guns withdrawn from the war museums. From Red Square the troops moved off back again to the fighting fronts.[1]

Meanwhile, during the first half of November, the West and Kalinin Fronts were being gradually strengthened, the West Front receiving more than 100,000 men.

At about this time Stalin, woefully short of anti-tank units, began, according to Voronov, to designate anti-tank batteries as regiments, insisting that these so-called regiments be commanded by colonels with full regimental headquarters. The dictator explained this apparently nonsensical move by saying that it was to be a temporary measure to raise the status of anti-tank units. It is possible, of course, that this was nothing more than a deception measure to impress German intelligence. It is possible, too, that this was the dictator's motive in retaining in being so many Red Army formations, bled by casualties and down to cadre strength.

Eventually the German intelligence service got wind of these deceits, and this sowed in Hitler's mind the suspicion that the enemy order of battle was a bluff as, to some extent, it probably was. As the war progressed, however, Hitler's suspicion became first a conviction and then an obsession, magnified out of all proportion, so that he began to regard his own intelligence chiefs as dupes of Soviet counter-intelligence. Then he, too, a victim of his own delusions, started to designate German artillery batteries as brigades and infantry divisions as corps, retaining an impressive order of battle by refusing to disband any burnt-out divisions on the Eastern Front. So the German as well as the Soviet fighting forces had inflated formation lists which could not be equated with their limited manpower.

To Stalin the most effective defense lay in offense. In the second week in November he telephoned West Front to propose a limited

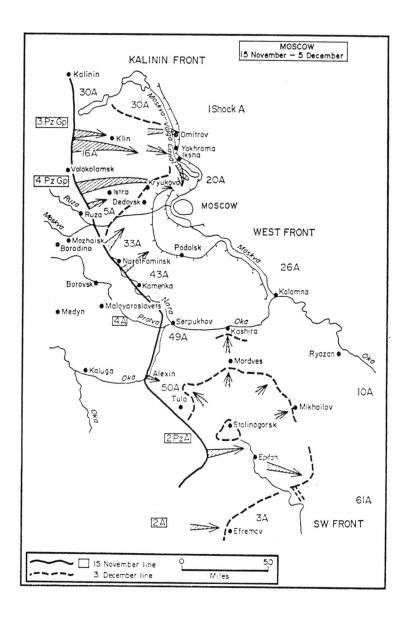

preventive offensive, thought up by himself and Shaposhnikov, to be made by Rokossovsky's 16 Army and Zakharkin's 49 Army. This was intended to disorganize the preparations for von Bock's new drive on Moscow and pin the forces on the German center.

When Zhukov had objected that he had no troops available for such an attack since every man was needed for defense in the coming battle, the reply was not well received by the dictator, who retorted angrily that the matter was settled and that he expected to hear Zhukov's plan for a counter-offensive that very night.

A quarter of an hour later Bulganin, the political member of the military council of the West Front, appeared in Zhukov's office. He was shaken and frightened. He had just been telephoned by Stalin, who told him that both he (Bulganin) and Zhukov were getting a bit too big for their boots but that he (Stalin used the impersonal Russian *my* as though he was acting for the Politburo) would soon bring them to heel. Bulganin had been ordered to go to Zhukov and set to work immediately on the plans. The offensive was prepared and mounted, according to Zhukov, with disappointing results.[2]

Golikov, formerly head of the GRU, the military intelligence directorate of the General Staff, returned to Moscow in October from a short tour of duty as head of the Soviet missions in London and Washington, to be given a field appointment. His new command was 10 Army, consisting of nine infantry and cavalry divisions, a formation which existed only in name as it had not yet been formed. Not even the army headquarters was in being.

The stocky and shaven-headed Golikov, an infantryman, was able and very intelligent, a somewhat unsympathetic character who was an ardent Party supporter, continually making a show of his political enthusiasm. He subsequently served as head of the Repatriation Commission for returning Soviet prisoners of war and, after the war, his protestations of political loyalty were rewarded when, although a soldier, he was made Commissar-in-Chief, an appointment usually reserved for commissars or particularly reliable political henchmen of the regime.

Golikov began to assemble and train his men but only one-third of his commissioned ranks were regular career officers of the active army, which meant that the remainder were over-age reservists or officers who had been inducted from civilian life or promoted from the ranks for the period of the war. Although divisional commanders and chiefs of staff were all regular officers who had graduated from the staff college, many of the infantry and cavalry regimental commanders did not belong to the active army; about eighty-five percent of the commissars were not professional soldiers. Only the artillery had a hard core of regular army officers with battle experience.

The Supreme Headquarters had issued a standing order that all newly formed divisions should have a total of fifteen percent Party and *Komsomol* members, but Golikov's men were so old (the majority being between thirty and forty) that there were very few *Komsomol* members in the ranks. Golikov was quick to ask the Supreme Headquarters to make up the deficiency, and a special reinforcement of 700 communists and a number of activist groups, all experienced officers and soldiers released from hospital, were dispatched post-haste to join 10 Army. Such was the importance attached to political awareness in the Red Army.

Golikov has said that his men had little or no combat experience. Training was still on a very low level, most formations having carried out only platoon and company exercises; in a number of divisions less than eighty percent of the men had completed even their basic firing tests. Some of the more recently arrived troops were civilians in uniform and had absolutely no conception of army life. Although it was already November many were still in summer uniforms and the supply and equipment position was not at all satisfactory. Three infantry and two cavalry divisions had no radio at all and the situation was not improved until Golikov sent telegrams to Stalin, the Politburo, members of the GKO and the Chief of General Staff.

Golikov's whole command numbered about 100,000 men but the total armament, so he has subsequently said, totalled 65,000 rifles, 2,000 machine-guns, 1,200 sub-machine-guns, 250 guns, 250 mortars and about 70 anti-tank guns. The difficulty with supply and equipment lay only partly in the temporary shortage of stocks; the main bottleneck was the overburdened railway system which was bringing up formations from the interior and the Far East and, at the same time, concentrating, supplying and equipping the nine reserve armies which were then being formed. Nor were matters made easier by the fact that many departments of government and a large part of the General Staff had been evacuated from Moscow. It was a wonder indeed that Golikov's army continued to receive quantities of equipment all the time it was *en route* to the front.

Golikov had arrived at the mobilization area of his new command on 27 October and the last of the divisions did not come in until 9 November. On 24 November, only fifteen days later, Golikov received a telephone call from the laconic Shaposhnikov telling him to prepare to leave for the front immediately, to which the bewildered Golikov could not forebear to exclaim, "So soon!" He was to entrain for the industrial city of Ryazan, about 150 miles south-east of Moscow, ready to take part in the battle for Tula. Shaposhnikov, friendly as usual, could do no more than wish Golikov every success, telling him that the written directive would arrive that evening.[3]

All the German formations were in contact and Moscow knew that there could have been no redeployment during the *rasputitsa*. Consequently it expected that the German offensive, when it came, would follow the same pattern as the preceding attacks, most of the panzer troops being on the flanks. Counter-action was to be taken by attacking these flanking forces before they could be reorganized for the offensive.

One Soviet tank and five cavalry divisions from the area near Volokolamsk to the north of Moscow began to thrust against the flank and rear of Reinhardt's 3 Panzer Group, but these troops, many of them Caucasians, were of low quality, and they failed in their mission. South of Stalinogorsk one cavalry and two tank divisions began to infiltrate with much more success into the rear of Guderian's 2 Panzer Army.

The scales of the coming battle were to be weighed, however, by the intervention of the reserve armies, of which Golikov's was one.

The German offensive was resumed on 15 November in clear and frosty weather.

Reinhardt's 3 Panzer Group and a part of Strauss's 9 Army drove in Khomenko's 30 Army on the left wing of Konev's Kalinin Front in an attack towards Klin.

Stalin's reaction was immediate. Lelyushenko, who was recovering from a wound he had received a few weeks earlier when his 5 Army command post had been overrun by German tanks, was ordered to go to 30 Army and replace Khomenko. Lelyushenko's arrival was the first inkling Khomenko had that he was to be relieved, this being Stalin's normal method of replacing unsuccessful commanders. Khomenko went off in disgrace and, Lelyushenko hints, to punishment. What form this took is not known but Khomenko reappeared two years later in command of 44 Army where, wounded and blinded, he died, so it is said, in German captivity.[4]

On 16 November Hoepner's 4 Panzer Group attacked Rokossovsky's 16 Army on the right wing of Zhukov's West Front and started to thrust towards Istra, and two days later Guderian's 2 Panzer Army took up the attack from the area of Tula.

The twelve divisions of Hoepner's 4 Panzer Group had gone into battle with only three-quarters of their first line ammunition and two and a half refills of vehicle fuel, sufficient for only 200 miles' normal consumption. Hoepner had been reluctant to attack without the co-operation of von Kluge's left flank, which was to stand idle, since an unsupported advance by the two panzer groups to the north of Moscow would give rise to a dangerously exposed salient. He was unsuccessful in his urging, however, and the OKH confirmed that von Kluge was not to participate. In consequence Hoepner was obliged to protect his own right flank, and the committing of formations to this task was to rob his main striking force of its impetus.

Hoepner's initial attacks against Rokossovsky's 16 Army had been made in thick mist, and in the very early stages of the offensive there had been some heavy fighting. *78 Sturm Division* of 9 Corps had good fortune when it hit upon a poorly defended locality; the defenders gave way to a short and sharp frontal attack and the attackers penetrated deep into the enemy rear and started to roll up the front. Red Army headquarters, artillery and reserves were taken by surprise, often still asleep, and were quickly mopped up. The count of Soviet prisoners was high, against negligible German casualties, and by the evening of the first day 9 Corps had reached a point five miles behind the enemy.

The second day was no less successful, although the enemy resistance was hardening so that each locality had to be fought for. The Moskva River and its tributaries were frozen and could be crossed but the usual difficulties were met in getting vehicles down the steep overhanging cliff-like river banks of the *balki*; these were impassable even to tanks. Mines had been sown everywhere. As Hoepner feared, the protection of his southern boundary, roughly along the line of the Moskva Rier, slowed the progress of 9 Corps.

Further to the north the other infantry corps made steady progress against a dogged enemy, and not before 26 November did 40 Panzer Corps take the city of Istra, known before 1930 as Voskresensk, with its famous New Jerusalem monastery, built in the seventeenth century after the model of the Church of the Holy Sepulchre. Istra, which had a population of only a few thousand, was about twenty-five miles from the original start line and only thirty from Moscow. The Germans held it against determined enemy tank and infantry counter-attacks.[5]

About a third of the German tanks had fallen behind because of breakdown or obstacles, and those still battle-worthy were beginning to run short of fuel. The maps were bad and many localities shown simply did not exist on the ground; all sign posts and place names had been removed by the Russians. Except on the beaten tracks the snow could not be crossed easily, for although its surface was frozen it would not bear weight, so that men and vehicles fell through into the two-foot-deep soft snow underneath.

On 16 November, 5 German Corps, part of Hoepner's force to the north-east of Moscow, had been counter-attacked by Caucasian troops but these were held, even though rifle company strengths were down to less than thirty men. Two days later 5 Corps itself went over to the attack to the south of Klin. By 22 November the Red Army troops facing 35 Infantry Division were withdrawing fast and for a short time it appeared that enemy resistance might be broken; there were numerous Red Army deserters and line-crossers. Meanwhile the extreme cold continued, the thermometer sinking at night to minus 40 degrees centigrade.[6]

Strauss's 9 Army and Reinhardt's 3 Panzer Group to the left of Hoepner stretched as far north as Kalinin, and only two corps, one an

infantry corps, could be spared for the eastward thrust on Klin and
Dmitrov. Schaal's 56 Panzer Corps, originally consisting of only one
panzer and one motorized division, made good progress, routing the
two Soviet cavalry divisions which were defending the area. Klin, once
a flourishing textile center but now a deserted ghost town, was taken
on 23 November, the area being heavily mined and booby-trapped.

On 24 November Reinhardt was ordered by von Bock to continue
his progress eastwards to protect Hoepner's left flank. Schaal's 56
Panzer Corps, the strength of which had been increased by a further
panzer division, attacked towards Dmitrov and Yakhroma, both on the
Moskva-Volga canal, against spirited ground resistance which was,
however, sporadic and uncoordinated. Although enemy air activity was
strong Reinhardt had formed the impression that Khomenko's (later
Lelyushenko's) 30 Army was unprepared for combat and was very
weak in numbers, as indeed it was; Reinhardt thought that with reinforcements he could have easily broken through, and he urged in
vain that the main striking force should be transferred from 4 to 3
Panzer Group.

This appeal fell, however, on deaf ears. Schaal kept up his rapid
movement and on 28 November crossed the bridge over the Moskva-
Volga canal near Yakhroma, a cotton-milling center on the east bank,
thirty-eight miles north of the capital. There, Reinhardt secured a
bridgehead.

The exploitation of this bridgehead was no part of the OKH plan,
since Reinhardt had been given what was, in effect, only a subsidiary
task, that of protecting Hoepner's flank. He was ordered by Army
Group Center merely to hold the line of the canal and advance southwards down the west bank to keep a closer contact with Hoepner. In
these circumstances there was nothing else to be done but give up the
bridgehead. Reinhardt ordered Shaal to hold the line west of the
Moskva-Volga canal while Model's 41 Panzer Corps, which had come
from the area of Kalinin to join Schaal, took over two of the 56
Corps panzer divisions and moved directly southwards in the direction
of Moscow.

The change of direction brought with it a change in the nature of
the fighting. Snow had begun to fall heavily and the temperature stood

at about minus thirty degrees centigrade. Artillery could not be relied on; the mortar, which has no working parts, being nothing but a barrel and fixed striker stud, had come into its own. Petrol was smeared continuously on the sliding parts of machine-guns to keep them from freezing. Motor trucks were left behind and even the tracked vehicles could not keep moving. The ground was sown with enemy wooden box mines with a particularly sensitive detonator which caused many a soldier to lose his foot.

So Model progressed slowly through a great area covered by luxurious *dachi,* the summer residences of the communist hierarchy. Prisoners and guns were taken, the latter usually being destroyed on the spot. A wounded woman in Red Army uniform, captured in a Russian tank, said she was a radio operator who had accompanied her husband to the war. Part of 23 Potsdam Division, one of the formations of 41 Panzer Corps, was surrounded by the enemy and Model had to take energetic action to free it. It was noted that as the strength of the German formations ebbed that of the enemy seemed to grow.

Farther to the south the advance of Hoepner's 4 Panzer Group had been beset by greater difficulties than those experienced by Reinhardt. The resistance of Rokossovsky's 16 Army had been considerably stiffer than that to the north. Although he continued to make progress eastwards, on 29 November Hoepner reported that the moment might soon arise when enemy superiority on the ground and in the air could bring the advance to a standstill.

When 35 Infantry Division, one of Hoepner's formations, eventually arrived at the town of Kryukovo, the Moscow suburbs were only fifteen miles away. Red Army infantry was making a poor showing but the enemy had plenty of tanks and artillery. Yet the German troops were already in a desperate state; the weapons were failing and the troops were without protection from the bitter winds. At dusk came the desperate scramble for the shelter of the villages.[7] Their neighbors a little further to the south, 3 Infantry Division, were in a similar plight.

In spite of the weather, Reinhardt's and Hoepner's advance was rapid, for in ten days they penetrated nearly fifty miles, almost to the northern outskirts of Moscow.

On one of the critical days during this time, a nervous Stalin, according to Zhukov's subsequent account, telephoned to ask the West Front Commander's opinion as to whether the front would hold and Moscow would be saved. Zhukov has said that he answered firmly and reassuringly that the capital was safe, although the grounds for his confidence are by no means apparent since Reinhardt was nearing the Moskva-Volga canal and Hoepner was already between Istra and Kryukovo and still moving forward steadily.

This vignette of a confident Zhukov and a nervous Stalin is oddly at variance with another from the same source which describes how, on 28 or 29 November, when Hoepner was less than fifteen miles from the western suburbs of Moscow, Stalin telephoned to ask whether Zhukov knew that the town of Dedovsk had been taken by the enemy. Zhukov did not know.

This answer irritated Stalin who tartly replied that it was the commander's job to know. Zhukov was to get down to Dedovsk immediately and personally organize a counter-attack. Zhukov tried to explain that the battle position was so dangerous that he could not leave his headquarters, to which Stalin replied: "No matter, do as you are told and leave Sokolovsky in charge." After a little telephoning, Zhukov found that the small cotton-milling town of Dedovsk, only 20 miles from Moscow, before 1941 known as Dedovski and before that Guchkovo, had not fallen and that it seemed likely that Stalin had either been misinformed or confused, both by the loss of a little village called Dedovo and by the frequent changes of name of Dedovsk.

Zhukov telephoned this information to Stalin, who flew into a great rage. Zhukov was ordered to go personally and retake the place, whatever its accursed name, and while he was at it he could take Rokossovsky, the Commander of 16 Army, along with him together with Govorov, the Commander of 5 Army who, because he had once been Director of Artillery of the Reserve Front, "could tie up the 16 Army artillery fire plan."

Zhukov did not care to argue further but when he told the Commander of 5 Army of his new task, Govorov, not unnaturally, objected that Rokossovsky had his own artillery commander and that he, Govorov, was in the middle of a fierce battle and could not leave

his troops. Zhukov cut off all argument with the dread words *prikaz
I. V. Stalina.*

So the three generals, one of army group and two of army rank,
proceeded to the hamlet of Dedovo where they had ordered the divisional commander, a Colonel Beloborodov, to wait for them. The latter,
little pleased by the arrival in his area of this high-ranking cortège,
explained that the Germans had seized a few houses on the other side
of a ravine and that he considered that there was no tactical advantage
to be gained by driving them out again. That was Zhukov's opinion
also, but he did not enlighten Beloborodov on the background. Beloborodov was solemnly ordered to mount a counter-attack with one
rifle company and two tanks, after which the three generals returned
to their more important duties.[8]

On the other flank, to the south of Moscow in the area of Tula,
Guderian's 2 Panzer Army, too weak for its task, was making slow
progress. For Guderian had only two panzer and two infantry corps
totalling about twelve divisions. On 18 November, 47 Panzer Corps
had taken Epifan, a straggling village on the headwaters of the Don,
and 24 Panzer Corps entered Dedilovo the same day, preparatory to
moving northwards in the direction of Venev on the road to Moscow.
17 Panzer Division began to advance through Venev towards Kashira
on the Oka.

On 24 November, 10 Motorized Infantry Division took Mikhai-
lov, a small city lying amid cement works and limestone quarries, once
a Muscovite fortress against the steppe nomad.

Meanwhile, however, 2 Panzer Army had become aware that
Siberian troops were detraining at Ryazan and Kolomna on the exposed
south-east flank and that one division had already arrived at the rail
junction town of Uzlovaya. Guderian managed to pin these troops, 239
Siberian Rifle Division, from the west using a German infantry division, while 29 Motorized Division encircled it from the east. The rail
track between Voronezh and Moscow was blown up by German long-
range demolition parties in order to prevent the arrival of further Red
Army formations, but an attempt to cut the most important Ryazan-
Kolomna line was a failure.

The Siberian division had been detraining on an open stretch of line when it was surrounded by the infantry division of 53 Corps to the west, 4 Panzer Division to the north and 29 Motorized Division from the east. The temperature was steady at minus thirty degrees centigrade, and the German troops were suffering acutely from exposure as all the hamlets and buildings (the countryside was open farmland) had been gutted.

It was impossible for the encircling troops to dig in and there were no explosives to break up the hard frozen ground. By night German outposts were put forward connected by telephone to the main positions; some of them were in strawricks and these were to set the straw afire on the approach of the enemy, alerting the troops in the main defensive line to the rear and, at the same time, illuminating the approaches and fields of fire. The outpost line failed in its purpose.

At about midnight the Siberian divisional headquarters, mounted in motor vehicles, moved across the front of 29 Motorized Infantry Division *between* the outposts and the main defensive line without being recognized as enemy or being fired on; but no sooner had it entered the sector of the neighboring German division to the south than it came under heavy fire and was destroyed, the Siberian divisional commander being killed. Then followed an uneasy quiet.

At two o'clock in the morning there was another alarm. But nothing could be seen by the German troops. Then came the long-drawn-out sigh as if of the wind, the muffled sound of the approach of hundreds of hurrying feet. Yet still the Soviet enemy could not be picked out against the background of desolate white fields, since they were cloaked in Arctic smocks, even their weapons being painted white; there were neither mines nor wire to stop them. Nor did the artillery defensive fire come down.

The attacking Siberians were not seen until they had broken into the defensive localities, firing from the hip with light machine-gun and machine-pistol as they hurled themselves forward. The German battalions, down to companies in strength, could not hold their ground. Unprotected even by weapon pits, groups were surrounded as they fought in close combat. Others ran away. Company commanders could not control their men and order broke down; many of the troops cowered behind the walls of gutted farm buildings to get some protection from the enemy fire.

Soon, however, discipline was restored as a few pairs of stouthearted light machine-gunners dragged their weapons into firing positions. It was too late, however, to prevent the Siberians from breaking out and they disappeared into the darkness.

The next day Guderian arrived to investigate the failure and to encourage the badly shaken German troops. A motorcycle battalion was sent off in pursuit of the Siberians but was unable to head them off. Although the Siberian division had left behind its equipment and artillery and a large number of dead, the price it had exacted from the encircling German troops had been high. For, after the engagement the motorized infantry companies were down to less than twenty men and the division had no further fighting value without refitting, reinforcement and rest.[9]

There and then Guderian made up his mind to take Tula and disregard his wider mission; in his mind there was no longer any question of reaching the deeper objectives or even of encircling Moscow from the east. Tula was still held by Boldin's reinforced 50 Soviet Army, and 2 Panzer Army tried to encircle it from the north in a short envelopment by using 43 Corps to thrust due east from the area of Alexin while 24 Panzer Corps moved westwards to meet it.

Even though the two spearhead divisions of 43 Corps had a frontage of twenty miles, the thrust westwards, helped on by sledges and air-dropped supplies, made steady progress. On 27 November Alexin was taken. But von Kluge's 4 Army to the north was still inactive and did nothing, not even pinning the enemy in front of it, in spite of the fact that it was becoming apparent that the enemy was moving troops away from the central Nara sector to bring Guderian's (and Hoepner's) attacks to a halt.

On 25 November a weakened 17 Panzer Division of Geyr von Schweppenburg's 24 Panzer Corps started to attack in a westerly direction about thirty miles to the north of Tula in order to meet up with 43 Corps, but made little progress in the face of bitter resistance. It became obvious that Tula was not going to be encircled; failure to take the city, coupled with the danger of the open east flank, meant that the area east of Moscow could not be reached by 2 Panzer Army unless von Kluge's 4 Army took an early hand in the battle.

Guderian's troops were very seriously weakened and in poor condition, their ration being no more than thirty grams of butter and one-fifth of a loaf a day. The wounded died where they fell.

On the afternoon of 23 November Guderian had visited von Bock to stress how tired and weak his men were and von Bock telephoned von Brauchitsch, Guderian listening in to the conversation on a separate earphone. It was plain to both of them that the Commander-in-Chief was not allowed to make any decisions. According to Guderian, further representations to Halder made through the OKH liaison officer were no more successful, and Guderian concluded, possibly correctly, that Halder was as determined as the Führer to get to Moscow.[10]

Von Bock, who, of course, needed no convincing that the longer-range objectives beyond Moscow were not attainable, agreed that Guderian should limit himself to improving his position about Tula. Up till then von Bock had been at his forward command post driving his troops relentlessly on, but by 1 December he had come to realize that even Moscow was no longer possible. He emphasized to von Brauchitsch and to Halder the weakness of his troops, who were by then having to attack well-prepared enemy positions frontally. Halder, by way of reply, could only reiterate that the difficulties were known but that it was the last reserves of strength which would count.[11]

Far to the south on the right flank of von Bock's Army Group Center, when Rudolf Schmidt's 2 Army began its advance, the only enemy was the weather. The Russian soon took a hand, however, his air force bombing and machine-gunning in skies absolutely clear of the Luftwaffe. Mines had been laid in profusion, many being sown in the hours of darkness by Red Army patrols which shadowed the German columns. Far from having evacuated the area west of the Don, every village and homestead had been prepared for defense by the Red Army, and these had to be cleared by bayonet and grenade. Booby-traps were everywhere. Although it was rare for the defenders to fight to the end, since they usually disappeared under the cover of smoke, these delaying tactics slowed the progress of Rudolf Schmidt's men; German losses mounted steadily.

45 Infantry Division, one of Schmidt's formations, complained bitterly about the Red Air Force attacks which were made in such unprecedented strength that it became almost impossible to move by daylight. The division had already covered 1,300 miles on foot since its first bloody encounters with NKVD and Red Army infantry in the garrison of Brest-Litovsk at the beginning of the war; it was not particularly cheered when it began to take warmly clad and well-equipped Siberian prisoners from 1 Far Eastern Division, one of many formations fresh to the fighting which had come in by rail to Elets a few days before.[12]

Tim was taken on 20 November, but the left flank of 35 Corps was held back by a number of enemy counter-attacks. Since Schmidt had been ordered to reach the Don as quickly as possible, irrespective of the situation on the flanks, indentations and gaps had to be accepted and in consequence the enemy began to infiltrate westward in large numbers through a vacuum to the north of the town of Livny. Not before 3 December was 45 Infantry Division to arrive at the rail junction of Elets, a textile center on the Sosna. This was only forty miles from its original start point; 45 Division never reached the Don at all.

By then the divisions of 2 Army were so scattered and strung out by the appalling weather conditions that they provided neither a threat to the enemy nor security for the southern flank of 2 Panzer Army or Army Group Center. They could not in fact defend themselves.

Meanwhile, von Kluge's 4 Army still stood on the Nara in those positions which it had reached at the end of the *Schlammperiode* before the onset of the cold weather. Von Kluge's force consisted of four corps of thirteen divisions, of which, however, only one was a panzer and one a motorized division. Many of these divisions had managed to dig themselves in, providing themselves with bunkers, dugouts, weapon pits with overhead cover, intricate fire plans and much of the paraphernalia associated with an organized defense.

At the end of October and the beginning of November a number of Red Army counter-attacks had caused several crises, particularly in the 12 and 13 Corps sectors, and for this reason, as has already been recounted, von Kluge was to be allowed to delay joining in the German offensive until Guderian's, Hoepner's and Reinhardt's panzer forces had begun to draw Soviet forces away from the Nara, west of Moscow, out to the flanks to the north and south of the capital. This was a reversal of the more orthodox methods which would have required von Kluge to engage and pin the enemy to his front in order to prevent the enemy from reinforcing the flanks. In consequence, in the last two weeks in November, 4 Army took no part in the battle aimed at encircling the Soviet capital. This inactivity did not inhibit von Kluge, however, from asking von Bock and without a touch of malice, "when he could expect the arrival of the promised reserve!"[13]

98 Franconian Sudeten Division was still in the line on the Nara, having had to give up one of its regiments and three artillery batteries to help clear up the position on the south flank where four enemy divisions had broken in. On the night of 23 November a special Red Army task force of 300 men, accompanied by female student *Komsomol* members and Party workers, all armed with machine-pistols, grenades and Molotov cocktails, infiltrated into the German rear to attack the village in which 12 Corps Headquarters was housed. The German guards were alert and the headquarters, when aroused, drove off the attackers who left fifty-eight dead and four prisoners behind. However, the German casualties of nineteen dead and twenty-nine wounded were not light.

The Red Army task force returned to its own lines by a zigzag and circuitous course to make interception difficult. But, in the early hours of that morning, the Commander of 282 Infantry Regiment was moving through the woods with his signaler on his way to his command post when he became aware of approaching movement; they took cover. Not thirty paces away there passed by a great column of men on skis, one behind the other in single file, armed to the teeth, quilted and silent, with lamb fur caps pulled over ears and face, each with his eyes firmly fixed on the back of the man in front and moving rapidly through the trees like a line of ghosts. This was part of the raiding party on its way home.

The area for a hundred miles behind 4 Army had been eaten bare by German foraging commandos, and 98 Infantry Division was forced to extend its search to the territory about a hundred and fifty miles away to the south-west beyond Kaluga. The main problem was to get hay and oats to keep the heavier West European horses alive. Parties of troops and Russian volunteer *Hiwis,* each about fifty strong, were sent off under an officer into the countryside to collect cattle, fodder and food.

98 Infantry Division was one of the many formations of von Kluge's 4 Army which was to take no part in the push on Moscow and it sat firm in its defensive localities. On 2 December it was itself attacked by an enemy which penetrated the sector held by the divisional anti-tank battalion, in the line as infantry; an immediate counter-attack restored the position, the enemy leaving 122 dead behind him when he withdrew.

On 4 December a warning was given out of a further lowering of the temperature below minus thirty degrees centigrade. Batteries were taken out of vehicles and even oil and glycerine and the water in the carbide lamps began to freeze; the accumulators on the radio sets became defective. The cold air stung the cheeks and made the eyes water; there was more frost-bite and even the hateful lice seemed to multiply. These could only be kept under control by pressing the seams of clothes with a hot iron; the scale of provision of irons was only one for each regiment.[14]

Like those of other formations, the divisional arms and vehicle workshop in Maloyaroslavets was idle for lack of spares and an order had been issued taking away motor vehicles from infantry divisions, even though these were in most cases captured Russian lorries. With them went the brave drivers, who by force of circumstances had become men of outstanding resourcefulness.

Reinhardt's 3 and Hoepner's 4 Panzer Groups were poised to the north of the capital but the newly arriving Soviet troops were fighting stubbornly. Hoepner, in white hot fury, telephoned von Kluge day after day demanding that he begin his attack west of Moscow from the area of the Nara. But von Kluge was still reluctant to act as he repeatedly talked the matter over with von Bock and Blumentritt, his own chief of staff; *78 Sturm Division,* one of Hoepner's formations, stood only twenty-five miles from Moscow waiting impatiently for 4 Army to go over to the offensive; meanwhile, for the first time in its experience, it was coming under sustained Red Air Force bombing attacks through-out the divisional area. On 29 November, much to its surprise, the division was told by the corps commander that 4 Panzer Group was itself going to resume the offensive on 1 December irrespective of the action taken by von Kluge's 4 Army.[15]

Not before 1 December did von Kluge begin his attack, and then with only part of 20 Corps and 57 Panzer Corps. On 30 November the weather had been clear and fine but the next day there were heavy snow storms and the temperature registered minus thirty-four degrees centi-grade. The cold was a far more terrible foe than the Russians, yet when 292 Infantry Division crossed its start line together with its neighbors, it began to make ground eastwards from the Nara. Then, together with part of 19 Panzer Division, it broke through the Red Army defenses and fought its way into the enemy rear, overrunning the headquarters of 222 Soviet Rifle Division and taking its commander prisoner. The flanking formations, however, were slow to support it. On 3 December the temperature was down to minus forty-two degrees centigrade.[16]

The 20 Corps operation, of which the 292 Infantry Division attack formed part, was a two-pronged assault, one of the thrusts being directed to cut the Smolensk to Moscow trunk route in the enemy rear. The other was made on to the main highway between Naro Fominsk and Moscow in order, as a preliminary operation, to take the city of Naro Fominsk and destroy the many enemy gun sites on both sides of the main road. 292 Division reached its objectives with a loss of 600 men, but some of the other troops of the corps returned to their start lines.

Naro Fominsk was a cotton- and paper-milling center, with a peacetime population of about 22,000. In spite of the fact that it was twenty-five miles from the capital, it was almost part of the Moscow metropolis and this was reflected in the manners and dress of its inhab-itants and in the improved state of its roads and buildings.

3 Infantry Division, part of 57 Panzer Corps, was one of the divi-sions earmarked for the 4 Army offensive; it occupied a difficult area near Naro Fominsk under observation from the Soviet positions, for Red Army snipers were in the chimneys of buildings and any daylight

movement brought down heavy mortar fire. 3 Infantry Division was too weak in strength to cover the frontage, and the enemy infiltrated into the German rear through the great gaps. Here, too, the bitter cold made it necessary to withdraw all soldiers after they had been in the open for an hour.

The divisional commander himself had reservations as to the likelihood of success, as he was opposed by fresh, well-equipped Siberian divisions with plenty of guns and tanks. His fears were justified, for when 29 Infantry Regiment began the attack with the support of a single armored assault gun company it immediately started to lose heavily in casualties. A reinforced and strong company of the regiment, numbering seventy men, by evening had only twenty-eight left. A battalion of 8 Motorized Regiment lost eighty men, a third of its strength, and had twenty-two battle and no fewer than fifty-eight exhaustion and frost-bite casualties. The division came to a standstill because its task was too great for it. The coordination between corps and army was poor and 15 Infantry Division was brought up too late to exploit 3 Division's gains.[17]

Some of the forward infantry companies of 3 Infantry Division had penetrated into the factory area and woodyards of the town when the Russians, who had taken cover in the nearby cellars from the German artillery fire, emerged once more and attempted to cut off the attackers from the rear. The German troops soon found that they were unable to move; nor could anti-tank guns and ammunition be got forward to them.

Two hours later white-painted heavy Russian tanks entered the woodyards and passed through the German infantry companies without opening fire, since they were obviously seeking out the German battalion and regimental headquarters. Some time afterwards they returned and began firing into the woodyards from the perimeter. The great symmetrical stacks of wooden planking gave good protection from the flat trajectory high-explosive shell and machine-gun fire, but not from the steep flight mortar bombs which were being lobbed into the alleyways between the piles. Red Army riflemen began to close up in support of their tanks and the German infantry companies were soon assailed on all sides; the position was no longer tenable but a withdrawal could only be made across the open snow-bedecked field over which they had come. Salvation came, however, by the accidental firing of the timber yards, which soon laid a pall of smoke over the area. Hardly able to credit their fortune, the German companies withdrew.

The Soviet High Command saw the thrust of Hoepner's 4 Panzer Group to the north of the city as the immediate danger to Moscow. As a counter, Soviet troops had been rapidly moved over from the Nara and from 24 and 26 Reserve Armies in the east, the first two divisions to arrive in the northern outskirts forming the nucleus of a new 20 Soviet Army commanded by Major-General Vlasov. This army was rushed to the northern outskirts of the city to stop Hoepner. Another new army, V. I. Kuznetsov's 1 Shock Army (a rifle army with additional artillery to equip it for breakthrough tasks), coming up from the area of Zagorsk, attacked Schaal's 56 Panzer Corps across the Moskva-Volga canal between Dmitrov and the Iksha Lake, pinning Reinhardt's 3 Panzer Group. These two Soviet armies, together with Lelyushenko's 30 and Rokossovsky's 16 Armies, brought the tired and understrength panzer troops to a halt about fifteen miles from Moscow.[18]

On the southern wing, Guderian's offensive had been brought to a standstill by the determined Soviet resistance in Tula, Stalinogorsk and Venev, which tied down so many troops that only one panzer division could be found for the final thrust on the Kashira bridges over the Oka. This attack, made by 17 Panzer Division, was repulsed. Meanwhile the new formations already noted by Guderian arriving from the east, 26 Army near Kolomna, Golikov's 10 Army in the Ryazan area, and F. I. Kuznetsov's 61 Army near Ryazsk, were approaching the 2 Panzer Army flank. Guderian's 2 Panzer Army and Rudolf Schmidt's 2 Army, further to the south, struggled on until 4 December, but their attacks became progressively weaker, spread out as they were over frontage of about 200 miles.

Von Kluge's 4 Army had its only noteworthy success when it breached Efremov's 33 Soviet Army line north of Naro Fominsk and tried to encircle Govorov's 5 Soviet Army. This thrust was the last of the German offensive and it was brought to a halt on 2 and 3 December by the reserves of Efremov's 33 and Golubev's 43 Soviet Armies near the railway town of Golizno. It was in any event too late to assist Hoepner. On 3 December von Kluge on his own responsibility ordered the withdrawal of 258 Infantry Division, since he could no longer be answerable for its safety, and he reported that "the bloody losses were quite colossal."[19]

By then it was clear to all that Moscow would not be taken.

The root of the German failure lay primarily in timing. If Hitler had listened to his professional advisers during July and August and had continued the Army Group Center offensive along the Smolensk-Moscow axis, instead of diverting his forces to Leningrad and Kiev, nothing could have saved the Soviet capital. In all probability he would have been able to extend his conquests to Yaroslavl and a line 150 miles beyond Moscow, but to have done this he would have been forced to forego his great victory at Kiev. The Eastern Ukraine would have remained unconquered. But even should he have reached the line 150 miles beyond the capital, the war would not have been won. In any case it is doubtful whether, having secured such a line before the arrival of the bad weather, German troops could have held it successfully during the winter months.

As it was, the German offensive had been made too late in the season. If it had been made only three weeks earlier, it is probable that von Bock would have escaped the *rasputitsa* and taken the city of Moscow. It is certain, of course, that in late October he could not have extended any further to the east. Mud, not snow, saved the capital.

Yet it would be wrong to attribute the German failure or the Soviet success merely to the weather, even though the onset of winter was the primary cause. The German defeat, like those which were to follow, rested on faulty war direction, inadequate intelligence and an insufficiency of material resources. German war direction never overcame the problems of climate, time and space.

In retrospect it can be said that there was some fault in both the strategic and the tactical planning of this last 1941 German offensive. Even in November the strategic concept still envisaged an advance on a broad front across the whole of Russia and the Ukraine, from Lake Ladoga to the Sea of Azov, forward to Onega, Gorki and the Caucasus. Such grandiose aims bore no relationship to the true situation on the ground, the seriously weakened state of the German troops and the apparently insuperable logistic problems. The best that could be hoped for was winter accommodation inside the capital and the German formations were far too dispersed to secure even this. Schmidt's 2 Army in the area of Orel and Kursk was so far removed to the south that it was of no *operational* benefit in the battle for the capital. Guderian was so weak that he could not achieve his mission and he was, in any case, nearly 120 miles to the south of Moscow.

The most controversial point, which was subsequently used by Zhukov as a criticism of the German handling of the battle and also by some German commanders as a reproach against von Kluge, was the employment of 4 Army on the Nara.

Until 1 December, 4 Army remained passive instead of attacking in the center and drawing on itself the Soviet reserves, so allowing Guderian, Hoepner and Reinhardt greater freedom to complete their envelopment tasks. As it was, the reinforcing Soviet formations, 1 Shock, 20, 10 and 61 Armies, were committed against the enveloping German pincers. Even worse, von Kluge's inactivity was such that Red Army troops were withdrawn from the Nara.

When von Kluge started his belated attack, Guderian, Hoepner and Model had expended their force. Even then, the 4 Army attack was made with only two corps.

The reason for von Kluge's inaction is not entirely clear; in any event, even if blame does attach itself to him, the responsbility was not entirely his, for von Bock, insofar as Hitler would allow, was the main coordinator of the battle. It will be recalled, too, that von Kluge had from time to time been under heavy attack, those same pre-emptive attacks thought up by Stalin and Shaposhnikov. It was on these attacks that the Soviet dictator had so grimly insisted. These offensives may not have been so unproductive as Zhukov now claims.

The I 153 single-engined
biplane with a maximum speed
of only 230 mph was one of
the standard service fighters.

The I 16 *Rata* radial-engined
monoplane with a maximum
speed of 285 mph was the most
numerous Soviet interceptor.
It was outpaced by German
medium bombers.

The Soviet T34 main battle tank, at its weight the best in the world. Its broad tracks gave it exceptional tactical agility and its well-sloped armour good protection. It had 45-mm front hull armour and a 76-mm (later 85-mm) high-velocity gun.

A KV1 heavy tank, weight 48 tons mounting a 76-mm high-velocity gun (later 85-mm and known as the KV85). Frontal armour 75-mm later increased to 105-mm.

The Mark III *(Panzerkampfwagen III)* 1940 model, weight 22 tons, with a 37-mm gun. The later '41 model had a 50-mm gun.

The Mark IV, weight 23 tons with 60-mm frontal armour, was originally a close support tank with a short barrelled low-velocity 75-mm gun. Later, equipped with a long-barrelled gun, it became one of the main battle tanks.

German infantry in burning Vitebsk.

Abandoned Soviet guns and tractors on the highway.

Soviet cavalry on the march.

Red Army motorized troops.

A cavalry charge of Red Army troops.

Soviet infantry, supported by tanks, improves its position.

Soviet sappers lay a minefield.

A Red Army scouting party crossing a river.

Red Army men attacking past a disabled German tank.

Red Army infantrymen charge with fixed bayonets somewhere on the Russian front.

Mud and the German *panje* wagon.

German motorized troops advance in the *Schlammperiode*.

Red Army mortar teams supporting advancing infantry.

A Soviet mounted patrol (not cavalry).

Under the cover of artillery fire, Red Army men dislodging Germans from a populated place during the great Soviet Winter Offensive.

Red Army troops counter-attacking on Mozhaisk, the great
monastery in the background.

A Soviet 76.2-mm field battery changes position, being towed and lifted by a T60 tank battalion.

The same field battery during a night engagement.

A Soviet mortar team in action. Note the overhead cover to the mortar pit.

A Red Army 152-mm gun howitzer opens fire. Note the fur caps, felt boots and quilted clothing of the gun crew.

A main road in West Russia during the thaw.

A main road in the south near the boundary between 2 and 6 Armies in April 1942.

CHAPTER EIGHT
THE FÜHRER IN COMMAND

THE FIRST DAY of December was a day of crisis in the German High Command.

In the Ukraine, von Rundstedt, acting on the Führer's orders, had already overreached himself and was in serious danger, for Army Group South was very widely dispersed; von Manstein's 11 Army was far away in the Crimea in front of Sevastopol; von Reichenau's 5 Army, on the border of the Ukraine, several hundred miles to the north, was trying to keep contact with Rudolf Schmidt's 2 Army of Army Group Center; Hoth, who had succeeded von Stülpnagel in early October as the Commander of 17 Army, had to extend his line both to the north to keep in touch with von Reichenau and to the south to support von Kleist's 1 Panzer Army. Since the arrival of the *rasputitsa* the supply system had failed and Army Group South, already too thinly spread, lay immobile in the mud.

With the coming of the frosts the scanty supply reserves had been pooled to allow von Kleist to continue his thrust with part of his forces along the northern shores of the Sea of Azov to Rostov-on-Don, the gateway to the Caucasus. The attack into Rostov was successful in spite of the determined resistance of Colonel-General Cherevichenko's South Front, but von Kleist's troops were precariously extended in a long salient with an open northern flank, which Hoth's 17 Army, left far to the west, could not cover. Red Army troops began to cross the frozen Don to envelop von Kleist's spearheads while others attacked 1 Panzer Army's exposed flank and rear. Hoth, von Reichenau and von Manstein were too far away to be of any assistance and, unless he withdrew, von Kleist was in grave danger of being cut off in Rostov.

Von Rundstedt had had a long and distinguished career under the Kaiser and in the *Reichsheer*. Entering 83 Infantry Regiment as a second lieutenant in 1893, he had at first risen in rank only slowly, not becoming a lieutenant-colonel until 1920. As a general officer he had commanded first a cavalry and then an infantry division and, at the time of his retirement in 1938, was a corps commander with the rank of colonel-general; he had been re-employed in 1939 and was promoted to field-marshal after the great victory over France.

Von Rundstedt had some reputation as a strategist but, although very able, it is doubtful whether he was a commander of first rank or an outstandingly strong personality. He had a very impressive presence and possibly for this reason he was highly esteemed by the Führer, who, in point of fact, scarcely knew him. Von Rundstedt was only a few days short of his sixty-sixth birthday.

Von Rundstedt had already come to the conclusion that it was impossible to reach the Caucasus and the lower Volga during that winter and, some weeks before, he had urged von Brauchitsch that all operations should stop at Rostov.[1]

Von Rundstedt's problems were little different from those faced by von Bock. His troops were tired, disorganized and much understrength, and very badly supplied. The mud and the cold had made movement most difficult and the functioning of the railway in the Ukraine, as in Belorussia and the *General Gouvernement* of occupied Poland, could only be described as chaotic. Because of the retracking, the capacity was limited. The *Reichbahn* engines could not operate on Russian coal and were quite unsuited to the very cold temperatures; the result was widespread mechanical breakdown, so that at one time during the winter eighty percent of the German engines were out of action. The railway situation became so near disastrous that a committee of investigation was eventually set up with the Führer himself in the chair.[2]

When Cherevichenko's South Front began to envelop von Kleist, von Rundstedt had, on 28 November, ordered a general retreat to the west of Rostov, the OKH being in agreement with his decision. The next day Halder noted that the withdrawal was proceeding smoothly in spite of the strongest enemy pressure, but he himself began to wonder whether a further retirement might not be necessary.

Events showed that Halder's fears were justified and that it was imperative to make a deeper withdrawal in one bound to the line of the

Mius in order to break contact with the enemy. This is what von Rundstedt proposed to do. When, however, the Führer heard of it, he became greatly excited and angered; he forbade any further movement to the west and ordered the troops to remain exactly where they were. He intended to restore the situation by using Hoth's 17 Army, a formation which was unable to move, to attack eastwards on Voroshilovgrad in order to take the pressure off von Kleist.

Halder was to bemoan that "'they' [meaning Hitler] just have no idea of the condition of our troops and indulge in fights of fancy in a vacuum." At one o'clock that same afternoon von Brauchitsch was sent for by the dictator and returned very shaken from what Halder described as a one-sided and thoroughly unpleasant conversation, during which the Führer, giving vent to his wrath, had issued impossible orders and heaped insults upon von Brauchitsch's head. Von Brauchitsch then sent out, under his own signature, the Führer's standstill order, but, when von Rundstedt's answer was received asking either that the order be rescinded or that he be relieved of his command, von Brauchitsch could do nothing but send the teleprints direct to Hitler.

At four o'clock on the morning of 1 Decemer the Führer himself issued three telegrams; the first removed von Rundstedt from his appointment, replacing him with von Reichenau, the Commander of 5 Army; the second ordered von Reichenau to stop the withdrawal of 1 Panzer Army and attack on Voroshilovgrad; the third ordered Fromm, the Commander of the Replacement Army, to send by *rail* fifty tanks to each of von Kleist's panzer divisions.

Then followed scenes, repetitions of which were to be commonplace throughout the whole war.

On the ground forward of the River Mius there was a most fearful confusion as all the motor transport which had arrived back in the position was turned round again and sent back eastwards. At eleven o'clock on that morning of 1 December Halder discussed the position on the telephone with General von Sodenstern, the Chief of Staff of Army Group South, with the calculating and unscrupulous von Reichenau butting in to say that the Führer's decision was quite right and that he (von Reichenau) would take the necessary responsibility, even though von Kleist was of the opinion that 1 Panzer Army would be defeated if it fought on the intermediate position. Von Kleist, however, regarded the intermediate position as useless and did not understand why his army should be broken only six miles forward of a much better line to its rear.

Both the Führer and von Reichenau refused to be convinced. At 2:00 P.M. Halder took the unusual step of bringing Jodl into the affair, asking him to reason with Hitler. At 3:30 P.M. Halder suggested to von Brauchitsch that he should go to see the Führer once more and, while the German Army Commander-in-Chief was actually talking to the dictator, von Reichenau telephoned Hitler *direct* to say that the Russians had broken through the *SS Leibstandarte* on the intermediate position and begged that he be allowed to fall back to the Mius. Permission was immediately given. "So," commented a rueful Halder, "we have arrived where we were yesterday evening. Meanwhile we have lost energy, time and von Rundstedt."[3]

In company with Colonel Schmundt, his military aide, the Führer then flew to Mariupol to see his former Party crony Sepp Dietrich, a strong-arm man who had once been his driver and bodyguard but was now the divisional commander of the *SS Liebstandarte,* to hear what he hoped would be a condemnation of the German Army field leader-ship; he was disappointed because the SS were convinced that they themselves would not have survived if they had remained in the forward positions. So this strange and unstable man returned to Rastenburg, his mind inflamed against von Reichenau. For Field-Marshal von Reichenau, once German Military Attaché in London, was unorthodox and none too trustworthy and he had, surprisingly, apparently incurred Hitler's displeasure by criticizing von Rundstedt and von Brauchitsch.[4]

Nor was the position in the north, near Leningrad, without its problems. Field-Marshal Wilhelm *Ritter* von Leeb, who like Halder was a precise Bavarian, was so cool and dispassionate in his judgment that, when in British captivity, he had surprised his listeners by scathingly condemning his own actions as though he were a third party. The extrinsic von Leeb had been ordered not only to encircle Leningrad but to drive north-eastwards, firstly to the bauxite-producing area of Tikhvin and then to the Svir to make a junction with the Finns. The country which he had to cross was for the most part heaily wooded marshland with very few roads and tracks.

At first von Leeb had made steady progress, but after von Richthofen's air corps and Hoepner's panzer corps had been removed to the area of Smolensk ready for the drive on Moscow, the offensive of Army Group North slowly came to a standstill. By 8 November, however, Colonel-General Busch's 16 Army, using the only panzer corps remaining to von Leeb, broke into the town of Tikhvin, scattering Lieutenant-General Yakovlev's 4 Soviet Army.

The Soviet line was soon restored; Stalin, alert, terse and practical, telephoned Meretskov, the Commander of 7 Army on the Svir, who was of course well known to him, having been the Chief of General Staff until the previous January. Stalin ordered him to give up his own 7 Army and take over the direct command of 4 Army together with all other troops in the area.[5] From this *ad hoc* arrangement a new Volkhov Front was to be born, Meretskov remaining as its commander for most of the war.

General Meretskov, another survivor from the concentration camp in the time of the purges, hastening to Stalin's bidding, took energetic action to counter-attack into Tikhvin. During the month of November von Leeb was gradually losing his initiative, an initiative which was never to be regained by Army Group North throughout the course of the Russo-German War.

Hitler's erratic and illogical strategy has subsequently been criticized by the German *Generalität* and General Staff, and rightly so. Yet the OKH operational and intelligence directorates were themselves not well informed at that time and their appreciations were often confused and contradictory, being based on little more than surmise.

Earlier the General Staff had believed that Stalin would hold on to Moscow and the Caucasus, using the line of the Don only as a connecting link between those two important areas. In due course this gave way to a somewhat contrary view that the enemy would defend Moscow at all costs even to the extent of draining troops from North Russia and the Ukraine to reinforce the threatened central sector. When von Leeb had protested against the removal of Luftwaffe and panzer formations from the Leningrad area he had, as already recounted, been told by the OKH that von Bock's thrust on Moscow would so ease the task of Army Group North that it would have no difficulty in securing its far-away objectives on the Svir and beyond.

So it came about that on 27 November Halder was to note with some surprise the weight of the Red Army attacks against von Leeb and was to marvel at the continued strength of the enemy artillery. Two days later the truth began to dawn when the pattern of the enemy counter-offensives over the whole Eastern Front indicated that, in addition to transferring troops to the Moscow area, Stalin was relentlessly driving all his armies forward into the attack irrespective of their weakened condition.[6]

This was exactly what was happening. During late November and December Stalin was desperately trying, in his efforts to save Moscow, to wrest the initiative from the enemy wherever Soviet troops were in contact, from Lake Ladoga in the north to the Straits of Kerch in the south. It came as an unpleasant discovery to the OKH when irrefutable intelligence was received that even the enemy in the flanking theaters was being reinforced, for on 2 December twenty-nine troop trains were counted on the move westwards towards Tikhvin, while three new armies from Iran had arrived on the shores of the Straits of Kerch ready to make a seaborne landing on the Crimea.[7]

From Halder's daily conversations with the chiefs of staff of the three army groups it is plain that, probably for the first time in the course of the whole war, the crisis felt by the army groups had at last communicated itself in part to the OKH; it was obvious that the Red Army, in spite of its very heavy losses, was still in being and, in places, was fighting strongly. Nowhere was there any firm indication of the promised collapse. The enemy still had plentiful reinforcements and resources and a good railway net with lateral tracks running the length of the battle area. The Germans were entirely without a north-south railway. The Soviet State Railway, unlike the *Reichsbahn,* continued to operate efficiently in the bitterly cold weather.

The OKH itself was in disarray. Halder gloomily discussed with Major-General Heusinger, the chief of the operations department, the Führer's recent fact-finding tour of 1 Panzer Army. This visit, it was suspected, had as its aim the collection of evidence of incompetency on von Brauchitsch's part, since no member of the OKH had been invited to accompany the dictator.[8]

On 4 December, on Hitler's return, Bodewin Keitel, the younger brother of the field-marshal and the head of the *Heerespersonalamt* responsible for senior officer appointments, broached to Halder the subject of a replacement for the Commander-in-Chief, since "there was a possibility that von Brauchitsch might be retired for health reasons." Halder wisely chose to keep out of such maneuvers.[9] He himself had more to do than he could cope with, for he was bombarded on all sides; von Leeb felt that the leadership was divorced from the situation on the ground and he did not like the way the campaign was being conducted for him from Rastenburg; von Reichenau had said that he *must* have more formations; and even the troops in Africa complained of high losses and demanded reinforcements which could not be sent.

On 30 November, the same day that the von Rundstedt crisis arose, von Bock, the Commander of Army Group Center, was in almost desperate straits in front of Moscow. That day he had a long telephone conversation with von Brauchitsch in which he reported the position as critical. The enemy was still bringing up fresh troops, well equipped for winter warfare, and these were being concentrated on the north and south flanks of Army Group Center. The situation, thought von Bock, looked decidedly dangerous. If the German attack was to be continued, Army Group Center had only one course open to it, to thrust eastwards frontally on to the Moscow defenses, ignoring the threat to the flanks; this was a type of battle which von Bock did not relish.

Von Brauchitsch, however, was an inattentive listener on that day and pathetically sought crumbs of comfort. "But was not Guderian over the Oka?" and "We have heard that von Kluge has already broken into the defenses west of Moscow." Yet the evasive von Brauchitsch made it clear that in no circumstances was he prepared to take von Bock's long tale of woe to the Führer; the Commander-in-Chief took the attitude that Army Group Center had received its orders and had better carry them out. The Führer was convinced, said von Brauchitsch, that the Russian was at the end of his tether, and the Commander-in-Chief reiterated that the sole responsibility for the taking of Moscow rested on von Bock's shoulders; he, von Brauchitsch, did not want to get involved as a go-between.

Von Bock, taken aback, became both worried and irritated, but with the exercise of much self-control he explained simply and clearly that Guderian's spearheads were without momentum or depth and could not hold. Von Kluge's behavior was a mystery, said von Bock, and he recounted to von Brauchitsch how the Commander of 4 Army, although pressed time and time again, had been reluctant to start his offensive.

From this he went on to winter equipment and he reminded von Brauchitsch that he had repeatedly reported to the OKH that his exhausted men were unequipped for winter warfare.

At this point, unbelievable though it may seem in retrospect, von Brauchitsch, sitting in East Prussia, contradicted von Bock, telling him that the winter clothing and equipment *had* been delivered to the troops. When von Bock demanded bluntly that the Commander-in-Chief should inform the Führer of the true situation, von Brauchitsch was struck with deafness and countered with the impertinent reply that he wished only to inform the Führer of the anticipated date when von Bock would take Moscow. Any further words by von Bock were answered by the same demand, repeated almost parrot-fashion.[10]

To such straits had the German High Command been reduced. Yet von Brauchitsch was a man of ability and in normal circumstances, freed from the overbearing presence of the dictator, he would probably have made an adequate Commander-in-Chief.

On 1 December, the same day that 1 Panzer Army was in danger of encirclement at Rostov and von Rundstedt had been relieved of his command, von Bock confirmed in a teleprint message to the OKH the views he had already given orally to von Brauchitsch. He was willing, he said, to continue the offensive but he had little faith in his ability to achieve his mission, for the troops themselves had lost confidence. All attacks had to be made frontally and at the best any advances would only be limited tactical affairs. Unless, however, he could be kept better supplied, he recommended going over to the defensive, making such withdrawals as were necessary to shorten his *700-mile-long frontage.*[11]

Two days later, when von Kluge had, on his own responsibility, already called off the attacks, von Bock, not trusting von Brauchitsch, telephoned Jodl at the OKW to make sure that the Führer was in possession of the full facts of the situation. This conversation is illuminating in that it took a different form from that with von Brauchitsch three days before. Whereas the earlier tendency had been to describe the situation graphically and forcefully, yet no less truthfully, presumably in an effort to compel the reluctant von Brauchitsch to take action, the conversation with Jodl, which, as von Bock knew, would be faithfully reported to Hitler, if anything rather understated the case. Indeed von Bock, surprisingly and somewhat weakly, ended on an optimistic note, holding out some slight hope that he might succeed in his task of taking the capital![12]

Yet, not forty-eight hours afterwards, von Bock acquiesced to what had already happened and, with the agreement of the OKH, called off the offensive. He would, he said, send news the following day on what withdrawals would be necessary. That day von Brauchitsch decided that he was going to give up his appointment and leave the Army; in this he was only bowing to the inevitable, for the Führer intended that he should go.

On 6 December Hitler held a meeting to discuss future action and the ideas he expressed and his decisions at this time were to set a pattern for the rest of the war, destroying three successive Chiefs of General Staff.

The Führer had read the OKH strategic appreciation of the relative strengths of the Russian and German forces and did not agree with a word of it. Statistics, he said, were en entirely unreliable guide to strength. But Hitler, who was never lost for a ready answer or convenient figure, usually conjured up from his fertile imagination to give support to his view, proceeded to base his argument on entirely false assumptions. He surprised his listeners by giving the German losses to date as only 500,000 against Red Army casualties of between eight and ten million. (In fact the German casualties were 830,000 and the Soviet losses probably not more than six million.) The enemy had lost so much artillery, Hitler continued, that it virtually no longer existed as an arm. If, concluded the Führer, German divisions were obliged to hold extended battle frontages of twenty miles or more, then *that* was conclusive proof of the weakness of the enemy.[13]

There could be little point in reasoning with a man whose logic was so devious.

At this meeting Hitler persuaded himself that all the advantages were on his side and he proposed a number of makeshift schemes to release German manpower to the Eastern Front. These included the raising of fighting formations from motor vehicle drivers, idle because of the great number of trucks derelict or awaiting repairs, the combing out of the rear services and the replacement of German civil labor by prisoners of war. There were, said the Führer, 65,000 men in Rumania and many more at home on leave. Under no circumstances would he permit any thinning out of troops from Scandinavia or Western Europe; those on the Channel coast in particular had to be ready to undertake the occupation of Vichy France should the situation go sour in North Africa. The Russian had held his ground in front of Moscow and so would the German.

Although he was to change his views a few days later, the Führer was not opposed in principle, so he said, to shortening the Army Group Center defense line, but there could be no question of pulling out before the rearward positions were prepared. He still had his eyes on Donets coal and Caucasian oil, nor had he written off the likelihood of the recapture of Rostov during that winter.

That same night General Brennecke, the chief of staff to von Leeb, came on the telephone to say that there was the gravest anxiety about the situation at Tikhvin. In temperatures as low as minus 35 degrees centigrade, cold so intense that, because of technical failure, only one in five German tanks could fire its guns, the enemy, after intensive artillery bombardment, had broken in and was about to encircle the town. The next day von Leeb was permitted by the Führer to withdraw, but only on condition that the area of Tikhvin was kept within range of artillery.

With Army Group Center, however, Hitler was already making difficulties about any withdrawal and Halder was to record the depths to which the Army High Command had sunk, for "the Führer himself dealt direct with the army group commanders." Von Brauchitsch, Halder said, was merely the postman.[14] At the time of von Rundstedt's dismissal and replacement, Hitler did not even bother to consult his Commander-in-Chief.

On 8 December the Führer grudgingly agreed that the Army Group Center offensive could not be resumed, and he covered this by a directive in which he gave as the reason "the unusually early severe weather."[15]

The Commander-in-Chief had not been to Army Group Center for at least two months and on 13 Decemer he paid a last fleeting visit. Von Bock noted how very ill he looked. Von Bock was in favor of a general withdrawal behind Smolensk, but von Brauchitsch told him that the Führer would certainly not agree to that. Von Brauchitsch in his turn sketched out a Winter Line only ninety miles or so to the west of the forward localities, this line following the north–south roadway just east of Vyazma through Zubtsov, Gzhatsk and Yukhnov. But he feared to authorize even this more limited withdrawal on his own responsibility, saying that the affair was a political matter requiring confirmation by the Führer.

The Commander-in-Chief then went on to Roslavl to see von Kluge and Guderian, and, if the latter is to be believed, sanctioned certain minor withdrawals by 2 Panzer Army. On 15 December von Brauchitsch returned to Rastenburg very dejected and low in spirits, for he could see no way by which Army Group Center could be extracted from its dangerously exposed position.[16]

The Führer of course placed no reliance on any briefing on the situation in front of Moscow that he might receive from von Brauchitsch. It is possible, too, that he had some doubts as to whether von Bock should be left in command. Within twenty-four hours of von Brauchitsch's arrival at Headquarters Army Group Center, Schmundt, the Führer's military aide, followed. Schmundt, only a colonel at the time, was on very close terms with Hitler. No other officer was more loyal or more subservient. Yet field-marshals were obliged to defer to him, for they knew that everything said went back to the Führer's ears.

From this time onwards von Bock ignored Halder and the OKH, but he went to extraordinary lengths to persuade Schmundt to telephone a report direct to the dictator, emphasizing the seriousness of the situation. The only responsible officer in the OKW who could be readily reached was Jodl, and to him Schmundt gave a briefing for onward transmission to Hitler. Shortly afterwards Hitler called back but would talk only to Schmundt, not to von Bock. Minor tactical withdrawals within Army Group Center *might* be permitted, the Führer thought.

The next day, however, Hitler had changed his mind again and, when he telephoned Schmundt, who was still at von Bock's headquarters, he forbade any withdrawal, however small.

During the remainder of that day which Schmundt spent at Army Group Center, the stiff and arrogant von Bock appears to have opened his heart; the consequences were to be of the utmost importance both for von Bock and for Army Group Center. The field-marshal made a verbal military appreciation of the situation for Schmundt's benefit and said that the Führer would have to make a choice. He could resume the attack towards Moscow, risking the danger that in doing so he might beat his own troops to pieces, or he could remain on the defensive. If the Führer chose to defend, he should remember that no defensive works had been prepared either in the present positions or in the rear and it was in any case doubtful whether the German troops could hold. Von Bock quoted as an example 267 Division, which had been forced to withdraw that very day at the cost of leaving all its artillery behind.

This conversation, carefully recounted by Schmundt the next day, had a profound effect on Hitler, for, when he heard it, he translated von Bock's musings into a course of action; his mind was made up. He had always been opposed, on the grounds of loss of prestige and countenance, to any withdrawal, but von Bock's military appreciation enabled the Führer to clothe the naked truth. He telephoned the Commander of Army Group Center and, taking von Bock's words as his own, said that, as no defensive positions had been prepared, there was nowhere to withdraw to; a withdrawal would entail the leaving behind of the artillery and heavy equipment; so the obvious answer was to stand firm and not withdraw at all![17]

From these conversations was born the "stand and fight" order which was to have such momentous consequences, not only during the retreat from Moscow but on Germany's fortunes during the whole of the Second World War.

It is hard to say exactly what was von Bock's state of mind at this time. During the second half of 1940 he had suffered from stomach ulcers and this had kept him away from duty until February 1941. The reverses in front of Moscow had put him under the severest of mental strain. He described his own health to Schmundt as precarious, knowing, indeed asking, that the details should be reported to Hitler.

It is very difficult not to arrive at the conclusion that von Bock wanted to be relieved of his appointment. Two days later the elder Keitel, the field-marshal, was on the telephone saying that the Führer had suggested that von Bock might take extended leave on account of his health, a proposal which von Bock appears to have viewed with mixed feelings: thankfulness, presumably in view of his health, regret, at leaving his command in such difficult circumstances, and suspicion, that he had not been relieved for the reasons given but had in fact been dismissed. All these feelings found place in his diary. Guilt was subsequently to be added, for afterwards he began to think that he should have stayed at his post.

Although the method by which von Bock was relieved was to set a pattern for many of the subsequent dismissals of higher commanders, that is to say, a telephone call from Keitel with the suggestion that the officer concerned should ask for his own removal on the grounds of ill-health, it does not appear that von Bock was out of Hitler's favor on this occasion. For, two months later he was recalled to the active list. It was not until July 1942 that Field-Marshal von Bock was to receive his final telephone call from Keitel suggesting that he should report sick. This time the Führer was indeed implacably hostile and von Bock was dismissed, never to be re-employed.

Von Bock was replaced at Army Group Center by von Kluge, the commander of 4 Army, it being at first understood that von Kluge was merely caretaking and holding the temporary command in von Bock's absence. Von Kluge, no friend of von Bock's, was more acceptable to the Führer, and by the New Year von Kluge had been confirmed in his appointment.

According to Keitel, the Führer had for long realized, however he might try to conceal it from his staff, that military catastrophe was near and he was searching for scapegoats; but it seems more likely that Hitler was convinced that his senior commanders lacked the fanaticism, willpower and even the professional ability to overcome their many difficulties.[18] Some of them were guilty of the graver fault of beginning to doubt the Führer's intuition and genius, and these were marked down for elimination.

Hitler had never held von Brauchitsch in very high esteem, but in 1938 he had chosen him as Commander-in-Chief because von Brauchitsch appeared to be loyal and an enthusiastic supporter of National Socialism. The Führer's opinion of his new Commander-in-Chief dropped sharply in 1939 and 1940 not merely because he recognized that the man had a flaw in his character, a certain weakness of will, but more particularly because von Brauchitsch failed to prove himself as Hitler's blindly obedient and ruthless executive. Caught between the upper millstone in the form of the Führer, and the lower in the shape of the army group commanders, von Brauchitsch, because he lacked both conviction and will, was unable to make his immediate subordinates obey orders in which he himself did not believe.

Nor did von Brauchitsch have the courage to make a stand against the dictator. Instead, he tried to divorce himself from all activity and responsibility. For this, the Führer, among whose less attractive traits was that of sneering at his absent subordinates, was to call von Brauchitsch "strawhead" and "a vain cowardly wretch and a nincompoop."[19] Von Brauchitsch's personality and health rapidly went to pieces under the pressure of the dictator's bullying.

As we know, Hitler had been considering ridding himself of von Brauchitsch from about 4 December and on the 16th of the month Schmundt told von Bock in confidence that the Commander-in-Chief was definitely to go. But the little matter of the dismissal was still dragging on and Hitler had not yet brought himself to the point of sending him packing. Finally on 19 December the two had their final acrimonious leave-taking, a very unpleasant meeting which lasted two hours. When von Brauchitsch came out from the interview he told Keitel quite bluntly that he had been sacked. Neither von Brauchitsch nor Keitel knew at that time who the new Commander-in-Chief of the Army was to be.[20]

The Führer had been closeted several hours that day with Colonel Schmundt, discussing the question of von Brauchitsch's replacement.

The views of Jodl or the two Keitels were not asked for and certainly not those of Halder. For Hitler had decided that he himself would take over the operational control of the German Army on the Eastern Front, and both he and Schmundt spent their time drafting an order of the day announcing the Führer's assuming of command. Von Brauchitsch's retirement was explained on grounds of sickness.[21] The time was particularly opportune as it could be implied, if not actually said, that the outgoing Commander-in-Chief was mainly responsible for the desperate straits in which the German Army then found itself.

Göring and Rader, the Commanders-in-Chief of the Luftwaffe and the German Navy, exercised the fullest command over their air and naval formations, irrespective of where these were operating, and, as Commanders-in-Chief, were subject only to the direct control of the Führer in his capacity as the Supreme Commander of the Armed Forces (Wehrmacht). Keitel, Jodl and the OKW had no jurisdiction or control over the air arm or fleet. With the German Army, however, the situation was very different.

By June 1941, von Brauchitsch had suffered a very serious diminishing of his responsibilities in that the operational control over the German Army formations in Western Europe, Scandinavia, Finland, the Balkans, the Mediterranean and Africa had been removed from the OKH. Hitler himself had assumed direct command over the German Army in these theaters. Planning and executive control was the responsibility not of Halder, the Chief of General Staff, but of Jodl and the *Wehrmachtführungsstab,* a part of the OKW. In 1941 there was no ground fighting in any of these so-called OKW theaters except Finland and Africa.

On 19 December, when von Brauchitsch was dismissed, Hitler had simply decided to extend the process of direct control by himself over the German Army, from the OKW theaters to the only OKH theater, the Eastern Front in Russia. When the Führer loosely stated his intention of taking over as Commander-in-Chief of the German Army, what he really meant was that he was going to assume direct *operational,* even tactical, control over the army group commanders, so that he could force them to do what they were told. In this, so Hitler thought, von Brauchitsch had failed him. In von Brauchitsch's many other functions as Commander-in-Chief Hitler had no interest and these he merely handed over to Keitel.[22] The taking over of the direct field command was merely an expression of the inner man. Hitler wanted to be a general as well as a head of state.

In June 1941 Hitler had already forfeited his standing as a world statesman and war leader when, willfully underestimating his enemies and believing that all problems could be resolved by force, he entered into a war on two fronts. He then incited Japan to enter the war, not against the Soviet Union but against Great Britain's eastern dependencies; Tokyo, however, attacked both United States and British Pacific bases. The Führer's penultimate folly, without good reason or cause and with little regard to the consequences, was to declare war on the United States.

The final madness was yet to be played out in Russia. For Hitler's overwhelming desire to display his military genius was to have a disastrous effect on the way in which he controlled Germany's destiny in war. His attention became riveted on the technicalities, the details, and even the trivialities of the fighting on the Eastern Front, so that when the territories into which he had so light-heartedly entered bogged down his panzers and soaked up the blood of his infantry, what was to have been an easily won summer campaign became instead, first a major war, then an all-consuming crusade against the Bolshevik, pursued with ever increasing fanatical fury, making the dictator blind to any other considerations.

Halder was sent for on that same day, 19 December, and informed of the changes with the words that "this little affair of *operational* command was something anybody could do."[23] Halder was to stay in office acting as the Führer's Chief of Staff for the Eastern Front. The young Keitel was shortly to give up his post as head of the Army Personnel Office, where, as Military Secretary, he had been responsible to von Brauchitsch for senior military appointments. In future the *Heerespersonalamt* was to be transferred to the direct control of the Führer with Schmundt as its newly promoted head. Hitler's control over the German Army and its senior officers was then complete.

In this first meeting in his new capacity of Chief of Staff for the Eastern Front, Halder was left under no illusions that von Brauchitsch and the OKH were regarded by the Führer as being responsible for the misfortunes in Russia. The German Army, sneered Hitler, compared most unfavorably with Göring's Luftwaffe. It had made inadequate preparations against the Russian winter and the troops had been most wrongfully misled by the concept of rearward defensive positions. These positions just did not exist and could not be built; for this reason, emphasized the dictator, *the order would be to stand and fight without regard to threats from the flanks.*[24]

CHAPTER NINE
WAR AT THE TOP

Up to the end of November the Soviet High Command had worked out no plan for a counter-offensive due west of Moscow.

Stalin had been frantically engaged with holding back the German advance and saving his capital and, as Halder so tardily recognized, the Soviet dictator's strategy throughout the month had been to attack everywhere over the whole of the thousand miles of front from Leningrad to the Black Sea. At all costs Stalin wanted to prevent the enemy from reinforcing Army Group Center by withdrawing divisions from Army Groups North and South. In this he was successful.

In the second half of November, however, it became apparent in Moscow that von Leeb and von Rundstedt were overextended and far weaker than had earlier been thought possible; gradually the tide of battle turned so that Red Army troops began to win the local initiative. The Axis advance was at first halted and then, bit by bit, the German formations, poorly supported and supplied, began to give ground. By the end of November the Red Army was probing and thrusting everywhere, except on the West and Kalinin Fronts before Moscow. There, to use Zhukov's words "the exhausted German enemy, although he had lost his momentum, continued to gnaw his way forward. Army Group Center was only nineteen miles from the capital and in spite of its severely weakened condition, could not be brought to a halt."[1]

Zhukov's tactical headquarters was hardly three miles from the forward defended localities; the army command posts were even closer, too close to the enemy for efficient functioning. In the first few days of December, at the time of von Kluge's breakthrough between 5 and 33 Armies, German troops nearing Zhukov's tactical headquarters, so he has said, had been beaten off by the NKVD security regiment responsible for its close defense. Only a few weeks before, the command post of 5 Soviet Army had actually been overrun by enemy tanks and motorized infantry and its commander wounded.

But for both practical and morale reasons there could be no question of removing these headquarters to the rear. The command system in those days depended primarily on field telephone, and the movement of higher headquarters often caused breaks in communication and much time and effort in relaying the field cable. And, although it was rather unusual at that time for the Soviet High Command to concern itself unduly with niceties of the morale of the rank and file of the Red Army, since any action likely to prove unpopular could always be explained away to order by the commissars, Zhukov has subsequently postulated that the final reason against the withdrawal of the higher headquarters and command posts was the disastrous effect that this might have had on the morale of the defending troops. For these had been ordered to die where they stood.

In the crisis of battle the commander's place is where he can best exercise control and this is usually at his command post and headquarters. Zhukov was all for this, and he was later to complain when he had been called away from his command post by Stalin's order and sent scurrying off with Rokossovsky and Govorov to the village of Dedovo. For it was while he was absent from his headquarters on 1 December that von Kluge had made his final attempt to penetrate the 33 Army area. Yet the outcome was bizarre. The new attack alarmed Stalin who, agitated and excited, demanded to know from Sokolovsky why the front commander had left his headquarters at such a time.[2]

What sort of a man was Zhukov at this period and what of his relationship with Stalin and the subordinate generals?

The odd account written by Belov, an old cavalry colleague of Zhukov's, describing a visit the two of them made to the Kremlin in November 1941, in which Stalin is portrayed as lacking assurance in the face of Zhukov's dictatorial manner, can only be dismissed as a fabrication probably intended to denigrate both the leaders. Every other description of the dictator, including, most important of all, those by independent Western observers, emphasize that Stalin's circle lived in mortal fear of him. Zhukov was no exception.

Nor is it likely that Zhukov was on the same plane as the members of the Politburo and the principal political members of the theater and

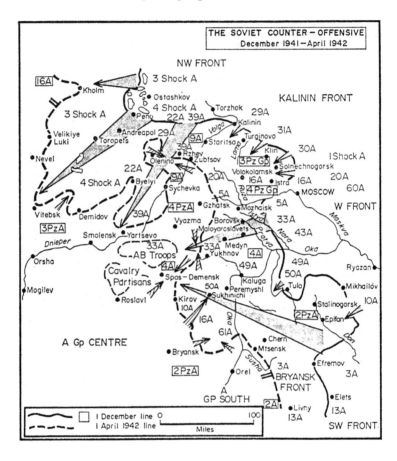

front military councils. Although he might have held his own with Bulganin, he was overshadowed by Molotov, Beria, Khrushchev, Zhdanov and Mekhlis. The role of the high-ranking command personnel of the Red Army in 1941, Zhukov's among them, was little different from that of the re-employed Tsarist officers, the military specialists, after the revolution. Real power remained in the center, with the dictator and those closest to him, the influential political members of the main military councils, Stalin's personal representatives. Zhukov was the highly trained military adviser and executive.

Yet it did not follow that his advice was necessarily asked for or, when asked for, acted upon. And Stalin and the political members of the military councils did not hesitate to interfere in the executive functions of any of the general officers, themselves abusing, upbraiding and commanding subordinate military commanders as the fancy took them. Most political members of the military councils were powerful enough to destroy the front military commanders to whom they were accredited. And these commanders knew it.

Zhukov had either failed, or had been found inconvenient, as a Chief of General Staff. He just did not fit in.

Yet he was a man of proven command experience, and Stalin found for him a fitting and essential role as a trouble shooter, a fixer, someone who could take command in moments of crisis. His strength apparently lay not only in his *operational* ability, but in his ruthless inexorable determination. For Zhukov was a true Russian with all the Russian's inborn respect for brutal authority. His responsibility was to Stalin, Party and self, in that order; like his fellow generals he felt himself in no way answerable to his subordinates or to his troops. The only criterion was success, and it was immaterial how this was achieved.

He who was so careful and diffident, even in the presence of minor political figures like Vishinsky, was frequently a bawling, raging tyrant in the field. When the mood so took him, everything was wrong and nothing could please. Yet he was not so stupid that he would not listen to his staffs and subordinates, keeping a careful note in his retentive mind of any good advice, even if, for the sake of form, he savagely contradicted them. For he was overbearing and contrary with his inferiors.

Yet this was not all, for if the testimony of Batov, Bychevsky and others is to be believed, a Zhukov inspection entailed the summary removal and degradation of corps commanders and the arbitrary arrest and dispatch of worthy divisional commanders to penal companies as private soldiers. These accounts written at the time of Zhukov's disgrace may of course be exaggerated. Yet the descriptions of Western observers in 1945 bear witness to the cold-blooded inhumanity of the man. His detractors say further that he was vain, self-seeking and anxious for fame and glory.

The counter-offensive of the West and Kalinin Fronts, which was eventually to imperil the very existence of Army Group Center, was not a masterly, carefully planned, strategic counter-blow, but simply developed from a number of counter-attacks aimed at saving the Soviet capital.

At about the beginning of December Zhukov telephoned Stalin, the Commander-in-Chief, and asked to be allotted V. I. Kuznetsov's 1 Shock Army and Golikov's 10 Army, still at that time at Stalin's disposal as part of the High Command Reserve. Zhukov needed these armies, he said, to stop the enemy and to restore the situation where there had been a break-in.

Stalin, after hearing him out in silence, showed wisdom when he replied that he was unwilling to release these two reserve armies unless the enemy had committed all his reserves and shot his bolt. It was Zhukov's opinion that Army Group Center had already done so.

The still-doubting Stalin said that he would talk to the General Staff. Zhukov, not slow to exploit any opening, instructed Sokolovsky, his chief of staff, to put the West Front case to the General Staff in Moscow before Stalin should consult it. By that evening the two armies had been allotted to the West Front, together with a third, Vlasov's 20 Army.[3]

As usual, the military council of the West Front was ordered to submit plans to Moscow explaining how they proposed to use the reinforcing armies, for Stalin always expected value, in terms of results, in exchange for any new troops allocated to the fronts from his carefully husbanded High Command Reserve. A few hours later Stalin was again on the telephone, suggesting to Zhukov that the time was opportune for "a counter-offensive." This Zhukov doubted, but it was agreed that the formations of the West Front in the line should try and pin the enemy in front of them, while Kuznetsov's and Vlasov's armies attacked from the north flank and Golikov enveloped Guderian's 2 Panzer Army from the south. West Front's outline plans were confirmed by Stalin without alteration.

Then followed a short lull while Zhukov's military council continued its preparations and planning, but on 2 December Stalin was back on the telephone, volunteering no information, but wanting to be briefed on the battle situation. In particular he required to know if the enemy had shown any hitherto unrevealed strength. He then rang off.

Stalin was a man who never wasted time or words, and Zhukov suspected that something new was afoot. So it was for, having given the plans further examination, Stalin had decided that he was not getting a big enough return for the allocation of three reserve armies. After some prompting, Shaposhnikov and Vasilevsky, the head of the operations department, had produced new plans and proposals. Konev's Kalinin Front was at right angles to the West Front and ran for 120 miles along the Army Group Center left flank; it was in an excellent position to probe into the enemy rear. The right flank of Timoshenko's South-West Theater could also attack in the area of Elets against the weak and extended 2 German Army.

This new concept was more to Stalin's liking. The offensives to be made by the two flanking fronts were to be carefully coordinated with that of the West Front. In this way the plans for a much more ambitious counter-offensive were quickly built up.

On 4 December Stalin told Zhukov that Konev and Timoshenko would definitely be taking part in the offensive, these flanking attacks to start on 5 and 6 December, and he allocated to West Front additional air formations from the PVO (Anti-Aircraft Command) and the High Command Reserves. He had no further tank formations left.[4]

Yet Zhukov has stressed that, even at this point in the planning, far from being the grandiose master stroke so often portrayed by historical writers, the offensive was still limited in its extent and had no aim other than that of making Moscow safe by pushing the enemy back and gaining room for maneuver; at the most it was hoped to gain forty miles of territory; the flanking attacks were intended simply to threaten the enemy's communications and force him to withdraw. No one at that time would have considered the destruction of Army Group Center as even a remote possibility. Nor did Stalin, Zhukov or the General Staff expect the remarkable success which was to follow. Because so many other ambitious counter-offensives had failed miserably in the past, the Soviet leaders were inured and accustomed to defeat.

The Red Army local counter-attacks continued in the first few days in December and the Soviet formations soon became aware of the surprising German weakness in the air and on the ground, for the enemy was much reduced in numbers and in firepower and his pitifully equipped troops were physically and morally exhausted.

Army Group Center, as the Soviet High Command was soon to realize, had advanced eastwards from Smolensk without a predetermined *Schwerpunkt,* the formations opening out like the ribs of a fan, intent only on covering ground. This had resulted in a grossly extended frontage of nearly 700 miles, from Ostashkov in the north to the Kursk-Voronezh railway in the south. Von Bock had neither *operational* nor tactical reserves and his troops were scattered and without depth. The OKW directive of 8 December, and Hitler's subsequent standstill orders over the following days, tied the handfuls of troops to the defense of ground in close, heavily wooded country, without prepared positions and without any form of continuous front. Far from being in contact with their neighbors, many of the German infantry divisions could only cover the roads and main tracks and the principal towns and settlements. Few Germans set foot in the intervening forests and frozen marshes, through which the Red Army troops and partisans began to infiltrate at will.

Already Hitler had begun to play into Stalin's hands, making a present to him firstly of the tactical and then of the *operational* and strategic initiative. But the Führer's determination to hold ground was an obsession which became a mania, until, in 1943 and 1944, a situation was to arise when Stalin's success, as the dictator himself confided to Churchill, was to depend on his ability to shunt sixty divisions of the High Command Reserve to and fro, from Leningrad to the Black Sea, mounting offensives in successsion first in one theater and then in another.

On the night of 5 December Konev's Kalinin Front attacked across the frozen upper Volga. At first resistance was fierce except in front of Major-General Yushkevich's 31 Army which, moving forward rapidly, penetrated Strauss's 9 Army and took Turginovo twenty miles in the German rear.

The next day the right flank of Zhukov's West Front took up the offensive and, after heavy artillery and aerial bombardments in which 700 tactical support aircraft took part, attacked Reinhardt's and

Hoepner's 3 and 4 Panzer Groups immediately to the north of Moscow. Kuznetsov's 1 Shock Army, Rokossovsky's 16 Army and Lelyushenko's 30 Army, recently reinforced by six Siberian and Ural divisions, began to move across the Kalinin–Moscow railway.[5]

To the surprise of the attacking troops, the Germans fell back about fifteen miles to the west and for the very first time it was borne in on Zhukov that the enemy was losing the initiative. By 13 December Kuznetsov had reached Klin. By then the pattern of the German defense had become apparent, for the enemy fought bitterly in defense of any town or settlement. Klin was only a small township with a peacetime population of about 10,000, yet it took two days to clear after particularly fierce fighting. The commanders of the advancing Soviet troops were quick to take advantage of the German tactics and to by-pass all centers of resistance, infiltrating into the rear as fast as their legs or ponies could carry them.

16 Army, well supported by Govorov's 5 Army on its left, began to move forward rapidly alongside the Istra reservoirs, crossing the ground over which it had so painfully retreated a month before. Its commander, the capable Rokossovsky, just promoted to Lieutenant-General, was once Zhukov's superior officer, but had lost seniority when in a concentration camp during the time of the Great Purge. He was a Russian, possibly of White Russian stock (since he had been born at Velikiye Luki), and not a Warsaw Pole, as was subsequently claimed by the Soviet Union. He was a quiet, cultured, well-mannered man who would always patiently hear out his subordinates. This, admittedly, was not a Russian characteristic.

On 12 December Vlasov took Solnechnogorsk.

Zhukov's center, made up of Efremov's 33, Golubev's 43 and Zakharkin's 49 Armies, was given only the secondary role of pinning 4 German Army, with which of course they were all in contact. They could do no more, for they themselves were severely weakened after the recent fighting; nor had they been reinforced or re-equipped.

It was to the south, on Zhukov's southern flank, that Stalin pinned his hopes. There Guderian's troops were in a sorry plight and very dangerously extended. The beginning of December had found 2 Panzer Army in a great salient to the east of Tula with a frontage of about

150 miles, stretching from Alexin to Efremov, without any pretense of depth or continuity. And, as Zhukov was to point out, Guderian was entirely without reserves. To Guderian's south, Rudolf Schmidt's 2 Army was similarly and perilously exposed.

Guderian was attacked by Boldin's reinforced 50 Army from the area of Tula, which already formed a threatening wedge in Guderian's rear. Boldin was supported by Belov's cavalry corps, held ready for pursuit operations. To the south of Boldin, Golikov's 10 Army, already detrained in the area of Ryazan, attacked Guderian from the east, having been ordered to take Stalinogorsk and Epifan. On Golikov's left flank, shock formations of tanks, cavalry and infantry had been formed by Gorodnyansky's 13 Army on the right of Timoshenko's South-West Theater, for penetration tasks into Rudolf Schmidt's rear.[6]

Boldin's attack had been made some days before those of the other armies, as early as 3 December, and was really designed to beat off Guderian's encircling movement on Tula and his thrusts towards Kashira on the Oka. Guderian's troops began to withdraw southwards to Venev, leaving seventy tanks bogged and broken down on the battlefield. On 6 December Golikov took up the attack in support of Boldin and the 2 Panzer Army men began to fall back rapidly; heavy artillery, prime movers, tanks and lorries were left behind. The Soviet advance on this southern flank began to gain momentum.

By 13 December the Soviet High Command had already realized that the situation had arisen where Army Group Center was defenseless against a deep envelopment on the south flank, and in order to strengthen the Soviet left wing, which at that time appeared to be on the point of breaking into the enemy rear, a new Bryansk Front was formed from Pshennikov's 3 and Gorodnyansky's 13 Armies, both removed from Timoshenko, and a newly arrived 61 Army under Popov. The new front commander was a cavalryman, Colonel-General Cherevichenko, the former Commander of South Front, fresh from his victory over von Rundstedt at Rostov.

The Red Army strength in the Moscow region at this time was sixteen armies, of which three formed the Bryansk and three the Kalinin Fronts. In all the Bryansk, Kalinin and West Fronts disposed of seventy-eight rifle and twenty-two cavalry divisions and nineteen rifle and seventeen tank brigades. The force was said to include 720 tanks and 1,170 aircraft.[7]

These early successes fired Stalin's enthusiasm and imagination. The counter-offensive plans were extended even further and the sector of operations was widened to a frontage of 600 and a depth of 200 miles. For he had decided that Army Group Center *was to be destroyed* by an attack on each shoulder of the German salient, one wedge being made by Konev's Kalinin Front from the area of Kalinin towards distant Smolensk, over 200 miles away; the left flank of Zhukov's front in the south, together with the Bryansk Front, was to drive in a great arc from Stalinogorsk to Sukhinichi and then on to Vyazma and Smolensk. In addition, Kurochkin's North-West Front had to make a secondary and yet deeper right encircling thrust, to the west and outside that made by Konev, from the area of Demyansk and Ostashkov roughly along the boundary between the German Army Groups Center and North.

The whole counter-offensive was designed to encircle a great German pocket, nearly 200 miles in depth, stretching almost from Moscow to beyond Smolensk, using one left and two right pincers one outside the other.

In this new plan the strong right flank of the West Front was no longer so important, since its task had been taken over by Konev and Kurochkin; its task was to be downgraded to keeping up a westward pressure and, in conjunction with the center, attempting to pin Army Group Center and prevent it from withdrawing. In fact, although this was not known in Moscow, Hitler had done its work for it when he issued his "stand and fight" order.

On 15 December, such was the optimism in Moscow, and so sure was the Politburo that the capital was no longer in danger, that the Central Committee and the main departments of government were ordered to return from Kuybyshev.[8]

In spite of the fact that all air operations were hampered by poor visibility and bad flying weather, the Red Air Force had achieved a decisive air superiority in the Moscow sector, since the total Luftwaffe strength in support of Army Group Center had sunk on 12 December to 160 fighters and 330 bombers.[9] Soviet aircraft bombed and machine-gunned enemy defensive positions and rear areas and made movement on the main arterial routes a hazardous business. Few Luft-waffe fighters seemed to be in the air. This newly won air superiority was put to good use by the Soviet High Command.

A thousand miles to the west in the East Prussian General Headquar-ters at Rastenburg, neither the Führer nor the German High Command had a close understanding of the conditions of the fighting in front of Moscow.

Nor was this ignorance confined to the OKW, for Kinzel, the head of Foreign Armies East, although a much wiser and more sober intelligence officer than he had been a year before, on 4 November had issued an intelligence appreciation in which he had said that "the strength of the Russian was not so high that he was capable of a major offensive without considerable reinforcement."[10] The intelligence and *OKH Lage Ost* maps of 6 December show that Kinzel was unaware of the presence of Kuznetsov's 1 Shock, Golikov's 10 or Vlasov's 20 Armies. Yet, in spite of this, Kinzel's enemy order of battle estimate issued the same day, putting the Red Army strength in front of Moscow at twelve armies, made up of eighty-eight rifle and fifteen cavalry divisions and twenty-four tank brigades, was not far short of the num-ber of Soviet formations actually in the area.[11]

There was, too, more than an element of truth in Kinzel's general assessment of the Red Army's fighting capabilities, for it *had* been severely weakened, and this is borne out by the German field forma-tion war-diary entries at the time. Even after the Soviet attacks had begun, the Army Group Center war diarist noted that the offensive spirit of the Red Army was not at all well developed, and the writer ascribed Soviet success to the poor physical and moral condition of the German troops whose strength had been so grossly overtaxed. He complained of the reduced fighting strengths, the lack of vehicle fuels and supplies and the severe shortage of good draught horses, which the little Russian ponies could not replace.[12]

Kinzel had not identified the three newly arriving armies but this was not of decisive importance. More damaging was the failure of the whole of the High Command, the Führer, the OKW, the OKH and the General Staff, of which Kinzel formed part, to recognize the relative weakness of the German troops. In December 1941 nearly all the high and key appointments in the OKW and OKH were staffed by officers who had no experience of fighting in the field in the Second World War, on the Eastern Front or elsewhere; this was a situation which was to continue throughout the whole of the war; by 1944 and 1945, with only one or two exceptions, Hitler's principal staff officers and advisers had occupied the same office chair for six or seven years.

So the position was to arise where the German Army Commander-in-Chief, von Brauchitsch, and the Führer himself, even as late as 17 December, were so divorced from the situation on the ground that they were to believe, not only that there was sufficient clothing and equipment for all the troops in Russia, but that it had actually been issued to troops in the field.

It became noticeable, too, during the first terrible winter in Russia, that the greater the distance from the front line, the more sanguine did German opinions and expectations become. The further away one was from the Russian the greater the tendency to underestimate him.

This was in direct contrast to the Soviet command and staff system at that time which, in spite of its many imperfections, was already developing a workable staff and field command relationship. With the exception of the aging Shaposhnikov, who held the appointment of Chief of General Staff for a year until mid-1942, many of the principal staff officers and advisers had recent command experience; others had been brought into the General Staff at Moscow from command or staff appointments in the field. All were expected to keep themselves abreast of conditions on the ground by frequent visits and by carrying out major planning at the subordinate field headquarters.

Then there was the question of age. Stalin was sixty-one, Hitler only fifty-two. But whereas the Führer's military commanders and staffs were a good deal older than he, the principal commanders and staffs of the Red Army were extraordinarily young. The three German army group commanders were all in their sixties, von Leeb and von Rundstedt being in their mid-sixties. Even those active panzer leaders Guderian and Hoepner were in their mid-fifties. But Timoshenko, Zhukov, Meretskov, Konev and Kurochkin were all between forty and forty-five. The only two old men of the Party were Shaposhnikov, who was fifty-eight, and Voroshilov, who was fifty-nine.

On 16 December, when the tension was mounting within the German High Command, it came to the Führer's ears through Schmundt that von Brauchitsch had discussed with von Bock, von Kluge and Guderian limited withdrawals and the setting up of a Winter Line to the rear. Tacit arrangements arrived at with von Brauchitsch were immediately cancelled. Any withdrawal was forbidden and troops were ordered to put up a fanatical resistance in their positions without regard to the situation on their flanks or to the rear. 4 Army in particular was forbidden to withdraw by a single step.[13]

Hitler's "stand and fight" order resulted in a division of opinion which has become more marked with the passage of time. Whether or not he was right in insisting on a rigid defense before Moscow none can be sure. A withdrawal made under heavy enemy pressure in the terrible winter conditions then experienced could easily have developed into a rout, for the smell of fear was in the air. German wounded lying helpless in the snow were usually finished off by Red Army bullet or bayonet, and sometimes prisoners were blinded, mutilated or killed in the most terrible and barbaric fashion.

Yet it is certain that this military factor of safeguarding against panic-stricken flight carried less weight with Hitler than personal considerations of prestige and the loss of countenance. Many, possibly the majority, of German commanders at that time considered that the Führer was right in his decision and probably saved Germany from a heavy defeat.

On the other hand, there was a very strong tactical argument for breaking contact with the Red Army at the most favorable moment and withdrawing rapidly westwards, even if it meant falling back as far as Smolensk. Failure to hold, or to break contact successfully and withdraw, could only lead to a running fight, a very costly and dangerous act of war. In spite of the desperate defense, Army Group Center hardly held any of its positions for more than a few days and was to be forced back everywhere during the next five weeks between eighty and 200 miles. Large numbers of guns and vehicles were to be lost, and exposure to the weather rather than fighting was to bring heavy losses. Even in mid-November, before the onset of the hard winter conditions, the Army Group Center casualties due to frost-bite averaged 400 a day.[14]

There were other even more convincing reasons for withdrawing at the beginning of December. The Army Group Center sector formed a great salient between 600 and 700 miles long. Against von Bock's wishes the Luftwaffe tactical support had been reduced to below the safety level. All the troops had been committed, and not a single division was in reserve. No successful defensive battle could be fought without mobile reserves being held at the disposal of the army group and army commanders and, since the OKH had nothing more to offer, these reserves could have been accumulated only by an extensive withdrawal and a shortening of the line.

Finally, there was the question of the over-extended supply lines. Army Group Center had failed in its October and November offensives, partly because of the weather, but primarily because it had been unable to overcome the problem of space and movement. For, as von Bock commented in his diary at the time, there were three main reasons for defeat: mud, the failure of the railway system and an underestimating of the enemy, in that order.[15]

When the exhausted, understrength and ill-equipped German formations, at the end of a 1,000-mile-long supply line which had in any case ceased to function, without shelter and winter clothing, were within twenty miles of the enemy capital, they were met by Soviet troops who, in spite of their shortcomings in training and field leadership, were adequately fed and well clothed and equipped, with ammunition and supplies dumped in their fighting areas. Their main bases, airfields and source of reinforcements were hardly more than fifteen miles to their rear.

In such circumstances, with every advantage in the Red Army favor, it would appear to have been wiser for the German troops not to have attempted to hold ground but to have fallen back immediately to the west. The Red Army man, well equipped and hardy though he certainly was, was scarcely able to wage an offensive at the end of a 200-mile-long follow-up. Deep snow and mud, caused by the occasional winter thaws, were as troublesome to the Soviet as to the German soldier. Separated from his bases, airfields and dumped munitions, the Red Army, like the Wehrmacht, rapidly lost its efficiency. This is exactly what was to happen over the next two months.

The battles before Moscow and Hitler's standstill order were to have a particularly damaging effect on the organization and efficiency of the German High Command.

In his arrogance and conceit, amid the acclaim of the whole German nation, the Führer had taken over the personal command of the German Army and henceforth regarded himself first and foremost as a soldier. He took the view that success in battle was a matter of willpower, *his* willpower; he had only to order a particular maneuver or course of action and he assumed that the mission was successfully fulfilled. Time, space, terrain, weather and relative strengths meant nothing to him, and he appeared to think that the enemy had no will of his own and must conform to that of the Führer.

For with the disappearance of von Brauchitsch, the writing of detailed military appreciations and the playing of war games within the operations department of the OKH to test the feasibility of military plans suddenly ceased. The Führer became the fountainhead of all plans and these were formulated without warning and in haste, following a cursory study of maps and a few telephone conversations.

Any failure of the German Army to fulfill the missions he gave it, however impracticable the orders might have been, was likely to be regarded by the Führer as a personal affront. He was suspicious of, and intensely disliked, the officer corps, particularly, as he called them, the gentlemen of the General Staff. When von Rundstedt, von Brauchitsch, von Bock, von Leeb, Guderian, Hoepner and Strauss would not or could not obey his orders or asked to be relieved of their duties, he got rid of them without compunction. Their successors he kept under very tight restraint.

In this way the more senior of the general officers were lost to the German Army in December and January of that winter. In addition, scores of experienced corps and divisional commanders were removed from their appointments or from the active list, many of them the Führer's scapegoats. The whole fabric of the German High Command was to be rapidly destroyed.

CHAPTER TEN
THE CRISIS

O N 3 D E C E M B E R, when 2 Panzer Division, one of Hoepner's formations, had come to a halt only nineteen miles in a direct line north of the Kremlin, 4 Panzer Group was told by 4 Army that von Kluge's three-day-old attack on the Nara, immediately to the west of Moscow, had failed.

Hoepner felt that he had been left in the lurch and had no qualms about saying so. If that was the best that 4 Army could do, he said, then the order should never have been given in the middle of November to resume the offensive on Moscow. He told von Kluge with some asperity that 4 Panzer Group could do no more, as it was at the end of its resources; the High Command should decide whether it would not be better to withdraw. Hoepner suggested that both 3 and 4 Panzer Groups should pull back westwards thirty miles from their exposed salient to the north of Moscow in order to straighten the Army Group Center line. Meanwhile, Hoepner added, until the High Command had made up its mind exactly what it was trying to do, he and his troops were going to have three days rest.

Not unnaturally the relationship between Hoepner and von Kluge deteriorated and the Commander of Army Group Center did not forget this conversation.

4 Panzer Group remained under the temporary command of 4 Army and two days later, on 5 December, Hoepner sent a situation report to von Kluge in which he estimated that nineteen enemy rifle, four cavalry and twelve tank formations were facing 4 Panzer Group. While he was prepared to admit that many of these enemy divisions had suffered great losses, it was also true that the German troops were outnumbered.

Hoepner went on to complain about the reports issued by the German Propaganda Ministry which described the Red Army as already

defeated and without courage or morale. In fact, the enemy in front of
4 Panzer Group was putting up a pretty tough fight *(wehrt sich sehr zäh)*.
The German troops, he said, marveled at the excellent quality of the
Red Army winter clothing, fur caps, felt boots, quilted trousers and
tunics, while they themselves had nothing but their summer uniforms.
The cases of frost-bite were increasing and making as heavy an inroad
on the reduced strengths as battle casualties, and it should be remembered that, while the Russian operated from prepared and covered
positions, the German fought where he lay in the snow, exposed to the
bitter weather.[1]

On 6 December at 5 P.M. the 4 Army order for the withdrawal of
the exposed salient back to the line of the Istra was received by
Hoepner, but its wording caused him surprise and anger. The order
applied to Hoepner but not to Reinhardt's 3 Panzer Group on
Hoepner's north flank since this was not under von Kluge's command
but came direct under Army Group Center. Army Group Center and
Headquarters 4 Army had made little effort to coordinate the withdrawal of the two panzer groups, 4 Panzer Group even having been told
to select its own intermediate withdrawal lines. Hoepner was to comment that whoever had drafted that particular order had absolutely no
understanding of General Staff work; his fears were well founded,
because 3 Panzer Group did not receive until later from Army Group
Center its own instructions to withdraw.

So, when every moment was vital, Reinhardt was to find himself
in difficulties as he was already being attacked in the flank and rear by
Kuznetsov's 1 Shock and Lelyushenko's 30 Armies. Hoepner's sharp
protests to von Kluge brought about some improvement when, on 8
December, 3 Panzer Group was put under Hoepner's command for
easier coordination and control.[2]

Hoepner began to fall back westwards; it was this fairly rapid
withdrawal which had been noted with surprise by the Soviet High
Command when Vlasov's 20 Army started its probes.

Hoepner was not without his problems, however. His rearguards
were being strongly pressed by the advancing enemy, and in the tiny
municipality of Istra he had a thousand wounded yet to be evacuated.
The French Legion, recruited from right-wing elements in France as

part of the crusade against communism, showed itself to be unsteady since it had received neither the training nor the equipment for winter warfare.

Under the strain and stress of the withdrawal tempers became frayed and there were mutual recriminations between the higher formations. Even the calm and level-headed Reinhardt reproached Ruoff's 5 Corps, Hoepner's flanking formation, for its lack of support, but Ruoff in reply could only stress that his infantry were at the end of their tether and that a short pause was essential so that they might get some sleep. The Red Army enemy, emphasized Ruoff, was fighting with skill and without regard to losses, and was crossing apparently trackless forests by night in temperatures as low as minus thirty degrees centigrade.[3]

By 12 December Hoepner was back on the Istra line formed by the river and the great fifteen-mile-long reservoir which ran from north to south; he had suffered equipment losses, for only half of the artillery could be moved due to the lack of gun towers and horses. The remainder was abandoned or destroyed; numbers of tanks were left behind, broken down or out of fuel. There was still no continuous front but Hoepner had managed to shorten his defensive perimeter and so was able to take 2 Panzer Division into reserve.

The field commanders reported that the men's morale was good in spite of the sudden reversal and the orders to withdraw. To the north Reinhardt was in difficulties, however, in his efforts to hold on to Klin; and, as it appeared as if his troops were in danger of encirclement, Hoepner was forced to hand over 2 Panzer Division, the only reserve he had, to extricate them. After this, the enemy pressure and the tempo of the battle quickened and Hoepner was unable to re-create a new reserve by withdrawing further formations from contact.

Having arrived on the Istra line, Hoepner found that he could no longer defend it. The left, held by Reinhardt, was in the air and in danger of envelopment, and Hoepner decided that he would have to withdraw further to the line of the River Ruza. 3 Panzer Group and the left flank of 4 Panzer Group gave up the little cities of Klin and Istra, over which they had fought so fiercely, and dropped back to the line Ruza-Volokolamsk-Lama, which they reached on 20 December. The withdrawal of 9 Corps, holding the north bank of the Moskva as part of Hoepner's right flank, had, however, nearly met with disaster.

78 Sturm Division, part of 9 Corps, had suffered 2,400 casualties between 28 October and 11 December and had disbanded two of its infantry battalions to reinforce the remainder. This brought the infantry companies up to fifty men each, but these were in poor physical shape and were suffering wretchedly from the cold, second-degree frost-bite, bowel disorders, boils and suppurating sores. The horses were so weakened that nothing could be asked of them.

On about 12 December Govorov's 5 Army to the front of 78 Division had made a number of probing attacks; these were beaten off without difficulty, but it was less easy to deal with the swarms of Red Army men who began to infiltrate under the cover of darkness into the German rear. The next day the division had been told of Hoepner's intention to withdraw 4 Panzer Group to the line of the River Ruza, about forty miles to the west, the movement of 9 Corps to begin on 14 or 15 December.

But on 14 December, before the withdrawal order had been issued from corps, there was great consternation in 78 Division when it was discovered that the enemy was already sitting in strength across the division's line of withdrawal and had begun to attack outlying detachments. The signal communications with 9 Corps had been cut and, although 78 Division did not know it, the other two divisions of the corps were in a similar predicament. There were fears in 4 Panzer Group that all the divisions were lost.

The danger became greater hour by hour; telephone communications within the 78 Division area began to fail, but line parties, sent to trace the breaks in the cable, were never seen or heard of again. The divisional commander became virtually *incommunicado* and soon ceased to have much influence on the situation. *78 Sturm Division* was then assailed on two sides, some of the attacks being supported by tanks. By three o'clock on the morning of 16 December the position appeared desperate and the decision was taken to abandon heavy equipment and weapons and break out by regiments westwards to the Ruza. Since there was no vehicle fuel, six tracked armored assault guns and all the motor lorries were among the equipment destroyed.

Daylight the next morning found the columns already on the march across open, wind-swept country, harried by the Red Air Force and by Cossack cavalry and tanks. The cavalry were no danger and the German flank guards soon emptied the saddles by long-range fire, but T 34 tanks emerging from distant woods caused great fear, for the columns had no anti-tank guns and little artillery. They were saved, however, by the arrival of Luftwaffe fighters, the first that the German troops had seen for a week or more. These, sweeping low over the plains, opened fire with machine-gun and cannon; the landscape and the skies rapidly emptied as all the enemy tanks and aircraft turned tail.

The westward movement then continued without interference but the losses in equipment had been very heavy. Men of the artillery regiment, refusing to be parted from their weapons, brought with them as many field guns and howitzers as they could drag along. The difficulty was to find any fit horses. But all their efforts were in vain. Having covered many miles the horses, overburdened and near death, halted. Nothing could induce them to move again. A junior leader from another formation was persuaded to lend the artillery regiment spare horses, and these were substituted for the played-out teams. But no sooner had the exchange been made than a senior officer, arriving on the scene, insisted on having his horses back again. All the weapons were then abandoned and the 78 Division artillery, without horses or guns, joined the withdrawing dismounted columns.

On 20 December the division arrived at the Ruza. Its equipment had gone, but all the wounded had been brought out. About a hundred men were missing and eighty dead had been left unburied on the road. The casualties in men were minor compared with those yet to come.[4]

One of the more remarkable aspects of the loss of German initiative in front of Moscow and the retreat was the leaderless state in which Army Group Center found itself during the months of November and December. It was almost entirely without purposeful direction. Von Brauchitsch had long since avoided responsibility, since he knew that anything he ordered would probably be countermanded by the dictator, and this gave rise to a paralysis of will within the OKH, a paralysis which spread to von Bock. Other than by urging on his formations, von Bock had exercised little personal control over the final offensive in late November and had been unable to compel von Kluge to get forward.

Von Kluge had eventually called off his own belated, almost half-hearted, three-day attack, and he did this on his own initiative. Hoepner and Guderian, on the outer flanks, had followed his lead. It was only at Hoepner's suggestion that 3 and 4 Panzer Groups made their tactical withdrawal north of Moscow; without his initiative they would have been left where they were by the High Command. Near Tula, Guderian was already giving ground of his own volition. All this time von Bock remained passive awaiting a lead from the Führer.

On 8 December, in his Directive 39, Hitler merely agreed to what had already taken place. He said nothing about withdrawals, except that these would only occur where it was considered necessary *after* rearward positions and shelter had been constructed. In reality, as we now know, Hitler had not made up his mind what to do, for although he had determined to be rid of von Brauchitsch, he was himself casting around for ideas and Schmundt was quizzing von Bock.

Meanwhile, between 5 and 18 December, there was much confusion and doubt in the lower formation headquarters.

On 18 December Hitler's "stand and fight" order, with its emphasis on fanatical will, arrived at 4 Panzer Group Headquarters. Firm orders had at last been given, but in Hoepner's view they were the wrong ones; for he read them with dismay.

That Christmas Eve, Hoepner carefully recorded his comment. The stress on fanatical will, he wrote, was hardly appropriate, for every German soldier had the will to fight; the trouble was that there were too few of them to do the fighting. A rigid defense would mean envelopment by the enemy and a cutting of the supply line. The logistic situation was already critical. Without replacements and spares, tanks, arms and equipment had become derelict; with no low-temperature lubricants the machine-guns seized up and the breech blocks of the artillery could not be opened. No defensive positions were ready or, said Hoepner, could be built, because of the lack of materials, tools and labor. The iron-hard ground was frozen a meter deep. A hungry and frozen soldier fought badly and his general efficiency was very poor.

On the other hand, the Russian had no lack of men, all remarkably well equipped for winter warfare, and if past experience was anything to go by, thought Hoepner, it was very doubtful whether the enemy's forces could be destroyed in costly battles of attrition.[5]

In retrospect, these opinions, so soberly recorded by Hoepner that winter's night, seem so obvious as to be hardly worth the recounting. They were too imperfectly understood in Rastenburg, however.

The Führer's conception of a rigid defense was based on his own experience and recollections of the static trench fighting on the Western Front in the First World War. In his mind's eye he could see once more the many parallel systems of continuous trenches, zig-zagging for mile after mile, prepared in tactical depth, trenches seven feet deep with A-frames and drainage sumps, fire-steps, deep dugouts, machine-gun nests and wire.

The examples, many of them fallacious, which he frequently quoted to confound his advisers, were all related to the conditions of the First World War. Never once did the Führer visit the battle area on the Eastern Front and he had little idea how far removed was the fighting there from that which he had experienced so long ago. For in Russia there was no form of continuous front.

Too often, during that winter retreat, the defense in the closely wooded country was based on understrength battalion or company localities, usually in isolation and out of touch with each other. More often than not, trenches were merely scrapes in the snow, little pits in which, unless they could get under cover at night, the men slowly froze to death. Battalions were commanded by lieutenants and companies by sergeants. There was little or no artillery or mortar support, few mines and no barbed wire. No position had any depth. Instead of the companionship of unit and formation and of the neighbors on the flanks, all around there was nothing but loneliness, emptiness and darkness. Visibility in the swirling snow was rarely more than a few yards and little could be heard above the everlasting howling of the wind in the trees.

By 19 December both von Brauchitsch and von Bock had gone, von Bock having been succeeded by von Kluge, a commander of somewhat narrow vision, who followed Hitler obediently and blindly, almost to the end. If scapegoats were needed, von Kluge could find them; if heads must fall von Kluge took good care to see that his would not be among them. Not without reason was he known as *der kluge Hans*.

Von Kluge added his own exhortations to those of the Führer, with the same menacing undertones, making all commanders in Army Group Center personally responsible to him that they did not give up one foot of ground without first obtaining his permission. Needless to say, this was merely a form of insurance, because von Kluge himself needed Hitler's prior authority. This resulted in a very odd situation in which von Kluge became a clearinghouse for the many urgent requests from lower formations for permission to withdraw. When von Kluge referred these to the Führer, many times a day, the dictator simply rejected them.

Von Kluge's vacant command of 4 Army was taken over by Kübler, the former Commander of 49 Mountain Corps in the Ukraine.

In the distant south Rudolf Schmidt's 2 Army was still responsible both for the protection of the right flank of Army Group Center and for keeping contact with Army Group South. Because Schmidt's extended formations had great gaps betwen them, they were unable to counter the probes and infiltrations of the three opposing armies which, on 18 December, became Cherevichenko's Bryansk Front. In response to Schmidt's urgent appeals, the OKH had transferred to 2 Army 56 Infantry Division from Guderian's 2 Panzer Army.

When, on 12 December, von Oven, the Commander of 56 Infantry Division, reported to the saturnine Schmidt in Orel to receive his orders, he was instructed to close a gap about thirty miles wide near Livny. Von Oven pointed out that his formation was still on the march fifty miles away, the division in any case consisting at that time of no more than one infantry and one artillery regiment and a signals battalion. Yet the situation was such in those critical days that Rudolf Schmidt, who was already in danger of losing 95 Infantry Division, which had been partly encircled near Livny on 9 December, merely shrugged his shoulders and answered von Oven that he had received his orders and had better carry them out! Yet Schmidt was neither an unsympathetic nor an unreasonable man.

The formations flanking this great Livny gap, 45 and 134 Infantry Divisions, were noted by Halder that same day as being unfit for battle as their supply had failed.[6]

The next day von Oven's only available regiment was in contact with the enemy, having the support of only two light field howitzers, some *Nebelwerfer* heavy mortars and two 88 mm flak guns, all hurriedly borrowed from other formations. At first, Soviet pressure grew rapidly, but von Oven was saved by patrolling Luftwaffe fighters which forced a temporary enemy withdrawal.

The situation and experiences of 56 Infantry Division were similar to those of other formations in the area. In a temperature of minus forty degrees centigrade it was impossible even to drive in wire pickets, and timber knife-rests were built as a substitute. Since the only places free from frost where the troops could break the frozen surface were inside the houses and farm buildings, positions were too often dug there without any thought being given to tactical layout and fields of fire. This problem could only be overcome by building weapon pits in the open, above ground, from hard-packed snow.

The snow drifts on the rearward routes made regular ammunition and ration supply impossible and without free-dropped supplies from the Luftwaffe the men would have starved.

By the next day 45 Infantry Division, on von Oven's flank, had been encircled by infiltrating Red Army troops and had to fight its own way out. Once again half of the guns, nearly all the vehicles, and 400 dead were left behind. The casualties in wounded and frost-bite were more than four times this figure.[7]

Immediately to the north, Guderian, the Commander of 2 Panzer Army which stood on 2 Army's left flank, had been ordered to transfer all available troops to help Schmidt, but in spite of this 2 Army continued to give ground and retreat westwards. Guderian, fearful for the security of his southern flank, hastened to conform and began to pull back further.

Just a few days before he retired, von Brauchitsch, on his last flying visit to Army Group Center, had met in Roslavl both Guderian and von Kluge, still at that time commanding 4 Army. Guderian had asked for von Brauchitsch's agreement to a withdrawal westwards to the line of the Oka and the Susha, where defensive positions had been prepared in the fighting earlier in the year. This permission, so Guderian subsequently said, was given; if von Brauchitsch did commit himself to giving such decisive orders, he was careful not to inform the Führer of what he had done. In any case, permission or no permission, Guderian would have withdrawn.

The open right flank to the south was only part of Guderian's worry, however, for his left flank had also been broken. Boldin's 50 Army in the area of Tula had forced a gap between Heinrici's 43 Corps and Geyr von Schweppenburg's 24 Panzer Corps. Both of these formations belonged to Guderian, and the breakthrough was without a doubt in 2 Panzer Army sector; but Guderian bickered with von Kluge, in front of von Brauchitsch, trying to blame him for the failure to close the breach. The only result of this meeting was that Schmidt's 2 Army was put under the command of 2 Panzer Army for better coordination of Army Group Center's southern flank.[8]

The next day Guderian went to Orel to see Schmundt, who was still in the Army Group Center area, to whom he made a long and gloomy report, begging him to take it back to the Führer. But Hitler's reaction was not what Guderian expected, for that night he received a telephone call from the dictator forbidding any withdrawal. The undisciplined Guderian ignored for the time being the standstill order, and probably rightly so.

Guderian had visited his corps commanders on 17 and 18 December to hear their views of the situation. All were agreed that the position was very serious and that something must be done immediately to regain mobility and combat strength. And where, they asked, was the promised winter equipment? For the first time, they said, the troops were beginning to question the judgment and ability of the High Command. Guderian, confident in his powers of persuasion, decided to fly to Rastenburg to put his case to the Führer.

Part of Guderian's account of his Rastenburg meeting must be treated with some reserve, yet much of it is undoubtedly true. For the first time in his life he saw the hard and unfriendly expression on the dictator's face, for the Führer already knew from Schmundt the purpose of the visit. He had no intention of being dissuaded from the course he had set himself. He made it clear to Guderian that no withdrawal would be permitted. When the army commander explained that he had lost twice as many men from frost and cold as from battle casualties, and that "any man who has seen the hospitals filled with frost-bite casualties must realize what that means," the Führer retorted that Guderian was too closely involved in events. He should stand back more, said Hitler, "for things then appeared in better perspective than when examined at closer range."[9]

It is certain that none could accuse the Führer of seeing the fighting at too close a range, for, like von Brauchitsch, the former Commander-in-Chief, he had no idea of the inadequate scale of provision of winter clothing and equipment. Nor did he know that none of it had arrived in the forward areas. Angrily he contradicted Guderian. Wagner, the Quartermaster-General, was sent for, and only then did Hitler accept that the clothing was still in the railway sidings in the *General Gouvernement*. This conversation resulted in the Nazi Party drive that Christmas to collect winter clothing and skis for the troops from the civilian population; none of it arrived that winter.

Guderian learned, apparently for the first time, that Hitler had no understanding of the problems of supply and space and that both the dictator and his immediate staff had no conception of the condition of the fighting troops in Russia. Guderian returned to 2 Panzer Army having achieved nothing. Von Bock had gone and Guderian's enemy, von Kluge, was the new Commander of Army Group Center.

The breach between Heinrici's 43 Corps, which was by then part of 4 Army, and 2 Panzer Army had still not been closed, and through this gaping hole swept Boldin's 50 Army, Popov's 1 Guards Cavalry Corps and, a little farther to the south, part of Golikov's 10 Army, all making for Yukhnov, Kaluga, Peremyshl and Sukhinichi deep in the German rear.

On the night of Christmas Eve, the small market town of Chern was lost to the enemy by 10 Motorized Division. Once again Guderian obliquely blamed 4 Army, although Heinrici's 43 Corps was over forty miles to the north of the area. Von Kluge on the other hand had no doubt at all as to who was responsible. On Christmas Day there were angry and violent arguments between the two men, ending in the

Commander of 2 Panzer Army sending off a telegram asking that he be relieved of his command. Meanwhile von Kluge had had Guderian removed from his appointment by an order from the Führer.[10]

It is probable that von Kluge was justified in taking the action he did, and that Guderian, although acting in the interests of the men under his command, was to blame. Guderian, brave, headstrong, violent, disloyal, capricious and petulant, was not a sympathetic character, and, in his own eyes, was never in the wrong. Although, after the war, he bitterly criticized and denounced Adolf Hitler and his war leadership, during the war years, until just before the end, he was, by and large, the Führer's man. No less was von Kluge. Although von Kluge was to add a rather weak little note to the Army Group Center record of the dispute, that "he [von Kluge] was basically in agreement with Guderian but that Guderian must learn to obey orders," none who flouted the Führer's orders could expect protection from von Kluge, least of all Guderian.

2 Panzer Army was taken over by that hostile critic of the Nazi régime, Rudolf Schmidt, formerly of 2 Army.

The position on the southern flank was indeed perilous. The little locality of Peremyshl, sixty miles west of Tula and well in the German rear, had been taken by the Red Army on Christmas Day and the city and marketing center of Kaluga a few days later. Stalin's left pincer had already covered a quarter of the distance to Smolensk, outflanking Army Group Center from the south. On this flank there was much movement but relatively little fighting.

The most bloody engagements during December and the beginning of January occurred in the center, for some of the divisions of 4 Army were to suffer grievously during the holding battles and the withdrawals which followed.

On 7 December, the same day that 98 Infantry Division, part of 4 Army and still on the Nara, received its first Knight's Cross, it began to snow heavily. A heavy stream of men, mainly cases of exhaustion and second degree frost-bite, continued to be evacuated to hospital. The snow settled and blanketed roads, tracks and trees. Even before the standstill order reached them on 10 December there was no longer any thought of resuming the offensive that winter. Yet Moscow was so near that on clear nights it was possible to see the searchlight beams and the shell bursts of the anti-aircraft fire above the city. Three days after the first fall, the strong winds brought heavy drifts and raging snow storms, cutting down visibility to only a few yards.

It was hoped that there might be a lull in operations so that the division, even though it was still in the line, could reform and reorganize; the anti-tank gunners and engineers, up to then used as infantry, were withdrawn from the forward localities and the engineer battalion was set to work constructing rest bunkers in the rear behind the Istya River. Yet in truth there was to be no respite, for numerous Russian line-crossers were coming into the divisional area bringing news of the preparation of new Soviet attacks.

Late on 13 December the divisional commander was called to corps and told, under the strictest secrecy, of the intention to withdraw the whole front nearly ninety miles to the west, a secret which, he wryly noted, had reached the other ranks earlier that morning in the form of a rumor. The very next day the troops were already aware that any withdrawal had been forbidden, even though the divisional commander had not yet been so instructed. From this time onwards the division, like all others, was to be plagued with uncertainty. Not before 17 December was the divisional headquarters categorically instructed to remain where it was. The advance parties which had been sent back to the River Protva were ordered to turn around and go forward again.

Almost immediately a new rumor arrived in the division, that the flanks of 4 Army were being turned by the enemy and that it was already threatened with encirclement, a rumor not far removed from the truth. Within twenty-four hours the division received a further order instructing it to prepare to withdraw. This chopping and changing and the repeated countermanding of orders led to the gravest disquiet and, for the first time during the whole war, confidence in the higher command was severely shaken. Three times in one day bridges were prepared for demolition and three times the division was ordered to remove the charges. Glass for the construction of the rearward winter bunkers was still arriving in the divisional area and yet the ammunition, without which no battle could be fought, was already on its way to the rear.

Not until the evening of 19 December were the troops finally told that there was no longer any question of withdrawal and that the division would remain where it was. The troops began to breathe again at having at last received clear orders.

The divisional commander was subsequently to applaud this decision. By then the snow was really deep, making large-scale movement very difficult, if not impossible, and a withdrawal in such conditions under the very eyes of the guns of the enemy was, he thought, out of the question. This general officer's opinions must be treated with respect, because only he could judge the conditions at that time. Yet within a matter of days, 98 Infantry Division, together with the other formations of 4 Army, had to begin the long retreat in blizzard conditions, harried by the enemy and rarely stopping for more than a few days in any one place, falling back over the next six weeks more than 100 miles to the west.

The men were not at all downcast by the news that von Brauchitsch had given up his command. Very much the reverse. The Führer was at the helm and faith in him was boundless; a new wave of optimism spread over the troops. Earlier doubts as to whether the Russian really was at the end of his tether, as the newspapers and radio claimed, or as to who was responsible for the winter clothing scandal, evaporated.

On 20 December the Red Air Force became active once more, bombing and machine-gunning along the whole front, and the next day the enemy artillery began its usual long-drawn-out preparatory bombardment. The air was filled with the noise of whining shells which, bursting against the tree trunks, vibrated and echoed throughout the vast forests. 98 Division was not, however, directly involved, but its neighbor to the right was penetrated by a very strong enemy force, supported by tanks. Bad news ran up and down the front. Immediately afterwards the division came under heavy attack from a guards and parachute division on its left. On 23 December, only four days after what was to have been the final standstill order, 98 Infantry Division was ordered to prepare to withdraw. It snowed as if it would never stop.

Of the army formations, 4 Army alone had been sufficiently static to make some preparation against the winter. The infantry, many of whom had occupied the same positions for nearly two months, left with heavy hearts, for they had managed to develop their weapon pits into little bunkers with overhead cover, giving some protection from the cold and snow. They knew the ground and had improved the defenses; most had some contact with their neighbors. Life had become a routine, particularly as the sector had been relatively quiet over the past few weeks. To withdraw meant to emerge into the unknown, the dark primeval, almost trackless forests open to the bitter weather. A withdrawal meant uncertainty, not knowing the whereabouts of friend or foe, or where the night's meal and shelter were coming from. On Christmas Eve the snow had stopped and, on a hard, clear and frosty night, the infantry began to move out, many of them thinking of 1812 and the great monument of Tarutino on the nearby field of Borodino.

Early on Christmas morning, just as it was getting light, the infantry companies, many less than thirty men strong and some mustering only two light machine-guns and hardly a dozen rifles, crossed the frozen Istya River and arrived at the edge of a great forest which marked the extent of their new positions. There was nothing there, just a great snowfield and the rock-hard ground.

At first the men stood disconsolately about, hungry and frozen to the marrow. Boots, gloves and greatcoats were tattered and torn and the icy wind blew straight through them. Some of the troops had lost their military jack-boots long ago and were wearing lace-up boots, even shoes. Others had taken to plaiting sheaves of straw round foot and calf, and all packed newspapers into their clothing for additional warmth. The artillery fared somewhat worse. As there were insufficient horses to move all guns and wagons, teams had to make the journey several times to bring the equipment back. A fully laden ammunition wagon needed twelve horses to move it and, although the distance from the Nara position to the Istya was only seven miles, many horses foundered and guns and wagons were lost. The anti-tank gunners moved their few remaining guns using teams of men instead of horses, sweating, cursing and falling in the waist-deep snowdrifts. More fortunate than most, 98 Infantry Division had broken clear of the enemy;

it was more than twenty-four hours before the Russians were to realize that they had gone.

By the morning of 26 December, however, the Soviet enemy was in contact again along the new Istya line but, except for isolated probes, made no attempt to attack. The flanking divisions were not so lucky, for, not being able to disengage, they were closely pursued by ski troops and tanks. On the night of 27 December, 98 Division was ordered to withdraw yet again, from the Istya to the line of the River Protva. This time the Franconian Sudeten Germans had a foretaste of what was in store over the coming weeks.

The retirement began in moonlight so bright that, in the forest clearings, a map could be read. The artillery and much of the infantry got clear away, but a battalion of 289 Regiment ran into an ambush prepared by Soviet ski troops deep in the German rear. The reactions of the cold, numbed and hungry troops were slow and the German battalion was shot to pieces. About sixty stragglers were eventually rallied but all the equipment was lost.

Times of great stress and crisis were to follow. The enemy seemed to be everywhere. German units and detachments on the line of march were overrun. The plight of the wounded and sick was desperate for these, together with the medical staff who volunteered to remain with them, were often butchered by the oncoming enemy. For the Bolshevik knew no pity. Where they could, the wounded and sick dragged themselves on until they could no longer put one foot in front of the other. At night, all around could be seen the glare of blazing villages in which bitter and bloody hand-to-hand fighting took place. In the hours of daylight there were frequent air attacks. Losses were heavy and the confusion such that all ranks knew instinctively of the imminent danger of disintegration, and that they were fighting for their lives. The divisional commander, who had led the formation with distinction, no longer felt able to cope with the situation and, like many others, asked to be replaced by a younger and fitter man.

On the night of 29 December, immediately before the division withdrew its badly mauled units behind the Protva, the divisional staff heard on the Berlin radio that the Nazi Party was asking the German public for winter clothing and ski equipment.

At three o'clock the following morning, in an icy wind and a temperature of minus thirty-five degrees centigrade, the last organized parties still in touch crossed over the Protva, and the order was given to the engineer demolition party to blow the bridge. Latecomers would have to take their chances over the ice. Battalions were down to less than eighty men. The troops had had no hot food for days and the infantry began to number in their ranks stragglers from other units and arms, clinging to any organized, disciplined units for protection; these stragglers were turned into riflemen. With them was the pitiful handful of reinforcements scraped together by 4 Army, army engineers, signal corps, medical and veterinary men, the field bakery, anybody in fact who could carry a rifle.

98 Infantry Division, which by then formed part of General Kirchner's 57 Panzer Corps, continued to withdraw, all the time putting out rearguards, many of which were overrun by the enemy and never seen again. There was no longer any pretense of holding lines or tactical ground or using the forest tracks. The division, like all others, was forced onto the main highways in order to keep up its rate of movement; for the forest paths were unusable except to tracked vehicles and ski troops. Besides which, the towns and settlements on the main roads offered the only protection for the sick and the wounded; without shelter, the fighting troops could not sleep. The main arterial *Rollbahn,* the same route along which Napoleon had retreated, was packed with the men, horses and vehicles of many formations, moving slowly southwestwards; 19 Panzer, 15 and 98 Infantry Division had to converge on, and pass through, the town of Maloyaroslavets on their way back to Medyn. Maloyaroslavets itself, full of headquarters installations and wounded, was bombed continuously by the Red Air Force.

Kirchner's 57 Corps was being hard pressed, and, on 30 December, 98 Division counter-attacked to force the enemy back. This attack was made across an open snow-covered waste by the remnants of a single battalion, reinforced by army engineers and over-age *Landesschützen,* who had been on guard duties in the communications zone; it broke up under the enemy artillery defensive fire with heavy casualties.

Battalions, even regiments, were frequently overrun or encircled, but they appeared again days later further weakened by losses in missing, wounded and sick. Much of the heavy equipment had by now been left behind. A battery of 198 Artillery Regiment, reduced in strength though it already was, at this time lost ninety-seven men through frost-bite, half of them being second and third degree cases. Detachments and units were left behind with orders to fight to the last since the safety of three divisions depended on their gaining a little time. Many of them did so, but in the bitter conviction that they were being senselessly sacrificed for no tactical advantage, since the oncoming enemy simply bypassed them.

On New Year's Eve the Soviet enemy began to infiltrate through the brickyards and railway repair shops into the main town of Maloyaroslavets which was still full of German wounded. The defenders were mainly engineer and signal troops. In a temperature of minus 40 degrees centigrade, in the glare of burning houses, there was close hand to hand fighting of the fiercest and most brutal kind. There was no quarter. Many of the enemy troops, fortified with vodka, massacred the German wounded or flung them out of the upper windows, the drunken hordes roaming around the suburbs of the town hurrahing and screaming, killing everyone in their path. Amid this inferno, 98 Infantry Division, which was scattered over the surrounding area, had to defend the town, keep contact where it could with all its outlying detachments and, at the same time, hold open the withdrawal routes. It was itself almost encircled.

On the bodies of fallen Soviet troops were found documents, wallets and trinkets which showed the fate of many of the German outposts and missing; but before morning the local Russian civilian inhabitants had appeared and stripped to the skin the Red Army dead.

On the morning of 1 January the divisional commander, together with a number of officers and noncommissioned officers, stood on the road leading out of Maloyaroslavets to catch the stream of stragglers who were coming away from the town. These were reformed into temporary units under new leaders and sent to defend nearby villages where they could at least be assured of some warmth. At all costs the *Rollbahn* had to be held, for that was the only means of movement and hope of salvation. Maloyaroslavets was lost the next day. A new and temporary line was drawn on the map, based only on the holding of the scattered little towns and settlements.

289 Infantry Regiment, which at full establishment should have had a strength of nearly 2,000 men, was re-formed as a battalion, since it numbered only 120 and was commanded by a captain. Between 4 and 11 January nearly 1,300 wounded and 300 sick from 98 Division were evacuated through the medical reception units in Medyn; other wounded and sick remained at duty. No check was kept on the dead and the missing.[11]

The plight of many of the isolated German stragglers was almost indescribable. Those overrun were obliged to keep to the forests since the Russians had already seized the roads and the settlements. Many of them died there. Parties, often of not more than a dozen men, trudged painfully in file through the deep snow. To become separated from the others, even for a few minutes, might bring disaster, for the steadily falling snow quickly filled all tracks and footprints. Their lips were cracked and faces frost-bitten, their legs numbed and without feeling; one by one men sat or dropped down to await death because they could go no further; no reasoning could make them continue. Some begged to be shot or shot themselves. Most had to be left to await their end by freezing or by Russian bayonet. Many of those who survived were permanent mental or physical wrecks.

Kübler, the new Commander of 4 Army, was in serious difficulties. His new command appeared in danger of falling apart and he could get little sense out of his immediate superior, von Kluge, the Commander of Army Group Center. On 3 January the Commander of 13 Corps said that he was mentally and physically exhausted and asked for someone else to take his place. That same day Kirchner's 57 Corps reported its position to be confused and critical; the fate of 98 Franconian Sudeten Infantry Division near Maloyaroslavets was unknown, as nothing had been heard from it.

Von Kluge could do nothing to help. He could only propose that 4 Army should fall back a short way to the line of a river called the Lusha in order to re-form the stragglers and withdrawing units. An attempt would be made to hold there. But Kübler was not so easily persuaded. He told von Kluge that this was all too late; the enemy was bringing up fresh forces and, with this continual procrastination and lack of direction, the German command would never regain the initiative. The Russians, emphasized Kübler, might be a rabble, but they at least could move, and they were coming up in considerable strength. His own troops—and this applied particularly to 98 Infantry Division—were only fighting in the towns and villages; all the vast wastes and forests in between belonged to the enemy.

At five o'clock on that dark bitter winter's afternoon the 4 Army Chief of Staff told von Greiffenberg, his opposite number at Army Group Center, that 4 Army could not long remain in its present positions because it was being enveloped from the north. Von Greiffenberg could only reply that it *must* stay there as it was a direct order from Colonel-General Halder that it should do so.[12] This telephone conversation was, however, reported to the OKH.

On 5 January the Führer's watchdog, Schmundt, arrived at Yukhnov airfield for a meeting with von Kluge and Kübler to discuss the plight of 4 Army. Kübler bluntly stated the position. If no reinforcements were received the position of 4 Army was untenable in view of the danger of encirclement and the frightening drop in German strength. 17 Infantry Division was at that moment holding an eight-mile frontage with a divisional strength of 1,400 men, of which 900 were fighting as infantry. The division would never have been able to break up the attack launched against it that day, said Kübler, had not the attackers been completely drunk. 4 Army held no positions as such; they were just fighting around the villages.

Admittedly 40 Corps had just retaken the locality of Meshovsk, but in case the High Command might snatch at this straw, Kübler stressed to Schmundt that Meshovsk had been defended by Red Army troops who lay in a senseless drunken stupor. Even now 40 Corps was asking permission to withdraw its three rifle companies as two of the company commanders were dead. 4 Army, said Kübler, was not commanding corps or divisions; it was down to siting individual rifle companies. The small arms ammunition in 43 Corps had been fired off or lost; all but one rifle clip had been collected from every man with a rifle and handed over to those troops actually in close combat; there was no more. If help did not come soon to 4 Army there would be a catastrophe.

Schmundt, carefully noting these words, could only assure Kübler that 9,000 vehicles were on their way to the Eastern Front. He had nothing more to offer.

At nine o'clock that same night, Heinrici, the Commander of 43 Corps, a rational and imperturbable officer who was to end the war commanding Army Group Vistula in front of Berlin, came to see Kübler. In plain words he asked how this battle was to be fought. Was he to instruct his commanders to fight as the enemy did during the last year; "for the Russian, never capable of learning, had simply stood his ground until he was surrounded." The present position, said Heinrici, was intolerable. First-rate regimental commanders were almost desperate. Everybody must be told exactly what was the plan and what was expected of them.

Kübler heard the corps commander out and decided to refer the matter, exactly as Heinrici had put it, to von Kluge.

The conversation which followed between Kübler and von Kluge is illuminating. Von Kluge struck an attitude. Such a mentality (presumably Heinrici's), he said, must be suppressed and nerves held in check. He assured Kübler that the troops would not be sacrificed and pointed out that he had already withdrawn 4 Army's left wing, a withdrawal which would be difficult to justify "to those up above." Kübler was not so easily mollified and he told von Kluge that in the not too distant future 4 Army would have no men left at all. To which von Kluge replied, somewhat inconsequentially, "That of course is *the* problem." He hastened to add that all 4 Army had to do was to keep going until mid-January, for 220,000 reinforcements were on the way. He (von Kluge) would not leave 4 Army in the lurch and he asked Kübler to tell Heinrici to continue to fight as boldly and skillfully as he had in the past.

Meanwhile Kübler became aware of a much greater danger looming up from the south, where the great Soviet pincer had broken through 2 Panzer Army and, enveloping the little German stronghold at Sukhinichi, was about to break into 4 Army rear.

On 6 January, in the middle of an atmosphere of heightening crisis, with commanders and staffs at the end of their reserves of nervous energy and deeply worried at the imminence of disaster, 4 Army received a telephone call from Paulus. The immaculate and fastidious Deputy Chief of General Staff and Chief of Operations who, except for a temporary command of a few months over an experimental motor battalion in the middle thirties, had commanded nothing larger than an infantry company, had heard something of Schmundt's briefing to Hitler on his recent visit. Paulus, speaking from the warm comfort of his OKH office, asked "whether there was not an air of pessimism within 4 Army." Today the written record of the conversation still conveys something of a sneer.[13]

The Führer appeared unperturbed by this new threat from the south and his only contribution towards countering it was to order the Sukhinichi garrison, which had already been by-passed, to fight to the last. This was too much for even the wily von Kluge to stomach and he expressed doubts to his staff as to Hitler's strategy. For, according to von Kluge, the Führer and Halder tended to disregard the threat on the southern flank, believing that the Russian would have to stop when he ran out of breath; since this was likely to be in Smolensk, behind Army Group Center, von Kluge found this cold comfort. He was certain that Army Group Center must be withdrawn, both to escape envelopment and, by shortening the line, to find the necessary forces to deal with this new threat.

The staff of Army Group Center itself was fully alive to the dangers of the situation and was amazed when von Tresckow, the chief of its operations department, returned on 7 January from a visit to Rastenburg and described the remarkable lack of tension *(Entspannung)* there.

That same day Schmundt was back again with 4 Army. Alarmed at von Tresckow's impressions, von Greiffenberg, the Chief of Staff of Army Group Center, told Kübler to speak out plainly and spare no details about the gravity of the situation. Kübler needed no urging. He opened by dashing all the Schmundt promises of help; the reinforcements arriving in the 4 Army area, said Kübler, were in a most unsatisfactory state since they had neither weapons nor equipment nor winter clothing. Tired of recounting his own views, he put before Schmundt the opinions of two of his senior officers. Kübler's chief of staff said that if any possibility remained of saving 4 Army, this could be done only by a decisive and deep withdrawal. Heinrici, the Commander of 43 Corps, explained to Schmundt that if he were permitted to withdraw in some great depth he could then break contact and collect and reorganize formations for a counter-attack. If, on the other hand, he was forced to continue withdrawing under heavy enemy pressure only a little distance at a time to unprepared sites in the middle of the forest, then his troops would simply mutiny.

Schmundt, having telephoned a situation report to Jodl, left the next morning on 8 January, his car being towed through the deep snow all the way to the airfield by a tractor.

Later that day 4 Army came under heavy attack and could not hold; Kübler asked permission to make limited withdrawals. Von Greiffenberg replied that a decision would be given in thirty minutes. Meanwhile von Kluge put the request to the OKH. The waiting was wearing on the nerves and in the interim the clamoring Heinrici had to be told that Army Group Center itself was sitting on a volcano. At eighteen minutes past five that evening Kübler was told that the Führer had *not* approved the withdrawal, but had suggested that 4 Army should concentrate troops in the area of Medyn and Yukhnov "to form pivots."

Kübler would not accept this decision and Army Group Center promised to refer the matter back to the OKH. At 7:30 P.M., as no further reply had been received from Rastenburg, Kübler told von Kluge that he must have an answer in five minutes. Three-quarters of an hour later the Führer had agreed, but only to very limited withdrawals, these to be made, in his own words, *step by step* and then only provided that there should be no heavy losses of equipment.

Two days later Kübler recorded his opinion that anyone who thought that the Russian had yet outrun his strength was on the wrong track. For, he continued, the Red Air Force was dropping leaflets far and wide over the German rear area telling the local Russian population that the Red Army would arrive within two or three days, instructing it to be ready with supplies of bread, butter and meat. Kübler noted despondently that to save 4 Army was hardly possible; a week later, feeling that his position was untenable, he asked to be relieved.[14]

Kübler, who had been in command of 4 Army scarcely thirty days, was replaced on 20 January by Heinrici.

The critical, at times desperate, situation of 98 Infantry Division, 57 Panzer and 43 Corps was similar to that of other formations in Army Group Center. Exhaustion, extended frontages and the chaotic supply and equipment position were common everywhere. The effects of Hitler's personal and close control, and his insistence on a rigid defense with no withdrawal, except when authorized by him, were to have the same results throughout the Eastern Theater.

292 Infantry Division, part of 4 Army, had also been on the Nara. It had originally felt great relief at the "stand and fight" order of 19 December, because it considered that it no longer had the strength to carry out a long withdrawal. But in spite of this, it did have to fall back, and on New Year's Eve was holding a divisional sector about eight miles wide with rifle companies which, although down to only thirty men, were still stronger than those of its neighbors.[15]

In early December, 6 Rhine-Westphalian Division, part of Strauss's 9 Army, was on the northern periphery near Kalinin when it came under attack from Konev's Kalinin Front. The first equipment to be lost was its heavy howitzer battery which could not be dragged clear for lack of horses. Some of the rifle companies were soon down to a few machine-guns, a mortar or two and about seven riflemen each. The light machine-guns had been carefully husbanded but these proved to be of little value in the closely wooded country with its limited observation and fields of fire. Men were needed, not firepower. Whereas nearly all the Red Army attacks were very heavily supported by artillery, the German guns could not fire for lack of ammunition.

Christmas Day passed without celebration, an enemy attack being repulsed quite close to the divisional headquarters, the enemy, apparently drunk, coming forward cheering and linked arm in arm. In the New Year the divisional headquarters was in a tiny hamlet where the fifty officers and men all got under cover in two single-roomed houses. There they dictated orders, radioed, telephoned, wrote, typed, ate, deloused and slept. Outside, Russian women, for payment in tea and food, kept the tracks free from snowdrifts.

This division noted that the intermediate withdrawal lines, laid down from above, were entirely unsuitable for defense and had no tactical significance, obviously having been drawn by someone miles away in the comfort of a map room in a much higher headquarters. The distance between withdrawal lines was rarely above three miles, not enough to make the enemy move his guns. Other divisions were to complain of this interference in operations by "the rarefied higher headquarters swine."[16]

So that the Russians should find no shelter, the Führer had ordered that all buildings were to be burned before retreating, and even the brick ovens, which formed the core of the peasant houses, should be destroyed. This order was ignored by German troops, as the first signs of smoke gave warning that a withdrawal was intended and brought the enemy down on their heads.

Ruoff's 5 Corps, part of 4 Panzer Group, fell back as early as 7 December in accordance with Hoepner's original withdrawal order. Moving westwards from the salient north of Moscow it covered at first seven to fifteen miles a day in temperatures of minus thirty degrees centigrade. Whenever the corps made a stand the enemy rapidly infiltrated into the rear. Over the next three weeks, if the troops were not fighting they were on the march, and during this time for the most part they went without sleep. The infantry in particular never knew whether there would be any shelter for the night or whether the Red Army would already be sitting waiting for them in the next village.

The strength of the corps drained away at a frightening rate but no help could be expected from neighbors or from those above. Everyone knew that he was fighting for his life. Between Christmas and the New Year the corps commander and his staff were juggling with little groups of men and single artillery pieces, trying to plug gaps, cajoling, threatening and court-martialling officers. Battalions were down to a strength of fifty men. Divisions had no anti-tank weapons capable of destroying the attacking T 34 tanks and the few remaining artillery howitzers were used as anti-tank guns. Enemy tank brigades were numerous in this sector. Battalions grouped round a single field gun were being sacrificed to the enemy in order to gain a few more days for the corps. Men, including officers, had become so exhausted and apathetic that, left in the open, they would gladly have slept and frozen to death.

35 Infantry Division of 5 Corps had only two 50-mm anti-tank guns and six field howitzers and, in the six weeks following Hitler's standstill order, it had lost over 2,500 men (of whom over a thousand had died of frost-bite), more than one-third of its casualties since the war began in June 1941. Yet these casualties were light compared with those of other divisions. 23 Potsdam Division, another of Ruoff's formations, lost a good divisional commander whose health could not stand up to the rigors of the campaign and climate. It had reformed its nine battalions into three. In all it had hardly a thousand infantrymen left, while its divisional artillery consisted of only one 50-mm anti-tank gun and three howitzers. 106 Westphalian Rhineland Division, once a first-class formation, had hardly any of its original leaders and was down to 500 infantrymen.[17]

Driven as they were, beyond the limit of endurance, there were no cases of refusal to obey orders and certainly no hint of mutiny among the men of 5 Corps. By then, however, the German troops had a deep-rooted fear of tanks and had become distrustful, even scornful, of those orders and situation reports from higher headquarters which stressed the inferiority of the Red Army.

CHAPTER ELEVEN
STALIN HAS HIS WAY

As SOON AS it was known that the Germans were in retreat, an extraordinary transformation came over the Red Army troops, and their morale and fighting spirit rose sharply. So did the Soviet casualties. For the Russians began to counter-attack without regard to losses, fighting their way into the strongly held towns and settlements and flinging themelves against the German rearguards. The toll in dead and wounded mounted, particularly in the fierce fighting around the little city of Klin. Zhukov was forced to change his tactics and order his troops to avoid and bypass all centers of enemy resistance. As soon as the many gaps in the German positions could be felt out, bold and deep penetration was to be the order of the day.

The Red Army men were well equipped for winter warfare and were consequently much more mobile than their enemy. But, as Zhukov admits, they were still poorly trained. Field commanders in particular, conditioned by harrowing experiences of the previous year, were still fearful of encirclement and they lacked the resolution to exploit the numerous and yawning gaps between enemy formations. For the German still appeared to be strong and there was no doubt that he was as determined as ever. The *operational* performance of the Soviet front commanders was hampered by the lack of strong concentrations of armored forces held in reserve for the deep envelopment tasks, for after the heavy summer defeats all mechanized corps and tank divisions had been broken up. Only the tank brigades remained. These, numering at the most only fifty tanks each, had been decentralized to the close support of infantry formations.

Unlike Timoshenko, Zhukov was not a theater commander at this time, for he exercised no control over Konev's Kalinin Front or Cherevichenko's Bryansk Front, both of which came directly under Stalin.

211

Zhukov's command consisted of only the West Front, admittedly a large one, made up of the ten armies sretching from the north of Moscow to the area of Tula in the south.

Zhukov's main talents probably lay in the sphere of *operations,* for he was a cavalryman and he had specialized in that level of study. He tended to take a somewhat narrow and parochial view, restricted to the needs of West Front. He professed to believe that the situation on the Volkhov and in the Ukraine offered little hope of immediate Soviet success and he saw no reason why the reserve armies, which he so badly needed, should be allocated by Stalin to Meretskov or Timoshenko. For he had come to the opinion that with another four armies from the High Command Reserve, West Front could reach the Bryansk-Smolensk-Vitebsk line. Stalin, however, had different views.[1]

On 5 January Zhukov was called to Moscow to attend a meeting of the GKO; Shaposhnikov, the Chief of General Staff, and Vasilevsky, the Chief of Operations, were also present. Shaposhnikov made a presentation outlining a proposed general offensive due to take place during the next two months. It was intended, said Shaposhnikov, to develop the present counter-blow against the German Army Group Center into a massive counter-offensive along the whole of the battle front from Lake Ladoga to the Black Sea. German Army Group North was to be driven back by two separate double envelopment operations; these would lift the Leningrad blockade. German Army Group South was to be assailed by a single envelopment which would free the industrial area of the East Ukraine and the Donets Basin. Meanwhile the troops from the Caucasus, who were already crossing over the frozen Kerch Straits, were to occupy the Crimea.

When the Chief of General Staff had finished his presentation, Stalin gave a brief summary of what Shaposhnikov had said, making his own views clear when he remarked that, as the Germans were in no condition to fight a winter war, the winter was the right season to smash them. The time was overdue, the dictator stressed, for the launching of a general offensive.

Stalin then asked if anyone else had anything to say, and the unsuspecting Zhukov, intent only on securing material advantages for his own West Front, took the floor. He said that he had strong doubts whether any success could be expected from further offensives in the area of Valdai and the Volkhov or in the Ukraine. Only in the center was victory ripe for the taking. There, the West, Kalinin and Bryansk Fronts all needed massive reinforcements. Zhukov, as he himself later admitted, should probably have realized by Stalin's testy interruptions that his views were unwelcome.

Worse, however, was to follow. Voznesensky, the Chairman of the State Planning Commission, a man presumably insensitive to atmosphere, then spoke out strongly in support of Zhukov against the general offensive outlined by Shaposhnikov, on the grounds that insufficient resources were available to undertake all the offensives concurrently. Stalin became increasingly angry. No one else dared to speak, except Malenkov and Beria, who hastened to agree with the dictator.

Stalin ended by saying that he had himself spoken to Timoshenko, who was all for the offensive in his particular sector. All that had to be done, continued Stalin, was to destroy the German while he was still benumbed by the cold. If a general offensive was too long delayed, the enemy would be back, as strong as ever, in the spring. On that note the meeting was concluded.[2]

Shaposhnikov told Zhukov after the meeting that the general offensive had long been decided on and that the General Staff directives were already prepared and awaiting issue, Zhukov gathering from this conversation that the plan for the great offensive was Stalin's own and did not originate from the General Staff. Both Shaposhnikov and Zhukov were puzzled by the dictator's motives in asking for other opinions, for this Stalin did only when he had not made up his own mind; Zhukov could only come to the conclusion that the Supreme Commander acted out of caprice and spite, being determined to show the military that he, Stalin, was the *de facto* Commander-in-Chief. Of this no senior Soviet general could ever have been in doubt.

Stalin had decided that Zhukov's strong right flank, made up of Kuznetsov's 1 Shock, Vlasov's 20 and Rokossovsky's 16 Armies, should continue their thrust against Reinhardt and Hoepner and, together with Konev's Kalinin Front, take Rzhev. Zhukov's center, that is to say Govorov's 5 and Efremov's 33 Armies, was to continue its westward pressure against Kübler. The left flank of West Front, and in particular

Boldin's 50 Army, which, benefiting by the earlier breakthrough at Chern, was already making rapid progress in its envelopment of Kübler's 4 Army from the south, was to move on Yukhnov, a small town on the Ugra about thirty miles south-west of Medyn. This movement was in support of Belov's cavalry and tank corps, which formed the great enveloping arc in the south. Belov was ordered to change his axis to a north-westerly direction and, striking between Vyazma and Yartsevo, join up with Sokolov's 11 Cavalry Corps from the Kalinin Front.

This double envelopment, meeting west of Vyazma, would encircle the larger part of Army Group Center. Golikov's 10 Army had the task of protecting Belov's far southern flank and preventing 2 Panzer Army, which was outside the pocket, from coming to the relief of the encircled German troops.[3]

The task of Konev's Kalinin Front was unaltered in that it had to provide the inner right enveloping arm directed on Rzhev, Yartsevo and Vyazma. Kurochkin's North-West Front, as before, was to provide the outer right arm which was to thrust on Velikiye Luki and Vitebsk, so driving a great wedge between Army Group Center and Army Group North. Cherevichenko's Bryansk Front was ordered to keep up its pressure against 2 German Army in the area of Orel, while Timoshenko's South-West Theater, crossing the Donets River, should take Kharkov and swing southwards to Dnepropetrovsk and Zaporozhe on the Dnieper. This movement, it was hoped, would free the East Ukraine and Donets Basin.

In accordance with the new directive, Zhukov ordered his right wing, Kuznetsov's 1 Shock and Vlasov's 20 Armies, to take up the offensive in the area of Volokolamsk against Reinhardt's 3 Panzer Army (after 1 January both Reinhardt's and Hoepner's panzer groups had been redesignated panzer armies). Together with Pliev's 2 Cavalry Corps and five ski battalions, this right flank of West Front started, on 10 January, to move steadily forwards. But on 19 January, to Zhukov's surprise and dismay, an order was received through the General Staff for the withdrawal of Kuznetsov's 1 Shock Army from West Front to the High Command Reserve, prior to transfer to the area of Demyansk, where it was to become part of Kurochkin's North-West Front.

Zhukov's appeal to the General Staff in Moscow met with only one answer—the transfer was being made at the order of the Supreme Commander. Plucking up his courage, Zhukov telephoned Stalin. On complaining that his frontage was very broad and his troops too few, he was merely contradicted by the dictator; when the front commander pleaded further, he was told to send off the army without any more back chat *(bez vsyakukh razgovorov)*. Zhukov attempted to continue the conversation. Stalin, without another word, simply put down the receiver.[4]

Two days later, Rokossovsky's 16 Army Headquarters and supporting troops were withdrawn from the West Front to the High Command Reserve for transfer to the southern flank. They reappeared there on 27 January, for Stalin was determined to strengthen the enveloping pincers rather than drive Army Group Center westwards out of the trap.

Vlasov was ordered to extend to his right and left, taking over the frontages formerly held by Kuznetsov and Rokossovsky; 20 Army became too widely spread and lost momentum, and in consequence the pressure against 3 and 4 Panzer Armies began to fall off.

Zhukov was subsequently to complain of the shortfall of ammunition deliveries to the West Front compared with the original planned allotment. There was of course some shortage of ammunition, and transportation difficulties caused a further bottleneck in supply. But, once again, the real grounds for Zhukov's dissatisfaction arose from the fact that a large proportion of the stocks was being diverted to the Volkhov and the Ukraine. Even so, forty-four percent of the planned allotment of artillery ammunition was delivered to West Front during January.

Zhukov's criticism of Stalin's strategy is probably not without bias, and his views in this particular instance possibly lack perspective. Stalin wanted to finish Army Group Center at a blow, and quick results could be expected only on the flanks. Four fronts were involved in the attempt to destroy von Kluge, and the North-West and Kalinin Fronts were ideally poised for a deep envelopment.

On the other hand, Zhukov's right and center were capable of only a limited rate of progress since German strong points and rear guards were proving extremely troublesome, causing heavy casualties and delays.

Kurochkin's North-West Front had been allotted two specially re-inforced shock armies, both commanded by eminent soldiers, to drive from the area of Ostashkov southwards and westwards deep into von Kluge's rear. 3 Shock Army was under Lieutenant-General Purkaev, who, like Tupikov, had once been the Soviet Military Attaché in Berlin. He was austere and grave and particularly well read and educated. 3 Shock Army was to strike towards Kholm-on-Lovat and Velikiye Luki. 4 Shock Army under Eremenko, yet to become famous at Stalingrad, was to move on Toropets and Vitebsk.

Purkaev and Eremenko began their offensive on 9 January, with Vostrukhov's 22 Army of the Kalinin Front covering the left flank. There were few German defenders except in Andreapol and Toropets, and the three armies began to make steady progress. As the country was heavily wooded and largely trackless, there arose great difficulties in supply and control. Vast gaps appeared between the armies as their axes ran out radially like the spokes of a wheel, westwards, south-westwards and southwards. Kholm could not be taken by 3 Shock Army in the face of the bitterest resistance by Scherer's 281 Security Division, but by the end of January Purkaev was on the outskirts of the railway town and industrial center of Velikiye Luki and Eremenko was nearing the great city of Vitebsk, which lies about fifty-five miles to the west of Smolensk. Eremenko and Purkaev had covered 170 miles in three weeks over some of the most difficult territory in Western Russia.[5]

Since Kurochkin was engaged at the time in another major operation in the area of Demyansk, not connected with the offensive against von Kluge's Army Group Center, the command of 3 and 4 Shock Armies was transferred on 22 January from Kurochkin to Konev's Kalinin Front.

To the east and roughly parallel with Eremenko's movement, Konev's Kalinin Front thrust south-westwards on Rzhev and Zubtsov, with the intention of turning the flank of 9 German Army and severing Army Group Center's rearward line of communications.

By 27 January Popov's 61 Army of the Bryansk Front, together with Golikov's 10 and Rokossovsky's 16 Armies on the left flank of the West Front, were hardly more than 100 miles east of Smolensk. The north and south pincers were closing like the upper and lower teeth of a great gaping jaw, with the German 9, 3 and 4 Panzer and part of 4 Armies inside the great horseshoe-shaped pocket. Only 2 Panzer and 2 Armies had escaped the encirclement, and this because they had been driven off to the south by the momentum of the Soviet break-in through the great Chern gap.

At the same time as the Soviet High Command was straining every nerve in its effort to encircle von Kluge's Army Group Center, the other major offensives planned by Stalin had already been launched between Leningrad and the Valdai Hills, in the Ukraine and in the distant Crimea.

Meretskov's Volkhov Front had, on 7 January, crossed the frozen Volkhov River immediately to the north of Lake Ilmen and started to move slowly but steadily in a north-westerly direction towards distant Leningrad. Although this offensive continued over the next two months and was to endanger the safety of 18 German Army (part of Army Group North), it was to offer no prospects of early victory. To the south of Lake Ilmen, however, Kurochkin's North-West Front had immediate success when, on 7 January, it developed a large-scale offensive and broke into 16 German Army defenses, partially enveloping 90,000 men of 2 German Corps in the area of Demyansk.

On 12 January, in a renewed air of crisis in Army Group North, von Leeb asked the Führer's permission to withdraw 2 Corps westwards out of the closing pocket. Hitler refused and countered with an argument, which he was to use repeatedly throughout the remainder of the war, that salients and encirclements of German troops tied down more Red Army than German forces, since the enemy was on the periphery whereas the defenders were fighting on interior lines. Since von Leeb could not subscribe to this novel theory, he asked to be relieved of his appointment. He was retired, reportedly on medical grounds, and replaced by von Küchler, formerly the commander of 18 Army.[6]

In South Russia and the Ukraine Stalin's offensives continued throughout January. Cherevichenko's Bryansk Front made only limited progress against von Weichs's 2 Army in its thrusts on Orel and Kursk, but Timoshenko had very promising success farther to the south in the Ukraine. Crossing the upper reaches of the Donets, Kostenko's South-West and Malinovsky's South Fronts secured a huge bridgehead on the west bank of the river near Izyum, about fifty miles deep, capturing the 17 German Army main supply base. Timoshenko then thrust from this bridgehead south-westwards to take the crossing places over the Dnieper at Dnepropetrovsk and Zaporozhe deep in the rear of Army Group South, and southwards to cut the Dnepropetrovsk-Stalino railway, this being the main supply artery for von Kleist's 1 Panzer Army. Army Group South was in danger of being cut off against the Sea of Azov. Its commander, the once so confident and ebullient von Reichenau, died suddenly of a stroke.[7]

On the far southern extremity in the Crimea, the Red Army occupation troops removed from Iran had arrived opposite the Kerch Straits.[8] From 26 December onwards two Soviet armies had begun to make landings on the Crimean coast. The Kerch promontory was defended by von Sponeck's 42 Corps, which consisted, however, of only one German infantry division. Von Sponeck asked permission to withdraw some miles to the east where he could shorten his line of defense, but this request was refused; so, taking the law into his own hands, he ordered the withdrawal of the German troops out of the Kerch Peninsula. For this, by Hitler's order, von Sponeck was arrested, court-martialled and sentenced to death.[9]

In more recent times Stalin's strategy during these critical days has been severely criticized. Yet in fact, far from being inconsistent or capricious, it was entirely logical. Nor was it without success. Stalin's fault was merely that of overestimating Soviet strength and underestimating German resilience.[10]

CHAPTER TWELVE
THE RETREAT CONTINUES

As PART OF the New Year's Honors the toiling and methodical Halder had presented a number of meritorious service crosses to the staff of the OKH; and, on that first day of the year, the Führer, in an effort to solve the calamitous supply situation, had removed the responsibility for the operation of the railways in Russia from the military transport organization to the *Reichsbahn*.[1] The day of 2 January, Halder noted in his diary, was one of furious fighting.[2]

At this time there were three main threats to Army Group Center. The first was on the far southern flank in the area south of Kaluga from what was known as the Oka bend. The second lay on the German center about seventy miles north of Kaluga in the area of Maloyaroslavets. The third was on the far left flank near Staritsa.

In the far south, in the Oka bend, the main enemy thrust was from Zhukov's left flank, made up of Boldin's 50 Army, Golikov's 10 Army and Belov's 1 Guards Cavalry Corps, the same force which had broken through Guderian's 2 Panzer Army near Chern on Christmas Day. Immediately after Guderian's departure, 2 Panzer Army had attempted to counter-attack from the southern flank with Geyr von Schweppenburg's 24 Panzer Corps, but both the preparation and the OKH approval had been too long delayed. By that time the enemy cavalry and tanks had clattered on westwards on their way towards the main German supply base at Sukhinichi and the more distant Yukhov on the 4 Army supply line. Both of these towns were hurriedly fortified by German part-formations, reinforcement march battalions, detachments and administrative units.

Heinrici's 43 Corps, as already recounted, had been caught in the torrent of the break-in and swept westwards, outflanked on both sides and at one time surrounded. 40 Panzer Corps tried in vain to seal the breach between 2 Panzer and 4 Armies, which were being rapidly pushed apart by the Red Army wedge.

Kübler's 4 Army was having its right flank turned by the Soviet envelopment to the south, but, at the same time, the pressure of Efremov's 33 Army on Kübler's left flank was increasing in the area of Maloyaroslavets. By probes and infiltration the Red Army attackers had, by 29 December, penetrated Kirchner's 57 Corps, making a fifteen-mile-wide breach between Maloyaroslavets and Borovsk. Although Kübler had been ordered to do so, it was beyond the strength of 4 Army to close the gap.

Further to the north 3 and 4 Panzer Armies still stood on the Lama and Ruza positions, virtually undisturbed since the third week in December. 3 Panzer Army continued under command of 4 Panzer Army, although Reinhardt's headquarters was to be shortly withdrawn to the area of Vitebsk, the 3 Panzer Army formations, 41 and 56 Panzer Corps, remaining in the line and being transferred to the command of Strauss's 9 Army.

The pressure of Konev's Kalinin Front on Strauss had been very heavy and by the New Year 9 Army had already fallen back nearly fifty miles from Kalinin to Staritsa. All the indications were that Konev could not be held.

On 2 January, von Kluge, the Commander of Army Group Center, being intensely worried about the situation of 4 Army in the area of Maloyaroslavets, asked Halder for permission to withdraw a number of formations. But when the Chief of General Staff had taken this request to the Führer it had caused an angry outburst; the front line, said the dictator, would stay exactly as it was without regard to the consequences. For Hitler was not in the best of moods since an unauthorized withdrawal by Strauss's 9 Army, which had come to light during the morning briefing, had led to a violent scene in which he had raged against Halder and the Army High Command. The OKH, said the Führer, merely took the side of the armies in the field instead of exercising any real control. Halder telephoned the news of his lack of success back to von Kluge, who replied angrily that he was at his wit's end and that a crisis of confidence had arisen between commanders, staffs and troops.[3]

Von Kluge then spoke direct to the Führer and was told that if the enemy had breached the line then he (von Kluge) had better stop the holes.

The crisis of confidence about which von Kluge complained certainly existed. Between the divisional commander in the field and Hitler, the Supreme Commander, there were four, sometimes five, successive headquarters or echelons of commnand. A division in desperate straits could not itself undertake a withdrawal, since the Führer's prior permission was necessary; this might take twenty-four hours or more to obtain. Commanders of all grades had been made personally responsible for holding their ground and the Führer had shown that those who failed to do so might, at the best, be removed from their appointments and prematurely retired, at the worst court-martialed and sentenced to death.

Not unnaturally, this resulted in a situation previously almost unknown in the German Army, where higher commanders were no longer willing to protect their juniors and where commanders and staffs dodged their liabilities when they allocated to their subordinates, or neighbors, tasks and responsibilities impossible to fulfill. In other words they simply passed the buck. In the case of failure and subsequent inquiry scapegoats could always be found, for the higher commander had simply to prove that he had passed on the order. The sacrifices were usually the unfortunate corps and divisional generals at the end of the line. One of the principal abetters of this malpractice was von Kluge.

Hitler's strategy, and indeed his peculiar newly found tactical concept, was based on the idea that all that was required was to keep one's nerve and hold firm up front, without giving up a foot of soil. These ideas, repeated many times a day for the rest of the war, were to hasten the destruction of the German Army. Already in January 1942 the formations fighting in the Russian forests were beginning to feel the ill effects of this fallacious doctrine. For although in some areas the Russian appeared to be everywhere, only limited numbers of Red Army men were in fact engaged in the close pursuit. But already they had the tactical initiative because they were relatively mobile and were not tied to defending or attacking ground. Because of this mobility they could be concentrated in areas of tactical importance.

On 3 January there were further angry scenes at Rastenburg when the Führer, shouting that he no longer had any faith in the ability of German generals to take hard and unpopular decisions, said, with that turn of logic peculiar to himself, that he was not prepared to listen to any more withdrawal proposals until those on the spot had taken action to plug the great gaps and bring Soviet movement to a halt. Since 4 Army was unable to close the Maloyaroslavets gap, Hitler instructed that the inter-army boundary between Hoepner's 4 Panzer Army and Kübler's 4 Army should be moved southwards, so that Hoepner would become responsible for closing the breach. 20 Corps to be north of the gap was transferred from Kübler's to Hoepner's command.[4] This decision did not please Hoepner.

Hoepner's troops were well dug in on the line of the Rivers Lama and Ruza. Christmas had passed quietly and only towards the end of the year had there been some enemy pressure in the area of Volokolamsk. Behind Hoepner's Lama-Ruza line no rearward defenses had been prepared, except that a main defensive line had been marked out, the so-called Winter Line earlier proposed by von Brauchitsch, running north to south from Rzhev to Gzhatsk and Yukhnov. The construction of defensive works there had been forbidden by Hitler, because he believed that prepared positions to the rear acted like a magnet on the defending formations, who were only too happy, on the slightest pretext, so he said, to fall back on them. This Führer Order was not, however, always obeyed and army commanders, where they could find materials and labor to do so, had begun the preparatory work of fortifying the area.

Hoepner himself had experienced no difficulty in holding his own forward positions on the Lama and the Ruza over the New Year, but the situation to his north and south was causing him great concern. On his left flank forty miles to his west, Strauss's 9 Army was still giving ground in face of the probes of Konev's Kalinin Front and was shortly to lose Staritsa. Further withdrawal on Strauss's part would bring Konev not only behind Hoepner but also behind the Winter Line. To the south of 4 Panzer Army was the Borovsk-Maloyaroslavets breach. Not only was Hoepner about to be enveloped on both flanks but, as if to add to his difficulties, Hitler had just made him a present of the responsibility for closing the Maloyaroslavets gap.

Since the time of Hoepner's violent outburst at the end of November, when the cavalry leader had so bitterly reproached von Kluge for leaving him in the lurch, von Kluge had never again visited 4 Panzer Army Headquarters. From that time onwards communications between the two men had been by signal or telephone or, more usually, through their chiefs of staff.

On 3 January von Kluge, carrying out Hitler's orders, transferred 20 Corps on the north shoulder of the Borovsk-Maloyaroslavets gap from 4 Army to 4 Panzer Army. Hoepner then found himself in a prominent and dangerously exposed position with the additional responsibility of repairing his neighbor's omission, while that neighbor, Kübler, whose main supply route from Roslavl was threatened, was slowly being forced back towards Medyn.

Nor was Hoepner to be left alone to solve his difficulties in his own way, for the Führer soon took a hand. Poring over his maps in Rastenburg, Hitler had worked out a solution as to how the Maloyaroslavets gap could be closed. And a facile conclusion it was. All the army commander had to do was to stand firm where he was without withdrawing a step, and at the same time thin out his troops to find a mobile reserve to close the hole. He went even further when he told Hoepner exactly how to do it. 4 Panzer Army was to move 5 Panzer Division from its northern flank over to its south, and attack into the gap.[5]

Hoepner, although irritated by these orders, which he regarded as entirely impracticable, nevertheless consulted the commanders of both 46 Panzer Corps and of 5 Panzer Division. Both were agreed that it would be impossible to move the division to the threatened area in time. The road conditions were bad and there was insufficient fuel in hand to undertake a journey of 100 miles. In any case the division was needed where it was, since there were indications of an imminent enemy offensive near Volokolamsk. A long and delayed move would result in the division being unavailable for either sector. Only if it were intended to disengage and withdraw 4 Panzer Army to the Winter Line could 5 Panzer Division be sent to the south, and even then not at such short notice. Hoepner's refusal to move the panzer division was very ill received by the Führer.

Hoepner, collecting a meager handful of reserves from the formations near the gap, prepared to counter-attack into the breach. He was not, however, permitted to use 20 Corps as part of the counter-attack force since this was tied to the defense of ground. Hoepner's operation failed while 20 Corps, which at that time was not even under attack, stood idle and uncommitted.

Von Kluge's personal position was a peculiar one. He was fully aware of the extent of the imminent catastrophe which faced Army Group Center and he well understood the impossible situation in which the "stand and fight" order had placed his army commanders. Daily he discussed with them their difficulties, even going so far as to work out verbally a program of withdrawal to the Winter Line. Yet he was unwilling to face any risk on their behalf and he continually stressed to them *their* personal responsibility should they withdraw without permission. Requests to withdraw he merely transmitted to Halder or to Hitler. Von Kluge had in fact replaced von Brauchitsch as the Führer's postman. Because of the strained relationship between himself and Hoepner, von Kluge had less close ties with 4 Panzer Army than with the other formations under his command.

On 1 January, 4 Panzer Army had sent a formal request to Army Group Center, proposing that the army should withdraw on Gzhatsk, the withdrawal to begin on 5 or 6 January. In the interim Hoepner had made his own prior arrangements with a withdrawal to the Winter Line should one be sanctioned.

Meanwhile, Efremov's 33 Army, advancing through the Maloyaroslavets gap, had changed its direction, and, instead of exploiting further to the west, had begun to curl round to the north to envelop Hoepner. 20 Corps, facing eastwards in a salient known as the Balcony, and holding the southern extremity of the 4 Panzer Army sector, was likely to be the first casualty, for the Red Army troops had already worked their way in behind it. One of 20 Corps' divisions was already isolated. The only course was to move the corps to the north, probably with the loss of much of its equipment, it being understood of course that such a withdrawal would widen the Borovsk-Maloyaroslavets breach. Delay in withdrawing 20 Corps might prove disastrous, and the danger in which the formation stood had been repeatedly pointed out to Army Group Center without, however, provoking a reaction.

Early on the morning of 8 January permission was asked once more from Army Group Center to withdraw 20 Corps, stressing that a decision could no longer be delayed. Von Kluge agreed with Hoepner's appreciation and said he would talk to Halder. A little later von Kluge rang back, but only to ask whether there was any other way out of the difficulty. Hoepner said not and he asked von Kluge whether the 4 Panzer Army request had been referred to the OKH. Von Kluge assured Hoepner that Halder was actually on his way to see the Führer. It was even possible, thought von Kluge, that agreement might be given to pull back not just 20 Corps but the whole of 4 Panzer Army to the Winter Line, so all arrangements should be made ready to carry this out.

Hoepner continued to wait. No answer came. In desperation he tried to telephone Halder, but could get no further than the Chief of General Staff's military aide, who promised that Halder would ring Hoepner back. The promised call never arrived. Early that afternoon Hoepner could wait no longer and, on his own responsibility, he ordered the code word to be issued for the withdrawal of 20 Corps.[6]

Although von Kluge did not hear that the corps was moving out until about 7 P.M. that night, the 20 Corps positions were still at this time firmly in the hands of the German rearguards. Two courses were open to him. Knowing, as he undoubtedly did, that Hoepner's action was the correct one, he could have backed Hoepner against a possible Führer inquisition and himself shouldered the responsibility in all or in part. Alternatively he could have ordered 20 Corps back to its positions, removing Hoepner from his command if he declined to comply. But he did neither. He telephoned Hoepner and heaped reproaches on his head. After all, he reminded Hoepner, *he had been warned* of the consequences of disobedience of the Führer's order.

There and then von Kluge spoke to Hitler. Whether or not, as Guderian subsequently said, von Kluge reported to the Führer the angry remarks, alleged to have been made by Hoepner, about the deficiencies of the civilian Supreme Commander, there must be some doubt. Yet it seems probable that von Kluge, heated and angered, aggravated the situation. For, far from tactfully breaking the news to the Führer or attempting to shield his subordinate, his opening words as he shouted into the telephone were, "My Führer, *that fellow* Hoepner has withdrawn," an approach which could not have been more calculated to drive the overtired and excitable dictator into a frenzy of rage. The reaction was immediate; Hoepner was to be flung out *(ausgestossen)* of the German Army "with all the legal consequences that it entailed."[7]

Hoepner took leave of his staff late that night in the big empty schoolroom at the industrial center of Gzhatsk. He said that he had no regrets at the manner of his going and, if faced again with the situation, would take exactly the same course of action. His duty, he said, was to the German soldier alone. So this man of courage and integrity departed the next day for Germany. Although it had been Hitler's original intention that Hoepner should be dismissed from the German Army without rank or retired pay, in this particular case sense and justice eventually prevailed, possibly due to the intervention of Schmundt. Hoepner remained thereafter with his family in the official residence of the Commander of 16 Corps in Berlin-Grunewald, with full pay, until June, when he was transferred to the reserve, and received retired pay until the time of his execution in 1944 for his part in the attempt on the dictator's life. After his death his widow was awarded a pension.[8]

Hoepner's place as the Commander of 4 Panzer Army was taken by Ruoff, the former Commander of 5 Corps. He could do no more than his predecessor to close the gap to his south and he too was to press von Kluge for permission to withdraw.

On the southern flank Red Army cavalry and tanks were rapidly approaching the great depot area of Sukhinichi, a rail junction and town with a peacetime population of 10,000, once engaged in flour milling and making bricks. There, the advanced elements of 216 Lower Saxon Infantry Division, just arrived in the theater from France, were clambering down from the train. The new arrivals consisted of nothing more than the divisional headquarters and headquarter company, including the divisional commander, *Freiherr* von und zu Gilsa, the band, two and a half battalions of infantry, all from three different regiments, a heavy machine-gun platoon and an engineer company. None of the men had seen Russia and most had never been in action before. The temperature stood at minus thirty degrees centigrade.

The Sukhinichi garrison, known as the Gilsa Group, totalled 4,000 German troops and about a thousand Russian *Hiwi* auxiliaries. There was no lack of ammunition because of the great munitions dump in the area; rations were not so plentiful, although a supply officer from the local *Kommandantur* static headquarters hurriedly combed the surrounding countryside with foraging teams in horse-drawn sledges manned by Russian drivers in a last-minute effort to find food and fodder. As Golikov's 10 Army and Belov's Guards Cavalry Corps closed in, a Führer Order was received ordering the Gilsa Group to hold its ground at all costs.

Von und zu Gilsa had only four doctors, one of them a surgeon, and these set up an advanced dressing station in a school, estimating that they would need accommodation for about 125 sick and wounded. The selection of the site was governed by the need for shelter rather than by tactical considerations, and the choice was afterwards to be regretted when the fighting threatened to envelop the building; the basis on which the casualty figures were calculated was to show that the newly arrived formation had little idea of the fighting on the Eastern Front. Doctors and troops were soon to learn.

On 3 January the Russians closed in fast, driving in the small perimeter. Yet, unused to battle and conditions in Russia though these troops were, the fighting soon became fast and furious, with much hand-to-hand combat and no quarter being given by either side. In spite of the lack of anti-tank weapons, the Red Army attacks were all held; but in the first ten days German casualties mounted frighteningly to 250 dead and over 1,000 wounded, from an original fighting strength of 4,000. Von und zu Gilsa's appeals for medical aid brought in only one more surgeon, who arrived by night in a glider.[9]

In the first week in January, Schmidt's 2 Panzer Army prepared to attack Golikov's 10 Army flank in the south from the area of Bryansk, using part of a panzer and two infantry divisions, to try to halt the rapid progress of Zhukov's left pincer towards Vyazma and Smolensk. Because of the iced roads and heavy snow the movement and concentration of the troops took a long time, and the attack was not made until ten days later. The nearby 4 Army was too weak to assist with concentric attacks from the north, and Schmidt's success was only limited.

Yet in spite of this, a wedge thirty miles deep was driven into the Red Army flank and this took the 2 Panzer Army troops into Sukhinichi on 24 January, from where the living among the garrison were evacuated. The dead were left in a great pit which was made to serve as a common grave. The flanks of the relief corridor came under counter-attack in their turn, and the following day, on 25 January, Popov's 61 Army, which was part of the Bryansk Front, opened a separate offensive against 2 Panzer Army due southwards towards Bryansk and Orel. Immediately afterwards, the headquarters of Rokossovsky's 16 Army arrived in the area, having been entrusted with the protection of this threatened southern flank. Rudolf Schmidt, when he had successfully evacuated the Gilsa Group, prepared to withdraw southwards from his exposed corridor.

The Führer did not agree. Sukhinichi must continue to be held; it was always possible that 4 Army's attack from the north to join Schmidt's troops might come to something, he supposed. Halder was told to telephone Schmidt direct and countermand any withdrawal orders; this was done, apparently too late, for willy-nilly 2 Panzer Army gave up Sukhinichi and withdrew to its original starting line in the south.[10]

A little farther to the north Kübler's 4 Army was still disorganized and disoriented, reeling towards the west under the pressure of Efremov's 33, Zakharkin's 49 and Boldin's 50 Armies. The encircled Heinrici's 43 Corps did not finally break into the open until 14 January and Heinrici continued to fall back westwards towards Yukhnov, an area which had been outflanked from the south three days before by Soviet cavalry posting forwards towards Vyazma.

On the north flank of Strauss's 9 Army events had not stood still. Maslennikov's 39 Army, part of Konev's Kalinin Front, had resumed its pressure from the area south of Staritsa and within a week was threatening Rzhev, twenty miles farther to the south. An attempt to hold the Red Army advance by flying in another two infantry divisions and an SS cavalry brigade failed when Shvetsov's 29 Army arrived unexpectedly in the area, having crossed from Maslennikov's left to his right. On 10 January the long-threatened attack by Kuznetsov's 1 Shock and Vlasov's 20 Armies against Reinhardt's 3 Panzer and Ruoff's 4 Panzer Armies developed near Volokolamsk and Purkaev's 3 Shock and Eremenko's 4 Shock Army had, the day before, begun their long march from the area of Ostashkov towards Velikiye Luki and Vitebsk, deep in the German rear. By the second week in January it was apparent, even in Rastenburg, that the inner Soviet pincers from Rzhev and Sukhinichi were about to close in on the area between Vyazma and Smolensk, encircling the larger part of Army Group Center.

On 9 January Halder spoke repeatedly to von Kluge, Jodl and the Führer about the rapidly deteriorating situation. An immediate withdrawal of Army Group Center was necessary to the Winter Line, thought Halder. Even the Winter Line itself had been partially enveloped by the most recent attacks of the enemy North-West and Kalinin Fronts. The Führer, as usual, could not come to a decision and wanted first to have a meeting with von Kluge, which, as Halder noted, could only lead to further postponements and the loss of so much valuable time. Von Kluge was due to fly to Rastenburg to see the Führer the next day, but on account of bad flying weather the meeting was delayed for forty-eight hours.[11]

That Sunday, von Kluge and Halder spent the whole day in the dictator's office. Hitler talked incessantly, ranging over a great variety of subjects which, although connected with the war in the east, were hardly relevant to the withdrawal to the Winter Line. Among the topics he discussed were army group boundaries, railway capacity, the evacuation of wounded, the raising of reinforcement battalions, the production of new tanks, and the movement of divisions from the west. He elaborated on the technical details of air and road transport, and lectured his audience on the strategic problems of getting into the Caucasus to stop up the Anglo-American aid entering the Soviet Union through Persia. Little was left unsaid. For Hitler used words to release his own pent-up emotions and habitually thought aloud and argued each point, whipping himself into hysteria, until he had convinced himself of the correctness of his views and the stupidity of those of his opponents.

Halder did not get back to his own office until the early hours of Monday morning, tired and depressed, having achieved nothing, while von Kluge returned to his Army Group Center Headquarters riled by the dictator's Parthian shot that matters were no worse for him (von Kluge) than for the others.[12]

The 13 January was what Halder called another difficult day. There were many desperate appeals from von Kluge. The Roslavl-Yukhnov *Rollbahn,* which was the main supply artery for 4 Army, was under attack and there was a crisis in the fighting near Medyn, enemy pressure being so great that von Kluge begged for permission to evacuate the town. This limited tactical withdrawal was agreed to only reluctantly by the dictator.

Von Kluge reported that 5 Corps, part of 4 Panzer Army, had been penetrated and that the enemy movement against 9 Army in the area of Rzhev was gaining momentum. A great gap had been forced between 6 and 23 Corps and the enemy 39 Army had got behind the Winter Line and had broken into the railway town of Sychevka, about thirty miles due south of Rzhev. The only supply line to 9 Army and the two corps of 3 Panzer Army had now been broken and, recorded Halder, the consequences did not bear thinking about, for 3 Panzer Army had supplies for only three days' fighting. Late that evening von Kluge was on the telephone again, saying that Strauss had ordered 23 Corps to fall back to the south.

The next day, von Kluge reported a still rapidly deteriorating situation. There was a real danger that the German defense in the area of Volokolamsk was about to give way; and the position south-west of Rzhev was perilous since he had three or four enemy divisions in his rear. Unless he got authority to pull back the whole of Army Group Center he could not possibly accumulate a reserve to deal with the Rzhev break-in. Still Hitler was reluctant to sanction a withdrawal, so that Halder was to note in his diary that there was no doubt that the Führer well understood the necessity for a withdrawal, but he just put off giving a decision. This sort of leadership, added Halder bitterly, would destroy the German Army.

Late that day Hitler did finally agree that Army Group Center should withdraw to the Rzhev-Zubtsov-Gzhatsk-Yukhnov line, after it had succeeded in closing the gaps near Rzhev and Medyn. This proviso was to prove impossible of fulfillment.[13]

On 15 January, Strauss, the Commander of 9 Army, asked to be relieved of his duties, the same day as the Commanders of Army Groups North and South were replaced. Model, the former commander of 41 Panzer Corps, replaced Strauss.

On Sunday, 18 January, Eremenko's and Purkaev's advance from Ostashkov towards Vitebsk and Kholm was creating what Halder called an awkward situation.[14] The Soviet High Command was in fact trying desperately to close the mouth of the great pocket. The southern pincer was still short of the area of Spas-Demensk, that is to say, nearly 100 miles southeast of Smolensk and about forty miles south of Vyazma. Konev's Kalinin Front was not yet close to Smolensk, but Maslennikov's 39 Army, with 11 Guards Cavalry Corps, were on the line of the Rzhev-Vyazma railway near Sychevka, about twenty miles west of the Winter Line position. Maslennikov's movement southwards had cut 9 German Army into three segments leaving four German divisions enveloped in the area of Olenino, other troops encircled south of Rzhev, while the rump of the army lay between Rzhev and Zubtsov. Sychevka, the point reached by the northern pincers, was forty miles north of Vyazma.[15]

In an effort to complete the encirclement of Army Group Center and close the entrance to the pocket, Soviet airborne troops were landed from 18 January onwards to reinforce and coordinate the activities of large numbers of partisans in the German rear near the open mouth of the great cauldron, roughly in the triangle Smolensk-Vyazma-Roslavl.

On 8 January, 35 Infantry Division, part of 5 Corps and 4 Panzer Army, stood on the Lama River facing east. On that day artillery observation posts had reported very heavy enemy traffic towards the area of the small and ancient city of Volokolamsk, but, because of the severe shortage of artillery ammunition which was aggravated by the fact that the railway line through Rzhev always seemed to be out of commission, these targets could not be engaged.

Two days later the enemy began a heavy artillery bombardment preparatory to attacking 5 Corps, the lorry-mounted *Katyusha* rocket launchers being particularly troublesome, since, as they moved immediately after firing, they could not be silenced by counter-bombardment fire. Red Army infantry then came forward in the attack, line upon line, wading through the deep snow, hurrahing and screaming like animals. These daylight attacks were beaten off by the German artillery and small-arms fire.

During the long winter nights, however, it was a very different story. In the pitch-black darkness the white-smocked enemy could not be seen in the snow fields, and, warmly clad and fed, could lay out all night in the snow, apparently without ill effects. These tense nightly vigils were very exhausting to the German defenders, for the enemy showed great ingenuity in infiltrating through the defenses. Yet the Soviet troops remained, for the most part, indifferently trained and unimaginatively led; for when a German battalion was pulled back a day or two later, closely pursued by cavalry, it saw a never-to-be-forgotten sight when mounted regiments attacked a tank company of 5 Panzer Division across open country. The massed machine-gun fire tore great gaps in the serried ranks of horses and men.

From 6 December this German division had lost eighty officers and over 2,000 men, half of these through frost-bite, and, on 10 January, the weakest infantry regiment had a strength of 270 men, while the strongest numbered no more than 390. Yet compared with other formations these strengths were not low. Although the troops were exhausted, the efficiency and morale of the division remained tolerably good.

When, on 13 January, Vlasov's 20 Soviet and Kuznetsov's 1 Shock Army, renewing their attacks with heavy artillery support, penetrated to the north and south of 35 Infantry Division, it became obvious that the forward Lama line which had been their home for more than three weeks could no longer be held. With heavy hearts the men made preparations to withdraw but, up to the last minute, the infantry of the division hoped that the withdrawal order would be cancelled. For the men were in some sort of shelter from the weather and from enemy fire; from these defenses they had successfully withstood all earlier attacks and they were reluctant to face the dangers of the open and the unknown. If they had indeed to withdraw to the Gzhatsk position, their only wish was that they should be allowed to stay there.[16]

The withdrawal, known under the code name of Winter Journey *(Winterreise),* was uneventful for the men of 35 Infantry Division and, since the enemy pressure fell off when Kuznetsov's 1 Shock Army had been withdrawn, some time was available hurriedly to fortify the new line with a number of splinter-proof weapon pits, observation posts and shelters. The artillery meanwhile dug itself in and began to register targets.

3 Infantry Division, also part of 4 Panzer Army, started to fall back on 18 January parallel to, and northwards of, the Mozhaisk–Gzhatsk highway, through a succession of intermediate lines which were from four to twelve miles apart. It reached the main defense line safely on 25 January.

A little farther to the south *78 Sturm Division,* near the right flank of 4 Panzer Army, was not so fortunate. The main axis ran along the Mozhaisk–Gzhatsk trunk road, but this was so deep in snow that it had to be marked out with poles topped with straw. Some units had been detailed off as part of the traffic control and recovery organization, and it was their duty to keep the traffic on the move, an almost impossible task since the horses, reduced to skeletons, died in harness where they fell.

The withdrawal began quietly on 16 January but the retiring troops soon came under heavy attack by enemy tanks and infantry. At one particularly critical moment it would have gone badly with 215 Infantry Regiment had not a withdrawing Luftwaffe flak battery, equipped with 88-mm and 20-mm flak guns, offered to put itself at the disposal of the regimental commander. The high-velocity 88-mm guns, which were capable of slicing through the turret of a T 34 tank, kept the enemy tanks at bay. Yet, in spite of this powerful support, casualties were not light and the strength of the weakened rifle companies ebbed even further, some being down to a dozen men.

Before the end of the month 78 Division had arrived back on the Winter Line near Gzhatsk on both sides of the *autobahn* and the Smolensk–Moscow railway line. The position was by no means ideal and little development work had been done on the defenses or shelter.

The men of *78 Sturm Division,* almost without exception, were in a distressed state. The troops' clothing was in a deplorable condition; underclothing, where they still possessed any, was in rags. Most of the regulation black leather *Kommiss-stiefel,* with which they had entered Russia, had long since fallen to pieces, to be replaced by Russian felt boots removed from enemy dead or prisoners. Some men wore looted footwear, even shoes of civilian pattern. There were few items of regulation uniform left and German troops on the march had taken on the appearance of columns of Russian civilian refugees.

Weapons were virtually beyond repair; the wonder was that the guns still fired. Whether shell and bullet found their target was quite another matter. The barrels were worn out, and those of rifle and machine-gun were fouled and distorted. The horses were done for and the vehicle engines were clattering away the last of their useful life. There were no vehicle spares and tires were down to the canvas.

Yet to the west of Vyazma lay littered the tens of thousands of good Russian vehicles, workshops and spares which had fallen into German hands the previous October. These were derelict and unsalvaged. So *78 Sturm Division* dispatched its own teams to the area under a heavy escort, for the roads were already under attack by partisans and airborne troops, and soon re-equipped itself with Soviet Ford motor trucks, much prized because of their good cross-country performance. These they loaded with brand new tires, unused replacement motor engines and spare parts still in their protective grease wrapping.[17]

In the first week of January the divisional commander of 98 Infantry Division was between Maloyaroslavets and Medyn, where our earlier account had left him, trying to net stragglers coming out of the town. He recorded the battle conditions at this time. The German forces were in retreat, he said, because they were played out and totally exhausted. There were no reserves; only willpower kept them going. Who, he wondered, was responsible for committing troops without any thought as to their real strength and capabilities; and who had so willfully underestimated space, climate and enemy? The roads were so poor that it was difficult enough for an army to campaign in Russia in summer. In winter it was well-nigh impossible.

Then there were the promises. Skis had been ordered. White combat smocks were on the way. Sledge columns would be provided. *Stukas* and bombers were coming to the rescue. None of these promises had been kept.

98 Infantry Division had fallen back to hold the town of Medyn on the main road to Yukhnov and the area had been fortified by what the divisional commander was ironically to call his three companies, so reduced were the infantry regiments in strength, and two independent SS police battalions. No sooner had the division taken up its positions in Medyn than the Bolshevik was on it.

At two o'clock that afternoon of 11 January the enemy was in contact, this becoming closer as the Red Army men actually began to shovel their way towards the defenders' weapon pits, coming through the deep snow like moles. The temperature was still down to thirty degrees below zero but, in the clear warm sunshine and windless air the conditions seemed mild. The battle around the town raged for three whole days in which the divisional anti-tank company, down to three guns crewed by one officer, one medical noncommissioned officer and six men, acquitted itself with great valor. Every hour there was a new crisis which threatened to engulf the survivors of the division.

On the morning of 13 January one of the SS police battalions which, having just arrived from Warsaw, was magnificently equipped with furs, skis and sledges, came under heavy enemy attack. Throwing away arms and equipment, it broke and ran in panic-stricken flight, hunted through the streets of Medyn by hurrahing Red Army infantry. An immediate counter-attack by the tattered remnants of 398 Infantry Regiment under the leadership of the regimental colonel threw the enemy out again and temporarily restored the position.

The second SS police battalion, commanded by a determined fifty-six-year-old major of police, continued to hold its ground.

On 14 January, the division was ordered to fall back to the Shanya position, based on a small river south-west of Medyn, which, the Führer had decided, was to be its final defense line. Few fortifications had in fact been begun, but, as the line was some distance from the main trunk route back to Yukhnov, the enemy activity in the sector was at first relatively light. Yet, in the remarkably clear daylight visibility, enemy columns, presumed to be Efremov's 33 Soviet Army, could be seen moving westwards through the twenty-mile gap to the north, outflanking the 98 Division defenses and obviously intent on joining up with the airborne troops which were being landed in the neck of the cauldron between Vyazma and Yukhnov. The enemy had made some contact with the division to the east and to the north, and to the west numerous infiltrators were moving through the woods behind 98 Division's positions.[18]

The supply situation was still bad and the incoming vehicles, which arrived only too rarely from the lines of communication, brought disturbing stories of the strength and activity of the partisan bands which were mushrooming everywhere. These were ambushing, plundering, robbing and murdering. Help came from heaven, however, when a deserted, crash-landed He 111 bomber was found to be loaded with petrol and winter clothing.

Between 12 and 27 January the divisional casualties totalled about 100 dead, 419 wounded and 1,178 evacuated sick. Only fifty-nine of the wounded and sick were to return to the division. Since the beginning of the war fifty-six officers and 1,916 men had passed through the rolls of 282 Infantry Regiment, and were now non-effective, dead, missing, wounded or sick.

On 26 January the temperature sank to 42 degrees below zero and the fine, clear weather gave way to raging snowstorms. It was by then obvious that 98 Infantry Division was filling no useful role on the Shanya River line as the bulk of the enemy was passing by to the north. The next day the division hoisted its few belongings onto its weary back and started westwards once more to the area to the north of Yukhnov.

Efremov's 33 Army, poorly supplied in its effort to get through to the airborne and partisan forces to the south of Vyazma, was already fast losing momentum. Yet the situation in the diamond-shaped area bounded by Smolensk-Vyazma-Yukhnov-Roslavl was becoming increasingly confused, with intermingled German and Soviet units fighting it out amongst the partisans, the battle there changing rapidly in kaleidoscopic fashion.

Gerrman supplies could not be got forward to 4 Army, or indeed into the pocket, as the Roslavl-Yukhnov road through the neck of the cauldron was being continually cut. 10 Motorized Division had the task of keeping the route open. From 29 January all convoys using this highway moved protected by tanks, and it was not a moment too soon for, according to prisoners taken by 10 Motorized Division on that day, three enemy ski battalions had crossed the road during the night on their way northwards. The trodden snow showed where some cavalry detachments had already crossed the road earlier, and captured maps indicated that the remainder of Belov's cavalry corps was to follow.[19]

About forty miles or so to the north, Efremov's 33 Army, moving from Medyn and keeping Yukhnov on its right, struck directly westwards towards Vyazma. In doing so it severed the communications between Heinrici's 4 Army, which was battling to hold the neck of the cauldron open, and Heinrici's neighbor to the north, Ruoff's 4 Panzer Army. At the end of January Heinrici and Ruoff both counter-attacked Efremov's flanks in the area to the north of Yukhnov, one to the north and one to the south, to re-establish contact between them and, at the same time, cut off Efremov's spearheads. It was in this fighting that 98 Infantry Division next became involved.

194 Soviet Rifle Division was in difficulties and immobile, some miles to the north of Yukhnov, and the liquidation of this enemy formation was the first task given to 98 and 268 German Infantry Divisions.

The first attack began on 29 January, but this was called off only 200 yards from the enemy-defended localities, since to have continued the slow advance in the breast-high snow would have been suicide. Some regrouping was necessary in order to change the axis of the attack and, due to the great difficulty in carrying out any movement, the assaulting troops were not in the new forming-up positions until 11 A.M. on 31 January. The second attack, made on a little locality of three houses called Plotika, by about 200 infantry, the remants of two regiments and the SS police battalion, succeeded.

Since Plotika sat astride the road used by 33 Army and its loss would stop up Efremov's supplies, the Soviet reaction was immediate. At 4:30 P.M. that same afternoon, newly arriving Red Army troops surrounded the tiny hamlet from three sides and launched a heavy attack on the defenders of the three houses. Anti-tank guns fired shot

and shell direct into the buildings, and a heavy mortar bomb, pene-
trating the roof, killed many defenders and wounded. In the five-hour
battle sixty percent of the German troops became casualties. Eventually the remainder were driven out into the darkness.

The third regiment of 98 Infantry Division, down to a company
in size, failed in its attempt to take a nearby village in a temperature of
minus twenty-five degrees, the enemy proving stronger, fitter and
better armed. In the wasps' nest into which 98 Infantry Division had
stumbled it had lost 210 casualties in barely two days' fighting. Those
remaining were exhausted and suffering badly from the cold. For the
moment 98 Infantry Division could do no more and the attacks on
Efremov's flank were taken up by 268 Infantry Division.[20]

For the first time since the long retreat had begun, the Luftwaffe
was active once more, operating from local airfields, bringing in supplies and taking out wounded, and keeping up a round-the-clock
bombing of 33 Army. Yet the Red Air Force was still in the air, fighting
doggedly, being particularly active at night.

Although 98 Division had been withdrawn from the battle with
Efremov's troops, there was no rest for these Franconian Sudeten
Germans. The surrounding area was full of enemy; complete battalions
of airborne troops appeared to be milling about without direction or
purpose; thousands of armed enemy stragglers, many of whom were
on the point of starvation, and partisans, seemed to be everywhere. The
headquarters of 290 Infantry Regiment, sheltering in a little village, was
attacked from all sides by a force estimated to be two or three battalions
strong. The headquarters consisted of only a handful of men, but everyone, from the commander to the medical orderly, seized a weapon and,
with the assistance of a nearby detachment, drove off the attackers.
These left over 200 dead behind them.

An enemy radio order instructing Soviet commanders to save their
ammunition but not their men was intercepted on 7 February.

98 Infantry Division, with the welcome support of armor, had
already begun the task of clearing the surrounding woods; in two days
of combing operations about 700 of the enemy were killed. Stocks of
arms and equipment were taken in hidden forest caches and these
included field kitchens, skis, sledges, about a hundred flame-throwers,
and forty-seven machine-guns, many of which were German.

Early on 20 January the divisional signal battalion watched the landing of part of a Soviet airborne brigade deep in the German rear near a place called Voronovo. There, during that night, the hidden watchers counted 162 twin-engined aircraft landings on an airstrip *which was brilliantly illuminated.* A large number of parachute descents were reported elsewhere from all over the rear area, together with descriptions of Soviet troops being dropped, without parachutes, into the deep soft snow from throttled-back aircraft flying at heights of about thirty feet above the ground.

A week later more enemy aircraft landings were made near the administrative area of 98 Infantry Division and, on 29 January, it was discovered that the Russian volunteer *Hiwi* doctors and nurses in the German field hospital in Snamenka, who, before their capture in the Vyazma encirclement of the previous October, had belonged to the Red Army, were in close touch with the Soviet parachutists and partisans in the area. The next day the administrative area itself came under attack by well-armed men, provided with skis and sledges; this attack was beaten off with heavy losses, the parachutists leaving 150 dead behind them.

The German troops in the administrative area sent out small assault groups to clear the neighboring villages, and at first the enemy fighting spirit was found to be low. A detachment from the divisional signal battalion routed out an enemy unit which fled leaving about fifty dead behind it. The signalers lost only two dead and two wounded. Later in the day, however, airborne troops and partisans closed in once more on the administrative area, which was by then completely cut off from the rest of the division. It went hard for many of the clerks and civilian officials, whether riflemen or machine-gun teams, for it required experience and expertise to keep the weapons firing in such bitter cold. But it was a question of live or die. Eleven of them died that day, twelve were missing and thirty-six were wounded; yet the Soviet losses were many times this figure. Not before 2 February did 98 Infantry Division succeed in relieving the surrounded administrative area.

The local villages often changed hands several times, the Soviet casualties being heavy. For these disproportionate losses there were a number of reasons not necessarily associated with lack of training. The

Red Army infantry of course were often without skill, but then, on the other hand, so were many of the German supporting and administrative troops. Most Soviet losses appear to have occurred when Red Army men were attacking or counter-attacking. For, fortified by vodka, and urged on or threatened by commissars, they often threw themselves senselessly into the German fire. Many were drunk. In a locality called Petrovo, held by German drivers, ninety attacking Red Army troops met their deaths against a German loss of four dead and eight wounded. Nearby, in the village of Lyadzy, the majority of the enemy dead were found to be in German uniform.

To the south-west of Yukhnov, 10 Motorized Infantry Division, still responsible for the security of the eastern shoulder of the bottleneck on the Roslavl-Yukhnov road, fought a series of grim battles against combat ski troops, cavalry, parachutists and partisans, and the forward elements of Boldin's 50 Army, which had just arrived after its long march from far-away Tula. Partisans were everywhere, but they showed a lack of enterprise unless closely supported by Red Army troops; they usually attacked only single vehicles or isolated and small detachments. Even though 10 Motorized Division's main task was to keep open the supply route to 4 Army, it could itself move only in convoy.

The foraging for fodder from the tiny farm localities became a hazardous and nerve-wracking duty and could only be carried out with strong protective escorts. But it had to be done, for there were no reserve stocks and the horses were near starvation.

Boldin's Red Army men had already broken through in some strength to join up with the airborne units, and, on 8 February, a big clearing operation undertaken by German troops near Ludya cost the Soviet defenders about 5,000 dead and 1,800 prisoners. Eight Red Army tanks were destroyed and eighty-seven field guns, seventy-nine mortars and hundreds of machine-guns were taken. Captured maps and documents showed quite clearly that it was Boldin's intention to envelop from the south that part of 4 Army which stood behind the River Ugra and, crossing the *Rollbahn,* make off northwards towards Vyazma.

Such clearing operations against a more numerous and better-equipped enemy, undertaken by German troops many of whom were not infantry by arm or experience, were to strain the German formations to the utmost. Movement and, on occasions, attacks had to be made through breast-high snow. Even the open farmland was broken by ridges and gullies; much was heavily wooded and entirely in the defenders' favor. Everywhere there was rumor, doubt, uncertainty, treachery and the lurking foe. Every civilian, every *Hiwi* was a potential enemy. Telephone lines were frequently cut and only the few radio sets could be relied upon.

According to the Soviet account, the first air landings had taken place as early as 18 January, when two battalions of 201 Parachute Brigade and 250 Parachute Regiment were put down to the south of Vyazma with orders to cut off the enemy withdrawal. Efremov, commanding 33 Army, had been instructed to extend his breakthrough as far west as Vyazma and, together with Belov's 1 Guards Cavalry Corps, join up with the airborne troops and partisans; he was then to connect with 11 Cavalry Corps, part of Konev's Kalinin Front, which was approaching Vyazma from the north by way of Sychevka.

Belov's cavalry began to cross the *Rollbahn* south-west of Yukhnov on 27 January and, three days later, had actually joined up with the airborne troops and partisans. On the last day of January Efremov himself arrived in the area south-west of Vyazma, about fifty miles to the rear of the German 4 Army, after his long march route from Naro Fominsk, Maloyaroslavets and Medyn, bringing with him three of his leading divisions which had bypassed Yukhnov to the north. These were further reinforced by troops of 4 Airborne Corps, but the shortage of aircraft had reduced the lift of this formation to little more than a brigade of about 2,000 men.

On 1 February, the same day that Stalin put Konev's Kalinin Front under the command of Zhukov's West Front, in this way temporarily resurrecting the West Theater, he ordered Efremov to storm and capture the important road and railway junction of Vyazma, on which 9 Army, 4 Panzer Army and 4 Army depended for their supplies. The road out of Vyazma westwards to Smolensk was already under attack and, from 29 January onwards, was broken for days on end.[22]

Efremov, however, was not without his own difficulties. Ruoff's 4 Panzer Army and Heinrici's 4 Army, about thirty miles to the east, were attacking from north and south into 33 Army's long supply line and salient north of Yukhnov, with the obvious intention of cutting the army's line of communications to the east. Belov's cavalry corps and part of Boldin's 50 Army had admittedly come up on Efremov's left, but they were well to the south of Vyazma and had become strung out and over-extended so that they no longer had any contact with their own firm bases; for the energetic measures taken by 4 German and 2 Panzer Armies to keep open the Roslavl-Yukhnov *Rollbahn* had cut diagonally across the supply lines of 50 Army and the cavalry corps. Efremov had heard reports, too, of fresh German troops from Western Europe arriving by rail in the area of Smolensk and Vyazma.[23]

On 4 February, when Efremov was no more than a few miles from the outskirts of Vyazma, the position was already critical in 33 Army rear; Efremov realized that he was not going to get into the city. He was already too far extended to the west and his neighboring formations could do nothing to help him. There was still no contact to the north with 11 Cavalry Corps or Maslennikov's 39 Army from Konev's Kalinin Front.

On the far left flank of Army Group Center, Purkaev's 3 Shock Army was near Kholm and Velikiye Luki. Major-General Scherer's 281 Security Division, an understrength formation with little artillery since it was meant merely for policing rear areas, had been ordered to get to Kholm by forced marches before the Soviets should occupy it. Although under attack by Red Army ski patrols, Scherer covered the seventy-five miles of snow-covered roads to Kholm in seven days. He only just got there in time, for on the same day that the division arrived in the small sawmilling center on the River Lovat, the town was encircled by Red Army troops. Except for a late-arriving machine-gun battalion which broke into the garrison, no further land reinforcement or supply was possible.

Scherer's main difficulty was in his lack of artillery, armor and anti-tank weapons. The only defense the troops had against tanks was their short-range hollow charge projectiles; the handlers needed great skill and courage. Soon the encircling Soviet troops began to press home their thrusts in strength, both by night and by day; all attacks were repulsed with bloody losses. The enemy dead, frozen stiff in grotesque attitudes where they fell, soon built up into great snow-covered mounds in front of the positions. At night, when the German fire slackened, Red Army foraging parties roamed over the grisly heaps of dead and dying, looking for arms to salvage.

Meanwhile, the Soviet artillery fire was growing in intensity, 175-mm heavy batteries systematically bombarding and destroying all strongpoints, headquarters and shelter. The town of Kholm was rapidly reduced to heaps of rubble. Divisional headquarters and the hospital were set ablaze and, in a temperature of minus thirty-eight degrees centigrade, it became impossible to find shelter for sick or wounded.[24]

Tank attacks were being repelled by a single anti-tank gun, an invaluable find from a disused ordnance store; since it had no sighting mechanism, it was aligned on its target by peering through the bore.

With the help of the Luftwaffe, the remnants of the garrison were still holding on to Kholm in April.

A little farther to the south-east, Eremenko's 4 Shock Army had taken Peno, a railway town and sawmilling center on the upper Volga, scattering 249 Infantry Division which held it. 189 Infantry Regiment, part of 59 Corps just arriving from France, was on the railway between Velikiye Luki and Peno; it hurriedly detrained near Andreapol and was immediately sucked into the battle. The riflemen had neither supporting weapons nor winter clothing and, in the defense of Andreapol and the forest fighting which followed, lost no fewer than 1,100 officers and men. Toropets next came under Eremenko's attack and fell within two days.

4 Shock Army then resumed its advance on a broad front towards Vitebsk, but was held on the line Nevel-Demidov by the newly arrived von der Chevallerie's 59 Corps of six infantry regiments from three different divisions.

Reinhardt's 3 Panzer Army Headquarters, which had been withdrawn out of the great pocket, took over the responsibility for the defense of the left flank of Army Group Center and, from 6 February onwards, began to counter-attack Eremenko's forces.

The beginning of February found Army Group Center back on the Winter Line where von Brauchitsch had wanted to withdraw it six weeks before. The great enveloping pincers had been held temporarily in check by Reinhardt's 3 Panzer Army on the left and by Heinrici's 4 Army on the right. Heinrici's troops, however, were in a near desperate state and the confusion was such in the mouth of the great pocket near Vyazma that none could be sure of the outcome of the battle.

Ruoff and Heinrici, both almost enveloped, were trying with their last reserves of strength to restore contact with each other. In doing this they were cutting Efremov's lines of communication and enveloping the enveloper inside the great cauldron. Heinrici's own supply line out of the pocket lay directly across those of Boldin's 50 Army and Belov's 1 Guards Cavalry Corps. Model, deep in the pocket to the north, had had his 9 Army cut into several segments by 29 and 39 Soviet Armies but, if he, in his turn, could re-establish flank contact across his enveloper's communications, 29 and 39 Soviet Armies would be doomed. Only Schmidt's 2 Panzer and von Weichs's 2 Armies, with very weak forces, still stood outside the encirclement.

Both the German and Red Army formations were nearly at the end of their strength. Both were inextricably interlocked with intercrossing supply lines. Both were flailing and striking at each other's flanks and communications, while at the same time trying to defend and keep open their own supply channels; the critical areas and the decisive battles were those which took place where the Soviet and German supply lines crossed. Although many of these engagements, in particular the daily forays along the Roslavl-Yukhnov *Rollbahn,* were only local affairs, their outcome was to decide the fate of Army Group Center on the one side and several Soviet armies on the other. The final decision as to the destruction or salvation of Army Group Center had yet to be settled in the main areas of Roslavl-Yukhnov in the south and Olenino-Rzhev in the north.

The situation of Army Group Center, as Halder was to say, was both *ernst* and *gespannt.* Most informed military judges would have said at the beginning of February that it was about to be destroyed.

CHAPTER THIRTEEN
BLOW AND COUNTER-BLOW

O N 2 FEBRUARY Halder, the Chief of German General Staff, had taken stock of the situation, putting himself mentally in the position of the Soviet High Command. But he could see no sense at all in Stalin's double thrust from Ostashkov, made by Purkaev's 3 Shock and Eremenko's 4 Shock Armies. For neither of the armies was very strong, considering the enormous task they had been set, and they were advancing on their feet over difficult country at the worst season of the year. They had few tanks and, already in difficulties over their supplies, were fast slowing up

Moreover the thrusts from Ostashkov formed only a single out-flanking arm without a matching pincer on which to close; earlier experiences in the war had proved that a single envelopment, because it was so much slower than a double envelopment and because it could usually be held or circumvented, rarely had much success. Halder was prepared to admit that Eremenko's and Purkaev's thrusts on a deep axis had forced the German High Command to deploy further forces to check the Soviet advance; but both 3 and 4 Shock Armies had been much weakened, not by the German resistance, but by the bad weather and the long line of communication. These shock armies, thought Halder, were sorely needed elsewhere and Stalin would have been better advised to have used them in the immediate area of the mouth of the cauldorn.

Halder could only describe the overall picture of the fighting around and in the great pocket as grotesque. Not only was the situation in the mouth of a horseshoe-shaped encirclement very confused, but inside the cauldron there were few recognizable forward defended lines or localities. He could only sum it up by saying that the fighting was entirely different from any other war and it had deteriorated into a slogging match or free-for-all, a *Prügelei*.[1]

The Chief of General Staff did not rate von Kluge's operational talents very highly. Whereas, in the eyes of his subordinates, von Kluge was a go-between with Hitler on the one side and themselves on the other, giving no orders or views which did not come from the Führer, Halder, on the other hand, saw von Kluge in a different light. The Commander of Army Group Center, Halder thought, was too much influenced by the day-to-day events and the hourly crises, voicing opinions based merely on his most recent impressions. Von Kluge, taking little account of long-term considerations and making no attempt to plan ahead, merely lived from hand to mouth. In any case, von Kluge was too strongly influenced by his own strong-minded army commanders.[2]

Model, the newly appointed Commander of 9 Army, was young by German standards, only fifty years old, and like most of his contemporaries, had been a professional soldier since he was eighteen. Entering Russia at the head of 3 Panzer Division, he had been promoted to the command of 41 Panzer Corps and the rank of general of panzer troops in October of that year.

An able rather than a popular commander, the secret of Model's subsequent success was bound less in education and ability than in inexhaustible energy and rigid determination. He was a man who wanted to see everything for himself, and his personality was mirrored in the way he exercised command. For, having given his orders, he went to see that they had been carried out; he toured the formations and the battlefield, quizzing and prying, and often knew more of what was happening on the ground than did his staff and subordinates. Some of his methods were foreign to the German Army standards of the time, since they were inquisitorial and destructive, impatient of the niceties of mutual trust and confidence. And so on his lightning, whirlwind tours he left behind him a trail of devastating confusion and countermanded orders. In choosing to act in this way he lost much of the respect of his subordinates but, in the short term, Model's fiery leadership produced results.

Model's personality and methods were to bring him the notice and favor of the Führer and, under Hitler's patronage, he was to be promoted two ranks from lieutenant-general to colonel-general in the space of three months. Within two years he was a field-marshal. Model was the first of a new school of senior German generals, a hardbitten, narrow-minded little company, blindly loyal to the dictator, who were to fight so tenaciously to the very end in Hitler's forlorn cause.[3]

Model's force consisted of three infantry and three panzer corps, since 9 Army was in the process of taking over the two corps of the outgoing 3 Panzer Army.[4] One of his corps, 23 Corps of four divisions, had already been cut off in the area of Olenino by the southwards thrust of Maslennikov's 39 Army, the spearheads of which were thirty miles to the south in the area of Sychevka; Model's first task on taking over his new command was to re-establish contact with this encircled pocket on his left flank.

Using one of his corps to attack westwards, Model ordered the encircled 23 Corps to force its way eastwards to meet it. 23 Corps was so hard pressed by the enemy that it could, in the event, provide only one infantry division and the SS Brigade Fegelein for the breakout. Success came rapidly, however, when, on 23 January, the two forces joined up; 23 Corps was no longer isolated and the rearward communications of 29 and 39 Soviet Armies and 11 Cavalry Corps had been broken. The tables had been turned and the Red Army besiegers were themselves encircled.

Two days later Model made von Vietinghoff's 46 Panzer Corps responsible both for the holding of the newly won area and for the coordination of the scattered groups fighting near Sychevka. Meanwhile he ruthlessly combed out from the German troops holding the perimeter as many formations and units as he dared; none of these was greater than a regiment in size and the bulk was in fact made up of numerous battalions and detachments. These Model welded together into temporary formations or into Kampfgruppen, ready to liquidate the enemy who had broken into the 9 Army rear area. On 29 January these Kampfgruppen, under the tactical control of 46 Panzer, 6 and 23 Corps, together with two panzer, three infantry and two SS divisions, began to drive a wedge between Shvetsov's 29 and Maslennikov's 39 Armies, both of which were deep inside the cauldron.

Here as elsewhere in the bitterly cold weather, German movement was hindered by the deep snow. The enemy did not lack determination and often fought bitterly; but by 5 February, 29 Soviet Army had been separated from 39 Soviet Army to its south and, twelve days later, the whole of Shvetsov's 29 Army had been encircled.

On 18 February Shvetsov and his troops were ordered by the Kalinin Front to break out of the envelopment and make their way to the south to join up with elements of 39 Army and 11 Cavalry Corps, but only 5,000 men were successful in doing so.[5] The German record claimed six enemy divisions destroyed and four scattered, 4,800 prisoners taken and an estimate of 26,000 enemy dead, together with 180 tanks and 340 guns captured or destroyed.[6] The German losses were said to be heavy.

Model had made his own army area secure by liquidating the enemy penetration and he had successfully cut the supply line to 39 Army and 11 Cavalry Corps. Yet these two enemy formations still remained to his rear, although they were, for the moment, no direct threat to 9 Army's communications to the south.

By 4 February Heinrici's 4 Army and Ruoff's 4 Panzer Army had finally re-established flank communication in the area of Yukhnov, across Efremov's rearward supply lines, while 5 Panzer Division was successfully wiping out Efremov's spearheads near the town of Vyazma. Farther to the south-east Schmidt, the Commander of 2 Panzer Army, mounted a concentric counter-offensive from the areas of Mtsensk, Orel and Bryansk, against Popov's 61 Army, this driving the Russians back to their original start line about forty miles to the north.

The situation of Army Group Center had suddenly and unexpectedly taken a turn for the better and yet it was still potentially dangerous. Except for Shvetsov's 29 Army, no Soviet formations had been destroyed and the enemy remained strong on the periphery of the cauldron and in the German rear. In the north Maslennikov's 39 Army and 11 Cavalry Corps were still inside the pocket, although they were moving rapidly southwards and south-westwards under the cover of the woods and darkness in an effort to join up with Efremov and escape the fate which had overtaken Shvetsov. The Red Air Force continued to land airborne troops in the area of Vyazma, and the Vyazma-Smolensk *Rollbahn* remained under enemy fire. In the south the Soviet

49 and 50 Armies were still trying to cross and close the Roslavl-Yukhnov highway and get to Efremov. Fierce fighting continued over the whole area during March and April.

After Ruoff and Heinrici had re-established flank communication between their armies, Hitler agreed to a further limited withdrawal in the area of Yukhnov to behind the River Ugra. The Ugra line had been prepared by divisional engineers and the *Reichsarbeitsdienst,* and between 3 and 5 March the divisions in the area, including 10 Motorized and 98 Infantry Divisions, fell back across the river.

The position was a bad one. The frozen Ugra, in spite of its steep, overhanging banks, formed no real obstacle. The river course was serpentine and the thick, dark woods on either bank came down to the water's edge; divisional frontages were wide and the country so close that the river line could not be properly covered by observation or by fire. A steadily sinking thermometer and a return of the bitter weather made the construction of further earthworks impossible and the troops set to work to build igloo-type block houses and fortifications out of the compressed and hard-frozen snow.

Only two days after 98 Infantry Division had occupied the new line, troops of Zakharkin's 49 Army followed up, crossing the frozen river and attacking one of its regiments. Further attacks followed at different points along the line over the next few days, and each time the enemy had to be thrown back by counter-attacks which involved hand-to-hand fighting.

Aerial bombing of the German positions became a regular nightly event and, as the enemy's medium artillery began to arrive, all localities and tracks came under heavy shelling. Tanks could be heard on the far bank; forward observation posts reported that attempts were being made to board over the ice with heavy wooden planking, and it was suspected that this was some weight-bearing test. The furious infantry attacks, usually of company or battalion strength, continued unabated, the enemy appearing to throw themselves, almost with indifference, into the defenders' fire.

In spite of their heavy losses, Red Army men continually succeeded in crossing the river; each time they had to be ejected by counter-attack.

Between 5 and 13 March a battalion of 282 Infantry Regiment had reported its losses as forty-four men, among them the last survivor of the old 10 Company, which had entered Russia the previous July; the number of seasoned *Ostfront* campaigners left in the regiment could be counted on the fingers of two hands.

In the early hours of 13 March about 150 enemy infantry once more managed to secure a foothold in the woods on the west bank, making a deep penetration into the line and separating the German forward defended localities. Since the divisional reserve was nothing more than the reconnaissance squadron, a totally inadequate force to deal with such a threat, a new counter-attack force was hastily scraped together, made up of the engineer battalion, part of the signal unit, and thirty men taken from divisional headquarters. But not before the afternoon of 14 March could this be welded into an effective battle group.

By then the enemy had got a further 400 men across the Ugra. During all this time, while enemy artillery and mortars kept up on incessant bombardment as if there was no end to their ammunition, the German artillery was silent.[7]

Just before dawn on 15 March, in a raging storm, the improvised counter-attack force moved forward against the enemy. Visibility was down to a few yards and the swirling, drifting snow had covered all tracks. Close artillery or mortar support was out of the question. With the assistance of two tanks and some assault guns, the attacking troops moved out of clearings in which they had formed up and, wading through the deep snow, plunged into the close woods. There they had to fight for every yard of the way, the tough, drunken, brutish enemy, so says the divisional account, fighting like the very devil. For in those somber forests tanks and the turretless assault guns were only of very limited help. Desperate and sick with fear, man fought against man, with machine-carbine and grenade, hewing and thrusting with bayonet, rifle butt, knife and entrenching spade. Bodies were re-stabbed before moving on for fear the unwounded or the lightly wounded, shamming death, should rise again and open fire from the rear.

Forest fighting has always been a most difficult and frightening affair, demanding self-reliance, strong nerves, stamina and the highest individual skill. At the best the man to the flank could be seen; if fortunate, there might be a cover man to the rear. There was always the danger of killing one's comrade; yet any hesitation in opening fire might be fatal. Visibility was too close for leadership, example or control. Usually there was none to see whether the soldier died a hero or a coward; whether he died at all or ran away. Yet most of the German counter-attack force, far from being highly skilled infantrymen, were drivers, telephonists, signalers, clerks and orderlies; but they all well knew that it was a matter of kill or be killed — there could be no turning back.

The condition of the Red Army men was little better. Factory workers, peasants and collective farm laborers, many of whom had only recently been rounded up from the fields, the length of their military service was rarely more than a few months. They believed that torture or death would be their lot if they fell into German hands and all knew that the fate of their relatives depended on their own conduct in the field. Becoming a prisoner, in the eyes of the Communist Party, was tantamount to being a deserter, and the family might atone in a concentration camp for the prisoner's guilt. Vodka and the bitter, emotional, race hatred preached by the commissar did the rest. There was no alternative to kill or die and this was reflected in the desperate resistance put up by the Red Army men.

Not until late that evening had the Soviet enemy been driven back, leaving 200 dead behind him. But although the Germans restored their broken forward localities, the enemy still hung on to the western bank. German losses again were heavy.

The next night was quiet but the left-hand neighbor, 268 Infantry Division, was under heavy attack and was soon reduced to such serious straits that the corps reserve was dispatched to its aid. Everyone was waiting desperately for the thaw, the *Schlammperiode,* or *rasputitsa,* which must bring enemy movement and attacks to a standstill.

The exhaustion of the German troops was in fact only matched by that of the enemy opposing them. All the Soviet armies were being relentlessly ordered forward into the attack, whatever their condition, but there was a growing realization among the Soviet field commanders that their men were too weak to achieve anything more. Further reinforcements had been allotted to West Theater, in Zhukov's opinion too late to be of any use, but the Red Air Force was suffering from a

lack of forward airfields, and the ground armies had been seriously
weakened by heavy casualties. The extended lines of communication,
too, made supply very difficult.

Zhukov, so he has subsequently said, knowing the weakened and
disorganized state of his troops, wanted to call off all attacks and go over
to the defensive.[8] This may or may not have been true. Certain it is,
however, that this was not Stalin's view, for on 20 March he demanded
the launching of a great new offensive. The German Winter Line was
to be broken open. Govorov's 5 Army was to take Gzhatsk and
Golubev's 43, Zakharkin's 49 and Boldin's 50 Armies were to resume
their attacks against Ruoff's 4 Panzer Army and Heinrici's 4 Army and
move on Vyazma, where Efremov was in danger of being destroyed.
Konev was ordered to thrust southwards once more, restoring land
communications to Maslennikov's 39 Army and splitting Model's 9
Army between Olenino and Rzhev. No one was to be left idle.[9]

On Palm Sunday, 29 March, the temperature was still twenty degrees
centigrade below zero, with a strong biting wind. Word had been
received in 98 Infantry Division that home leave could begin again, up
to eight men in each company being allowed away at one time, provided that commitments and strengths would allow. The strengths in
98 Division would not allow, for the enemy continued to attack all
along the line.[10]

On 2 April, a little further to the north, 3 Motorized Infantry
Division was locked in close combat, in an effort to stem the Soviet
offensive, the troops fighting in the open for the third night in
succession without weapon pits or cover from shot, shell and cold.
Many were pinned to the ground by enemy fire, in a temperature of
fifteen degrees below zero. Numbers froze to death. The shelling and
machine-gunning by enemy tanks caused heavy losses among the
infantry, a battalion of 8 Infantry Regiment being almost wiped out.

In addition to holding the enemy to its front, 3 Division had to
keep up an incessant running fight against partisans in its rear, for
aggressive measures were essential even to keep them in check. Patrols,
still without proper winter clothing and still relying on newspapers
and straw for protection against the icy winds, were mounted on

horse-drawn sledges to race through villages and settlements, so advertising the German presence.[11]

Although the storm of Stalin's final winter offensive had not yet broken over 98 Infantry Division, the Ugra divisional sector had never been quiet since it had been occupied; the daily drain in casualties and sick continued. Yet there were some hopeful signs. Although the troops were tormented with lice and covered with scratches and scabs, the cases of typhus had dropped due to recently introduced three-stage injections. There was a further reduction in the sick rate, which the medical officers could only associate with the coming of spring and the arrival of fresher reinforcements, less prone to disease and sickness than the exhausted *Ostkämpfer*.

On the other side of the Ugra at least eighteen places had been counted where the enemy was tunneling approach roads through the deep snow into what were obviously forming-up areas for a new attack. But not before 29 March did Red Army prisoners tell of Stalin's directive to join up with Efremov in the 4 Army rear.

98 Infantry Division numbered only 900 men in the line. The positions had no depth and could easily be penetrated. The weakness of the defending troops lay not only in their lack of numbers but in their unreadiness for battle, for there was a shortage of leaders, particularly experienced noncommissioned officers, and of trained support weapon specialists, infantry gunners, anti-tank detachments, mortar men and machine-gunners. Even the rifle sections lacked training and combat confidence since many of the rank and file had just arrived with the formation. The divisional reserve consisted of only two rifle companies.

The division had not long to wait. On Good Friday, the first Friday in April, every worthwhile target within range of the Soviet guns was engaged. Ammunition appeared to be unlimited, for the bombardment continued for hours at a time. German movement was pinned and the forward defended localities began to disintegrate as the weapon pits were pounded to pieces under the overwhelming weight of the shelling. Then, from the edge of the woods, came masses of hurrahing khaki-clad infantry, advancing, line after line, disregarding casualties as they passed through the standing barrage of the German artillery. Time and time again they reached and penetrated the German localities and, after each break-in, they were thrown out again.

The change of wind to a westerly direction had brought a steady rise in temperature and the snow slowly began to melt. So the wretched infantrymen fought on, cursing the inopportune thaw, which had filled the weapon pits with ice-cold water.

The enemy was across the river to stay, however, and he had dug himself in near the locality of Pavlovo on the west bank. A fresh counter-attack group was called for to throw him out but, as no help could be expected from corps, another divisional *ad hoc* force had to be collected. The divisional engineers went into the line once more to relieve infantry withdrawn for the counter-attack.

By 10 April, Pavlovo had been cleared of the Red Army enemy. That same night, however, further enemy troops had crossed the river and infiltrated back into the town. To renew the German attacks could only have led to a further loss of life without gain, for it seemed to be impossible to counter the enemy's infiltrating tactics; so he was left where he was, holding a stretch of the right bank. It was just hoped that the information given by prisoners that further Soviet troops were about to cross over the river was not true.

The heavy enemy artillery fire continued and, within a matter of hours, German outposts were reporting large concentrations of troops on the far enemy bank waiting to cross over the ice. By then 98 Division was too weak to put in even local counter-attacks and, in the early morning of 11 April, the divisional commander reported to corps that although his division was still capable of holding ground, it no longer had any offensive capability at all. The corps commander handed over to 98 Infantry Division his tiny corps reserve together with *Alarmein-heiten* formed from corps troops. He had nothing else to give.

Then followed days of anxiety and crisis. Two heavy Russian attacks on the first morning were pushed home relentlessly by infantry and artillery, without regard to losses. In the afternoon there followed two more determined attacks. They were all beaten off, but the casualties were heavy on both sides. 289 Infantry Regiment, which a week before had only had 300 men in the line, lost eighty men on that single day. The spirits of the tired and despondent troops were temporarily restored towards evening, however, by the sight of fourteen *Stukas* attacking the enemy concentration areas on the other side of the river.

The following morning, after a two-hour artillery preparation, the enemy came forward once more, driving in part of 289 Infantry Regiment, by then reinforced by detachments and men combed out from the other two regiments. There had been many flanking probes throughout the divisional sector, and yet it was obvious that the enemy axis lay through Pavlovo and 289 Regiment sector.

Flexibility and originality in thought were characteristics rarely encountered in the lower levels of the Soviet field command at that time and no Red Army commander had any qualms about reinforcing failure, whatever the casualties. So 98 Infantry Division kept repairing its defenses in front of Pavlovo and reinforcing the badly mauled 289 Infantry Regiment. This fifth attack on the second morning was repulsed and the enemy driven back again. No more infantry could be found and 289 Infantry Regiment was joined by the signal battalion, the divisional headquarter company and a motley collection of drivers, telephonists and clerks. These took part in the final defensive engagement when the sixth attack was beaten back on the afternoon of 12 April.

By then 98 Infantry Division was no longer fit for any further fighting. In two days one battalion and seven company commanders had fallen, together with a large number of junior leaders.

On 17 April, over a space of hours, the snow and ice began to disappear. The Ugra started to move once more, the ice cracking and breaking into floes which began to drift faster and faster downstream on their way to the Oka and the distant Volga. The level of the water rose quickly, over six feet in as many hours, and the starlings, those harbingers of spring in Northern Europe and Russia, arrived in great flocks on the warm west winds.[12]

Meanwhile only a few miles to the German rear, 4 Army had been engaged in breaking up part of 33 Soviet Army encircled to the south-east of Vyazma. For Efremov's troops were already on the move, streaming back eastwards towards safety. Most were desperate and near starvation. Nearly 5,000 were accounted for, over 1,600 in prisoners, immediately to the rear of 98 Infantry Division. Eighty guns, seventeen tanks and 300 horses were captured together with a great mass of other booty.

The thaw struck the death knell of 33 Army, for Efremov relied on the sledge and the ski for all supply. Motor vehicles and carts had been left a hundred miles to the east on the Nara. Without the food foraged for him by the partisans he could not exist, and the *rasputitsa* robbed even the partisans of their mobility.[13]

Efremov and Belov were then ordered from Moscow to escape eastwards and make their way by woods and darkness to rejoin Golikov's 10 Army in the area of Kirov, the route laid down for them by Zhukov being circuitous, swinging far to the south towards Roslavl, through areas where few German forces were to be found and where partisans were active or had much of the countryside under their control.[14] Belov's cavalry corps and part of the airborne troops, abandoning their equipment, held to their route instructions, and a large proportion of them, according to Zhukov, reached safety.

Efremov did not agree with Zhukov. Because he believed that the starving and exhausted men of 33 Army were no longer in condition to cover so long a journey, he radioed the General Staff in Moscow asking for permission to move eastwards on the shortest direct route over the Ugra. Stalin was informed. When the dictator asked Zhukov for his opinion, the Commander of West Theater spoke against Efremov's proposal. But Stalin that day was capricious and contrary. After all, he said, Efremov was a man of great experience and if that was his opinion, he must have good grounds for it; one must defer to the man on the spot.[15] A rational enough view, except that, when the dictator wanted *his* own way, he never deferred to anyone.

Lieutenant-General Efremov's attempt to cross the Ugra through the rear of Heinrici's 4 Army ended in disaster. Efremov's own fate is uncertain, but he is said to have committed suicide in order to escape capture. So died a soldier of great promise, who had been fighting continuously without a break since the previous July, commanding first 21 Army and, for a short time, the Central Front.

If the German troops on the Ugra thought they were due for a well-earned rest, their expectations were sadly shattered when 268 Infantry

Division was ordered by 12 Corps to destroy the Soviet bridgehead west of the Ugra at Aksinino. The German division had already been burned out and the attack failed.

The next day, 24 April, 98 Infantry Division was instructed to prepare an offensive to throw the enemy back over the river at Pavlovo, and the pattern and chronology of events is of particular interest since it shows the new technique of command which was rapidly transforming the German Army.

The divisional commander was ordered to report to corps, where the corps staff discussed, over the space of several hours, the details of the coming attack, tediously and repetitively ranging backwards and forwards over scarcely relevant details. What really mattered was the relative strengths, the fighting power of 98 Infantry Division compared with that of the Pavlovo defenders.

The divisional commander, who was dismayed at the thought of the new offensive, stressed to corps the weakened and disorganized state of his commnand. His men were tired out and his fighting strength had dwindled almost to vanishing point. This had been reported, he pointed out, repeatedly to corps headquarters over the past few weeks. Graessner, the corps commander, put an end to all objections with the words: "The attack has been ordered. You will get reinforcements." These were the replacements which rarely materialized.[16]

The divisional commander received no reinforcements, as such, to assist him in the offensive. Instead, he was given elements of three other infantry regiments and part of two motorized regiments from panzer divisions; these were in no better condition than his own men. Worse still, only a few days before, they had taken part in the unsuccessful offensive made by the neighboring 268 Infantry Division, during which they had suffered further casualties. Tired and dispirited, their morale was not of the highest.

The attack against the Pavlovo bridgehead was to be supported by bombers, but the additional artillery consisted of nothing more than a 100-mm battery, a heavy mortar and some *Wurfgerät* multiple rockets, the German equivalent of the *Katyusha*. Only two tanks were to assist in the operation.

With a heavy heart the divisional commander made his plan and this was sent on to 12 Corps, where it was corrected and altered; from there it was forwarded to 4 Army for yet further amendment. When the plan finally came back to him, he could hardly recognize it as his own. The corps and army headquarters continued to breathe heavily down his neck, making a further three alterations, the last one only a few hours before the attack was due.

The plan imposed on 98 Division, on paper at least, appeared to have taken account of all possible contingencies. The fire program in particular was one of the most comprehensive that the divisional artillerymen had ever seen, with a preparatory and harassing fire bombardment, extensive use of smoke and a very detailed covering fire timed schedule aimed at pinning the enemy, neutralizing his fire and masking the observation posts. What was not taken into account was the debilitated state of the German troops, the condition of the waterlogged ground, or the defensive techniques of the Red Army.

At twenty minutes before seven o'clock on the morning of 28 April the preparatory bombardment began, this being timed to last for thirty minutes, a very short bombardment measured by Soviet standards. Twenty minutes later seventeen *Stukas* joined in the bombardment, and the effect, particularly of the carpet fire of the *Wurfgerät* rockets, appeared to the onlookers to be so devastating that it looked as if the Red Army defenders must be either destroyed or so severely shaken that they would be incapable of putting up any defense. Even the tired German infantry felt, as they entered their forming-up places, that, with such support, this was an attack which *must* succeed.

At ten minutes past seven the two divisional assault groups crossed the start line on their way towards Pavlovo, accompanied by the two tanks. Both tanks sank down into the waterlogged morass and could not move. The infantry struggled on alone, up to their knees in mud and water. Twenty minutes after the assault group on the left flank reported that the stiff resistance and mounting casualties made further success unlikely, it was ordered to dig in where it was. Shortly afterwards the other group was forced to a halt, for the enemy, far from being demoralized and shell-shocked, were actually coming out of the woods to counter-attack.

By eight o'clock the divisional attack was stuck fast everywhere. Enemy mortars and artillery were causing many casualties, the infantry lying on their faces in the mud and melting snow trying to scrape holes for protection against the flying fragments. The resolution of the enemy and the energy of the defense had come as a most unpleasant surprise. Another *Stuka* attack was called for.

At 10:30 A.M. the single-engined Junker 87 bombers were overhead once more and, together with the artillery, began pounding away at the woods immediately to the German front. The attack lasted only fourteen minutes but it put some heart back into the German troops.

As soon as the last *Stuka* aircraft had dropped its bombs and flattened out from its dive, the infantry rose to their feet and with a ragged cheer plunged into the woods before the Russian defenders had time to collect their wits. Success was immediate. Many of the enemy were dead or wounded and the others were numbed by shock and fear; the woods were speedily taken. But when the German infantry emerged into the open on their way to Pavlovo beyond the fringe of the forest, they came under heavy artillery and small-arms fire which forced them to earth once more.

Casualties began to rise again, particularly among the junior leaders; meanwhile the terrified troops lay in the water and soft wet snow, pinned to the ground. The heavy rain and sleet made it impossible for the German artillery officers to pick out their targets.

By an almost superhuman effort the battalion commanders, captains or lieutenants, got the unwilling infantry on to their feet once more and forward into the attack. But the thin line of men was met by a veritable hail of fire as it attempted to pass through the standing barrage, shells and rockets plowing up the ground all round them. Many of the German troops turned back, and panic, rapidly spreading, took hold everywhere. In spite of the efforts of their leaders to hold them, the men streamed off the field, running back through the stricken woods to their rear, until they reached the positions from which they had started.

The attack on Pavlovo was at an end and the enemy remained in control of the bridgehead. The German divisional losses during the few hours of the attack had mounted to twelve officers and 450 men.

The next morning von Kluge, the Commander of Army Group Center, wanted an immediate report as to why the attack had failed. Yet von Kluge was fully aware of the state of this division since this was the formation which he, as the former commander of 4 Army, had visited at the beginning of the previous November. Even then it was at the end of its resources. Since July 1941 it had had no rest and had only been out of the line during its long march from Army Group South to Army Group Center.

On 30 April an inquiry was ordered by Army Group Center to find out the responsibility for the failure, it being clearly understood by its terms of reference that a court-martial was intended. The divisional commander could only answer that the blame and responsibility lay with whoever had brought the troops to that condition.

The subsequent investigation, however, did bring a number of unexpected facts to light, and these were to give some indication of the characteristics of the Red Army defenders. It was gathered from prisoners that about a thousand fresh troops were brought into the Pavlovo bridgehead on the night before the German attack, and this made it probable that the Soviet field command had some prior intelligence of the German intentions. It was discovered, too, that the remarkable way in which the Red Army defenders stood up to the fierce bombardment had less to do with training and resolution than with their skill and energy with the spade. For they dug everywhere above the waterline, not just weapon pits, but bunkers and interconnecting galleries, in the steep sides of the Ugra bank and in every sandy mound and hillock.

Although many of these Red Army men may have been poorly trained and indifferent soldiers, given a spade and a few hours' respite, they simply melted into the earth. Defense was the operation of war for which they were best suited and, once dug-in, they could only be routed out at the cost of heavy casualties. During the worst of the bombardments they would leave their weapon pits and make their way underground by interconnecting trench or gallery. Any delay in launching an attack after the bombardment had lifted allowed these Red Army defenders to return to their weapon pits in time to meet the onslaught.

The Commander of 98 Infantry Division was called first to 4 Army and then to von Kluge to explain the failure. Although he succeeded in persuading the Commander of Army Group Center that the fault lay neither with the leadership nor with the troops, the pattern of the inquiry was to become a common procedure for the German Army on the Eastern Front. Moreover, as German fortunes waned the Führer was wont to vent his spite on the commanders in the field.

By 30 April Army Group Center had gone over to the defensive everywhere and the Soviet enemy did the same. For the Red Army and the German Army in the East were both at an end of their strength.

CHAPTER FOURTEEN
EPILOGUE

A T T H E E N D of April the North-West, Kalinin, West and Bryansk Fronts, fully extended and incapable of further effort, were bogged down in the spring mud. The longest advance had been made by the left flank of the West Front from near Stalinogorsk north-westwards to Spas-Demensk and Vyazma, a distance of nearly 240 miles. The Kalinin and North-West Fronts had covered about 180 miles, while the least progress, in terms of distance, had been made by the center and right flank of the West Front. This had pushed the enemy back about sixty miles.

The German line remained in the big horseshoe-shaped salient formed when Stalin had attempted to envelop Army Group Center. The airborne troops and partisans together with elements of 33 and 39 Soviet Armies remaining in the mouth of the pocket to the south and west of Vyazma were not cleared by Army Group Center until after the mid-summer of 1942. The great pocket continued to stand, otherwise un-altered, for the next eighteen months, in the form of the Rzhev salient.

Hitler refused to give up this salient, in spite of the fact that it took three armies to hold it, reasoning that it offered a springboard for a new offensive, should he at a later date decide to reopen the campaign towards the Soviet capital. In fact he never did so. Even in March 1942 he had lost all further interest in Moscow and was feverishly planning the gigantic offensive in South Russia and the Ukraine which was to take the German armies down the Don to the Caspian and the Caucasus.

The Rzhev salient was not withdrawn until March 1943, after the failure at Stalingrad and in the Caucasus, and then only in order to shorten the line and make troops available for the final German offensive of the Russo-German War at Kursk.

When the Führer had decided to invade the Soviet Union, he had intended only to occupy, in a short summer campaign, its western territories as far east as Archangel, the lower Volga and the Caspian, this line being, of course, well to the east of Moscow. What was to happen after he did not know.

Germany was strong enough in 1941, even without the assistance of allies, to have destroyed the USSR as a political state, but it could have done this only if it had mobilized the whole of its resources. There could have been no question of waging, at the same time, a costly air and sea war against Britain, or of leaving fifty divisions behind to garrison Western Europe. And it would have been necessary to gear the whole economy of the Reich to total war. Even if Hitler had done all this, the margin between the war strengths of Germany and the Soviet Union was not great. In any case, the USSR could not have been destroyed until after it had lost the Caucasus and the Urals, and German troops could not have overrun so vast an area in 1941.

When Hitler ordered his armies eastwards against the Soviet Union he had already entered into a war on two fronts and, not six months later, in a fit of megalomania and caprice, he had added the United States of America to Germany's enemies. Against such odds Germany could not win.

To the Führer, war meant little more than a succession of land campaigns and battles. Because he wanted his name written in the pages of history beside those of Alexander, Caesar and Napoleon, he had taken too close a hand in those details of command which are normally the province of soldiers. Yet he had already failed as a war leader and head of state by not providing his Commanders-in-Chief with a master plan elaborating the political, economic and strategic aims of the new war. His military commanders and staffs had restricted their war planning to the destruction of the Red Army in the western regions of Russia and the Ukraine; no one had any clear idea how the area between the Dvina-Dnieper and Archangel-Astrakhan lines was going to be occupied, or of the aims and priorities involved in that task.

The occupation of the Ukraine, the Baltic States and Leningrad was more important, so the Führer had said, than a rapid advance in the center in the direction of Moscow and beyond. None of his senior advisers could be sure on what he based this premise, but it was generally assumed that the dictator had good reason for what he did. They were not to know that his views were founded neither on intelligence nor logic but merely on the chance idea picked up from Jodl and the *Lossberg Studie.* But once Hitler had accepted an idea, however grotesque, nothing could shift him, and, instead of taking the rational course of amending his opinions according to changed circumstances, he obstinately stuck to his original view and tailored intelligence to fit it.

So he maintained that the Baltic States and Leningrad must be taken and the Ukraine occupied before an advance was made from Smolensk eastwards on the Moscow axis. Sometimes he supported this view by the forecast that the enemy would defend strongly in the north and south, so form flanking threats to an extended German salient in the center. At other times he was disinterested in simple arguments based on the narrower aspects of military strategy, but emphasized that his predominant interest in the north and south rested on economic considerations alone. At least once he engaged in a form of political obscurantism when he justified his actions to a doubting questioner, giving as his opinion that the mere fall of Leningrad would bring about the complete collapse of communism throughout the Soviet Union.[1]

Many of Hitler's ideas were illusory, and the evidence provided by the Führer's statements and actions during the summer of 1941 supports the view that the dictator's war direction at this time was becoming increasingly fumbling and uncertain. Hitler had not made up his mind what to do and he attempted to conceal this uncertainty from his subordinates. Anything served as a screen, and the excuses which came most readily to his tongue and could not be confounded by his generals were based on economic, political or security considerations. It seems more likely that he was, in fact, just hoping and waiting for the Soviet leadership and system to collapse.

Von Bock's Army Group Center had reached Smolensk by mid-July 1941, and the Red Army troops encircled in the Smolensk cauldron had been destroyed by 5 August. At that time von Bock had estimated that he would take Moscow by the end of the month. If he had been permitted to keep the panzer corps of Guderian's 2 and Hoth's 3 Panzer

Groups, there can be little doubt that Army Group Center would have been in Moscow by the beginning of September. No Red Army force could possibly have stopped it. Provided that von Bock had kept his armies concentrated on comparatively narrow fronts, it is likely that he could have penetrated even further before the onset of winter, up to 200 miles east of the capital beyond Vladimir and Ryazan, so cutting the north-south railway which connected Yaroslavl with Voronezh.[2] On the other hand, Budenny's South-West Theater would have remained in being and it is doubtful whether von Bock could have held on to his conquests during the winter.

Hitler's decision in the fourth week of August, after several weeks of vacillation and argument, to detach all but one panzer corps from Army Group Center and send them to Leningrad and the Ukraine meant that the capital would never be taken by German troops for, when they reassembled in the area of Smolensk and Glukhov at the end of September, with the muddy *rasputitsa* in front of them, it was already too late in the season to cover the 200 miles from Smolensk and the 300 miles from Glukhov to Moscow.

Even if any of the German troops should succeed in getting as far as Moscow, it was certain at that late stage that none of them would hold it. Yet Moscow was not Hitler's objective for that winter for, although it was so late in the season, the dictator still had his eyes on attaining the Archangel-Astrakhan line several hundred miles beyond the capital; all his three army groups, from Leningrad to the Black Sea, had been ordered eastwards to reach it.

In retrospect it may seem remarkable that the German generals took the Führer's orders seriously and continued to have faith in him. For the field commanders knew only too well that their formations were already tired and understrength, without replacement or reserves, and at the end of a long and uncertain supply line. That the generals accepted this situation reflects both on themselves and on the German military system as a whole. Yet it also emphasizes the extraordinary ascendancy which Hitler had established over nearly all who came into contact with him, even those normally regarded as doubting and critical. It brings, too, into clear relief the lack of understanding on the part of the High Command and General Staff of the simple truths of the geography of Russia.

Von Brauchitsch, von Bock and Halder were all officers of great experience and ability and two of them, on occasions, voiced to Hitler their disagreement on the strategy of the campaign. But neither they nor their opinions mattered, for the conduct of the war in the East was completely in Hitler's hands, even the day-to-day battle moves being controlled from the dictator's desk.

Von Bock was allowed no latitude and the axes of his armies and panzer groups were drawn on the map for him at Rastenburg. He might, and sometimes did, disagree with the orders which came down to him from above; from time to time he remonstrated, but the OKH orders were only once varied as a result of his objections. Hurt and resentful, the complaining von Bock was obliged to conform.

Von Bock had no confidence in von Brauchitsch, but it was not until the autumn that he began to realize that the Commander-in-Chief of the German Army was merely the Führer's mouthpiece. It followed that von Bock was to become critical of the dictator's field leadership, but he did not express this openly to Hitler or to anyone else. Nor did he ask for his own removal or retirement in protest against the way in which operations were being conducted on his behalf. For von Bock was an ambitious man. He finally went only when his health could no longer sustain him. Later he was pleased to return.

Although the Führer was on cordial terms with von Bock and had some respect for him, he does not appear to have rated his ability very highly. Nor did von Bock enjoy Hitler's fullest trust, because the dictator was continually seeking second and third opinions, even from von Bock's subordinates, von Kluge and Guderian, thrusting men who were not unwilling to criticize their absent commander.

Nor was von Bock's successor more fortunate, for von Kluge, when he took over the command of Army Group Center, was to become little more than the unwilling link between the Führer and his own army commanders. Both of these field-marshals had an inglorious and minor part to play in the tragedy; the principal role was reserved for Hitler.

From the beginning of September onwards, amid a complexity of hidden aims and changing priorities, the pattern of Hitler's military strategy began to emerge, and it amounted to little else than an eastwards advance across Russia and the Ukraine, the progress to be made uniformly on a broad front without indentations or salients in the north-south line. The troops no longer had *Schwerpunkte,* or areas of main thrust, and the Führer attempted to clear what he imagined to be flanking pockets of resistance and to occupy all ground before pressing on to more distant objectives.[23]

On the strategic plane this had some bearing on his decision to divert troops from Army Group Center to the north and to the south, where concentrations of Red Army troops in the Pripet Marshes and in the area of Velikiye Luki were proving troublesome to Army Groups South and North. Other enemy concentrations near Valdai, on the right flank of Army Group North, were to assume an importance in the Führer's imagination far outweighing their numbers, and for this reason he was to order Army Group Center, even as it was advancing on Moscow, continually to extend its left north-eastwards towards Vyshniy Volochok and Kalinin to get behind Valdai.

Similarly von Weichs's 2 Army on the opposite right flank of Army Group Center was ordered by Hitler to make ground to the south-east towards Voronezh in order to support von Rundstedt's Army Group South.

It was at Hitler's insistence that all formations were continually feeling to their flanks to keep close contact with their neighbors. In this way the frontages became over-extended, the thinly spread troops lost depth and the whole momentum of the advance slowed down. By 30 October, when von Bock had been engaged in heavy fighting for a month in the battle which, according to Hitler, was finally to destroy the Red Army, Army Group Center, because it was moving on widely divergent axes, had extended its frontage to over 600 miles.

Hitler had already overreached himself when he set out, without proper logistic preparation, to get to his final Archangel-Astrakhan line objective so late in the year. He failed to reach this line and take Moscow, and the cause lay in the weather, in his own faulty strategy and in the inadequacy of his resources.

Yet the loss of the capital, however damaging it might have been to the Soviet Union from a political and a morale point of view, would not have put Russia out of the war, since much of Soviet industry had its basis in the Urals and Siberia. Nor would the loss of the Moscow industrial complex have robbed the USSR of its main source of armaments.

Moscow was, of course, a nodal point for most of the Central Russian railway system, and its loss would have been serious to the Soviet Union on this account, but even so, the railways from the Urals were still connected with Vologda, Murmansk, Archangel, Iran, the Caspian and the Donets Basin, together with all the main theaters of war. Nor should the Soviet powers of improvisation be lightly disregarded, for Soviet railway construction, though primitive, was both very rapid and effective. New loop lines had already appeared in the wilderness connecting Murmansk to Archangel, bypassing those cut by the Finns.

There is no reason to suppose that Stalin would have made peace with Hitler if Moscow had been lost, and there was perhaps even less likelihood that Hitler would have treated with him.[4] Defeat for the Soviet Union would have meant complete submission to Hitler and in all probability the overthrow and liquidation of Stalin and his communist hierarchy. In such circumstances there can be little doubt that Stalin would have continued the war whatever his territorial losses, particularly when he had been assured of the support of the United States.

Hitler was not alone in his determination to drive on Army Group Center towards Moscow so late in the year, for von Brauchitsch, Halder and von Bock were no less eager to get forward. So it came about that, by the beginning of December, Army Group Center was stranded in the heavy snow in an extended, vulnerable, almost desperate position.

Whether or not, in the circumstances, Hitler's "stand and fight" order was the correct one, must remain a point of conjecture. Hitler was primarily concerned in saving both his face and equipment; in fact, the equipment was already forfeit, for any movement, even of a few miles, led to the loss of guns, vehicles and horses, so abominable were the going conditions. The determination to hold in a rigid defense, never withdrawing more than two or three miles, and then only when under the heaviest pressure, made a present to the enemy of both the tactical and the strategic initiative; even worse, it forced the German troops to fight in the open from unprepared positions. This resulted in over a quarter of a million frost-bite casualties, a large proportion of whom became unfit for any further military service.

In the five months from 22 June to 26 November 1941, 187,000 men had been permanently lost to the German armed forces over the whole of the Eastern Front in killed and missing. The wounded for this period amounted to 555,000, of whom two-thirds might be expected to return to duty.[5] The killed and missing for the whole of the theater during the period of the retreat, from 27 November 1941 to 31 March 1942, were put at 108,000 and the wounded at 268,000, a total of 376,000 men. To this figure, however, must be added 228,000 frost-bite cases and over a quarter of a million other sick, mainly from exhaustion, exposure, typhus, scarlet fever, jaundice, diphtheria and stomach and skin complaints.[6] These were caused by the terrible conditions under which the forward troops lived, for nearly all these casualties occurred not in the rear areas, but among the divisional and corps formations. These casualty figures and the contemporary views of the field commanders, recorded in the war diaries, all tend to cast serious doubts on the Nazi Party claim that the Führer was the savior of Army Group Center.

The figures tell the story for themselves. The actual battle casualties of 376,000 for the four months of the winter withdrawal were significantly lower than those for the five summer and autumn months of 1941. But for every battle casualty during the great retreat two men were evacuated on account of frost-bite or serious sickness, and this brought the total fallout for the period to over 900,000 men, more than the German Army could afford. Only half of the 900,000 could be replaced and the overall deficiency in the East still stood at 625,000 men at the beginning of April.

If Army Group Center had broken contact at the beginning of December and, as von Brauchitsch had suggested, fallen back a hundred miles to the west to the Winter Line he had sketched out for it, most of the sickness casualties might have been avoided.

Be this as it may, the retreat could not be reckoned as more than a serious setback. It certainly was not a heavy defeat and must be measured against a Soviet loss between 22 June 1941 and 20 March 1942 of 3,461,000 men in prisoners alone.

At this time German material losses were possibly easier to bear than personnel casualties, but even so, the equipment wastage was not light. A quarter of a million horses, half of those which had entered Russia, had been lost, together with 2,300 armored vehicles, of which 1,600 were Mark III or IV tanks or assault guns. Although many of the artillery losses were replaced, the artillery and anti-tank arms were still deficient in April of 2,000 guns and howitzers and 7,000 anti-tank guns.

The Soviet Union's success in halting the German invasion was due in the first place to the accident of geography, to the vastness of the Soviet Union, to its undeveloped road and wide-gauge railway system, to the vagaries of its climate and the bitterness of its winter. The second most important factor was probably Stalin's brutal determination as a war leader and the third the resistance put up by the Red Army during this first year of war.

As head of the Soviet State there was little of real importance which escaped Stalin's attention. The direction of foreign and home affairs, of Soviet industry and economy, all were under his tight control. He alone was the supreme controller and coordinator. As a war leader Stalin dwarfed all his contemporaries.

In addition he was, like Hitler, the Commander-in-Chief of the Armed Forces, a military and field commander, following, and sometimes directing, operations. The control he exercised over the General Staff and subordinate field commanders was personal, close and threatening, for as the *de facto* Supreme Commander he was greatly feared and his wish was law. The words "you will answer for it with your head" and "or we will shorten you by a head" were commonplace adjuncts to his orders. No joke was intended. None dared to disagree, far less argue, though, if the opportunity occurred and the occasion was auspicious, some might discuss or plead their case.

Stalin had neither military education nor any experience of war, but common sense, a ruthless and brutal determination, a good head for detail and a lively, inquiring mind stood him in good stead. He understood, probably better than most of his generals, the necessity for creating and husbanding strategic reserves, both of men and materials. These he organized into a High Command Reserve made up of armies, corps and divisions, together with artillery and air force equipment

parks, keeping them entirely under his own hand. The details of the
state of the reserve, recorded on tally boards by his desk, were not dis-
closed to the front commanders in case they should vie and wrangle
with each other for the allocation of men and material. For Stalin himself doled out formations and equipment for specific operations, mark-
ing up his own lists as he did so. No Armenian or Jewish usurer ever
safeguarded his capital so diligently, or called in the loan so swiftly
when it was failing to bring him advantage.

Front commanders were deliberately starved of men and materials
until the need for allocations should arise, and in this, in great measure,
lay the secret of Stalin's success. For, in spite of his lack of military experience, Stalin was able to divorce himself at will from the detail of the
tactical battle and see the thousand-mile theater, even the Soviet Union's
titanic war effort, as a whole. Neither tactical threat nor tactical defeat
could force him to disgorge his precious reserves and he held on to
them tightly until he could be reasonably sure that the enemy had
committed all his forces.

Never did Stalin allow himself to be forced by circumstances into
the unhappy position of the German Führer, whose strategic intention
was governed by the tactical situation, who had to resort to what
Halder called *Flickwerk,* patchwork cobbling, to try and redeem a situation or restore a broken defense by withdrawing from the line a division
here and a division there, always too little and always too late.

Yet it would be entirely misleading to portray Stalin as a military
genius. It is indeed doubtful whether, in the narrower sense, he was
even militarily gifted. He was able and he learned as he went along, but
his earlier control of the forces in the field had nearly brought disaster.
Stalin's faults were those associated with the untrained and uneducated
commander molded in the communist pattern, with undue emphasis
on a rigid military and political discipline enforced by Draconian
punishments.

In that first year Stalin had been obsessed with the obstinate defense of ground, being convinced that only in this way could the Red
Army defenders bring the German invasion to a halt. This was of
course a fallacy. For although a rigid defense, tied to ground, increased
the German casualty rate, the final cost to the defenders far outweighed

the first temporary advantage. Strategy and tactics based on such a defense could have but one end, the encirclement and liquidation of great numbers of Red Army troops.

Stalin's mentality and character still remain somewhat in the shadows, and the descriptions of him which have come out of the Soviet Union are contradictory and not without bias. When Stalin first came to power he had the history of the Civil War rewritten, giving himself credit, probably undeserved, as a military sage. During and after the Second World War a new flood of historical literature appeared in the Soviet Union eulogizing the dictator's military leadership in the most extravagant and flattering terms.[7] This was generally disbelieved in the Western world, and rightly so. It must of course be remembered, too, that Stalin won because he was on the winning side.

Yet the Soviet High Command did in fact display military leader-ship of a high order, particularly from 1942 onwards, and historians began to speculate as to the master mind, the *éminence grise* on whose advice the dictator relied. The old marshals, Voroshilov, Budenny and Kulik, the cronies of former times, were of little account. Timoshenko was a man of ability for whom Stalin appears to have had some respect, but he was a hardheaded, obstinate field commander whose strength best lay as a trainer of men and in the conduct of the defense. After the first week of war Timoshenko was rarely in Moscow.

Shaposhnikov, the last of the marshals, the former Tsarist staff colonel, was much closer to Stalin, whom he served faithfully from July 1941 to June 1942 in his second tour of office as Chief of General Staff. As has already been recounted, Shaposhnikov was to Stalin what Jodl was to Hitler: adviser, tutor, executive and, as far as the dictator would allow, confidant.

It had been widely assumed, particularly in Germany during the war, that Shaposhnikov, a very able staff officer and a theorist and writer of distinction, was the real architect of Stalin's victory. This view, which can be given no greater credence than that of surmise, has been reproduced in immediate postwar United States literature. Shaposh-nikov certainly played an important role, but his importance should not be exaggerated. For Shaposhnikov was something of an anachro-nism in that strange communist company, made up largely of former noncommissioned officers and commissars.[8] Well mannered, friendly, gentle and fatherly, he was merely Stalin's executive and adviser.

Although Stalin undoubtedly made good use of Shaposhnikov's experience and brain, there could never have been any question of the Chief of General Staff initiating any action or attempting to persuade the dictator to undertake anything against his inclination. For no Red Army general ever did that; nor did any show much moral courage in the presence of the dictator. Shaposhnikov had a reputation for being clever but pliant, something of a reed which bent in the storm. He had much in common with Vasilevsky, the Chief of Operations, who, although only a major-general, was quickly promoted to colonel-general and appointed Chief of General Staff in June 1942, when Shaposhnikov finally had to give up the post through sickness.

The only other Soviet general close to Stalin during the winter of 1941 to 1942 was Zhukov, the former Chief of General Staff, and he, more recently, has been acclaimed in the Western press as the commander to whom the credit was due for the victory in front of Moscow. Recalled from Leningrad, he had taken over from Konev the command of the shattered West Front in the second week in October.

A man of great talent and energy, and, when assured of Stalin's support, a hectoring bully who would drive his subordinates to the limit of their endurance, Zhukov soon restored some order and cohesion to West Front. Yet at this time Stalin presumably rated Zhukov's ability and experience as inferior to that of Timoshenko for, whereas Timoshenko had commanded West Theater, made up of a group of fronts, and had been transferred in early September to South-West Theater in an attempt to restore the situation in the Ukraine, Zhukov was given the command of only the West Front. Kurochkin's North-West, Konev's Kalinin and Eremenko's (later Cherevichenko's) Bryansk Front, all of which were used in the defense of Moscow and the subsequent counter-offensive, were kept independent of Zhukov and directly under Stalin.

Although there is no doubt that Stalin consulted Zhukov frequently and discussed with him the operations on the West Front sector, there appears to be no evidence that Zhukov was asked for his opinion or recommendations on the activities of the other three neighboring fronts. Indeed, when Stalin and Shaposhnikov were hatching the embryo counter-offensive, Zhukov received no intelligence of it but could only infer that something was going on behind the scenes. West Front was merely telephoned from time to time and instructed to provide information, and Zhukov remained in ignorance of the new plans until they were completed. When the final plans were presented by Shaposhnikov at the subsequent conference, Zhukov disagreed with them on the grounds that his own West Front was not receiving a sufficiently large share of the High Command Reserve.[9]

These, and other accounts, may or may not be true, but they come from Zhukov's own pen and they do at least agree in tenor with the descriptions of Stalin by other Soviet generals and by Western observers.

It is difficult to escape the conclusion that Stalin was the sole military commander and that plans for the defense of Moscow and the subsequent counter-offensive were drawn up at his direction. Except that he was the commander of the largest of the four fronts, Zhukov took little or no part in the planning of the counter-offensive which threw Army Group Center back over a hundred miles and at one time threatened to destroy it. Far from being dependent on any of his generals, Stalin, caustic and insulting, treated them little better than serfs.

Soviet historical accounts written immediately after Stalin's death are generally agreed that the counter-offensive plan was Stalin's own, but the dictator has come in for some severe criticism for allocating such a large part of his reserve to the distant Volkhov and South-West Fronts, for these received three of the nine armies available. The Kalinin, North-West and Bryansk Fronts were each given an army and the other three went to the West Front.

Soviet historians argue that if all nine armies had been allocated to West Front von Kluge would probably have been trapped. In view of Hitler's insistence on a rigid defense this might indeed have occurred. But it seems that the excitable, mercurial and highly strung Stalin had taken it into his head that the Austrian, like the Corsican conqueror of 130 years before, had over-extended himself and was already at the mercy of the Russian. Stalin had conjured up a picture of the routing and pursuit of a panic-stricken enemy back to the Berezina and beyond, perhaps even ending the war in one blow. It was for this reason that

Eremenko and Purkaev, to Halder's surprise and wonder, were directed so deep into the German rear on Vitebsk and Velikiye Luki, without obvious aim or gain.

Stalin made the mistake of underestimating German stamina and resilience and he demanded too much of his own troops, many of whom were disorganized and poorly trained levies. These were goaded and harried into battle piecemeal. Yet when one takes into account the lack of mechanization and the condition of the Red Army forces at that time, the counter-offensive in front of Moscow was a remarkable feat of arms. This would have been impossible of achievement under a less ruthless and more humane Supreme Commander.

All Soviet historical accounts of the victory extol at great length the part played by the Communist Party "as the inspirer and organizer of all victories of the Soviet people and their Armed Forces." This is neither propaganda nor overstatement.[10] For at that time Stalin and the Communist Party were indivisible; the Party was Stalin; it was his tool, his sounding board, some of his eyes and ears, and one of the organs by which he ruled and oppressed the Soviet peoples. Together with the NKVD secret police, the Communist Party, through its commissar representatives with the Red Army, was the guardian of the morale, efficiency and political reliability of generals, officers and troops.

Incomprehensible though it might be to freedom-loving peoples, the most remarkable aspect of this commissar organization, repressive though it was, was its effectiveness. The more desperate the deteriorating situation, the more harsh and bloody were Stalin's counter-measures in the face of inefficiency, failure or misfortune. Such was the Russian and the communist mentality that these repressions achieved their object.

GLOSSARY OF TERMS

Alarmeinheite — units hurriedly raised or nominated for immediate emergency action

armoured assault gun — a German tracked and armoured fighting vehicle, like a turretless tank, mounting a close-support gun in the hull

balki — ravines made by Russian rivers

colonel-general — in Germany the rank above that of full general; in the Soviet Union the rank below that of full general

dachi — Russian country cottages usually for summer use

ernst and *gespannt* — serious; tense, tight (pg. 244)

Feldherr — a tried and proven senior general officer experienced and successful in field operations

Feldzug — a campaign

Flederwisch — feather duster

Flickwerk — cobbling, patchwork or botched work

Flittergelehrsamkeit — tawdry, shallow, tinsel-like learning

Freiherr — a German baron

Führer — literally "leader"—the title Hitler bestowed on himself

Führerbefehl — a Führer order

Generalität — the body of German generals on the active list

GKO — the Soviet state committee for defense

Gruppenkommando — originally German corps headquarters in peacetime, many were eventually upgraded to army or even army group status

Gutsherr — the lord of the manor

Heerespersonalamt — the German Army directorate responsible for officers' postings and administration

Kampfgruppen — battle groups

Kluge Hans, der — "clever Hans," a play on von Kluge's name

Kommiss-stiefel — the regulation issue half-length leather army boot

Landesschützen — reserve and generally elderly or low-category troops

Landser — the colloquial term for a German private soldier, the equivalent of G.I. or "Tommy"

Luftwaffe — the German air force

Machtkampf — fight for power

Nebelwerfer — a large mortar capable of throwing smoke canisters or high-explosive bombs

Oberquartiermeister — the head of a group of German Army general staff directorates

oblast — a Soviet district

Ostkämpfer — the east fighter (a German soldier on the Eastern Front)

panje cart — a Polish or Russian farm cart

Politburo — the bureau or senior committee (dominated by Stalin) that controlled the communist party and, by extension, the Soviet Union

prikaz I. V. Stalina — J. V. Stalin's order (pg. 141)

Prügelei — a free-for-all fight

rasputitsa — the fall and spring "breaking up of the roads" in Russia through rains, frost and snow

Reichsarbeitsdienst — the Reich labour service

Reichsbahn — the German state railway

Reichsheer — the Weimar German Army

Reichswehr — the armed forces of the Weimar Republic

Ritter — title of German nobility (knight)

Rollbahn — a main motor road

Rüstungsamt — German armament and equipment office

Schlammperiode — periods of mud after thaws or heavy rains in Russia

Schwerpunkt — in offense, the sector or direction in which the main thrust is to be made, or the centre of gravity in defense

SS Leibstandarte — "Adolf Hitler's Bodyguard"; one of the original *Waffen SS* divisions that fought in Russia

Stavka — in tsarist times a GHQ in the field; under Stalin it meant little more than a number of names (mainly generals) accredited to Stalin or the GKO as advisers

Stuka — German single-engined dive bomber (Ju 87)

Wehrmacht — the German armed services

Wehrmachtführungstab — Hitler's OKW staff (under Jodl), responsible for strategic and operational war plans

Wi Rü Amt — a military office dealing with both armaments and war economy

Wurfgerät — German mortars or rockets, usually multiple-barrelled

zu preussisch oder zu kaiserlich — too Prussian or too imperial (i.e., conservative) (pg. 4)

NOTES AND SOURCES

Chapter One

1. Keitel, *Memoirs*, pp. 119–23.
2. Halder, *Kriegstagebuch*, Vol. 2, p. 49 and note 14.
3. Compare, for example, Souvarine, *Stalin*, p. 512; Trotsky, *Stalin*, pp. 17, 18 and 417.
4. Stalin's speech to the 18th Party Congress, 10 March 1939.
5. *Polish–German* and *Polish–Soviet Relations 1933–39*, p. 183, No. 163; also Beloff, *The Foreign Policy of Soviet Russia*, Vol. 2, p. 273.
6. *Ibid.*, pp. 366–67.
7. Hitler, *Mein Kampf*, Chapter 14; and Hillgruber, *Hitlers Strategie*, p. 29.
8. *50 Let Vooruzhennykh Sil SSSR*, p. 235; Sherwood, *The White House Papers*, Vol. 1, pp. 328–43 (Stalin's briefing to Hopkins).
9. *Speer Papers FD 2690/45 Vol. 10 (Flensburg Collection), Statistische Schnellberichte zu Kriegsproduktion.*
10. Marcks, *Operationsentwurf Ost*, 5 August 1940.
11. Von Bock, *Tagebuch*, 3 December 1940 and 3 February 1941.
12. Warlimont, *Inside Hitler's Headquarters*, p. 136; Greiner, *Die Oberste Wehrmachtführung*, p. 295; *Die Lossberg Studie WF St Op H 905* of 15 September 1940.
13. *OKH Gen St d H Op Abt III Schematische Kriegsgliederung*, of 18 June 1941.
14. Von Bock, *Tagebuch*, 27 March 1941.
15. *Die Kriegswehrmacht der UdSSR, OKH Gen St d H O Qu IV Abt Fremde Heere Ost (11) Nr. 100/41g*, of 15 January 1941, p. 66.
16. Halder, *Kriegstagebuch*, Vol. 2, pp. 257–60.
17. Rendulic, *Gekämpft Gesiegt Geschlagen*, p. 22.

Chapter Two

1. *OKH Gen St d H Op Abt III Schematische Kriegsgliederung*, of 18 June 1941.
2. *Kriegstagebuch des Oberkommandos der Heeresgruppe Mitte*, 12 March 1941, shows that von Bock's intention was to bypass Minsk and close in the area Borisov–Orsha; see also von Bock, *Tagebuch*, 27 March 1941; Guderian, *Panzer Leader*, pp. 158–66; Halder, *Kriegstagebuch*, 23 June 1941.

3. See also von Manstein, *Lost Victories*, p. 185.

4. Von Bock, *Tagebuch*, 25 June 1941.

5. Halder, *Kriegstagebuch*, Vol. 3, p. 56; von Bock, *Tagebuch*, 8 July 1941. *Istoriya Otechestvennoi Voiny Sovetskovo Soyuza*, Vol. 2, p. 37, admits the loss of eleven divisions and "parts of others."

6. Halder, *Kriegstagebuch*, Vol. 3, p. 38.

7. Von Bock, *Tagebuch*, 26 June 1941.

8. Hoth, *Panzeroperationen*, p. 78; Guderian, *Panzer Leader*, p. 166.

9. Rendulic, *Gekämpft Gesiegt Geschlagen*, pp. 25–26.

10. Hoth, *Panzeroperationen*, p. 92.

11. Von Bock, *Tagebuch*, 25 and 26 July 1941.

12. *Kriegstagebuch des Oberkommandos der Wehrmacht*, Vol. 1, pp. 451–54; Halder, *Kriegstagebuch*, Vol. 3, pp. 98, 128 and 150. Contemporary records support that this number of prisoners was taken although Soviet accounts deny it.

13. Halder, *Kriegstagebuch*, Vol. 3, p. 163. Soviet sources merely admit loss of part of 6 and 12 Armies without giving further details; e.g., Platonov, *Vtoraya Mirovaya Voina*, p. 217.

14. Von Bock, *Tagebuch*, 4 August 1941.

15. Directives 33 and 34, see Hubatsch, *Hitlers Weisungen für die Kriegführung*, pp. 140–47.

16. Conversation with Heusinger, 18 August 1941.

17. Von Bock, *Tagebuch*, 24 August 1941; Halder, *Kriegstagebuch*, Vol. 3, pp. 194–95.

18. See also Zhukov, *Vospominaniya i Razmyshleniya*, pp. 243–44.

19. *50 Let Vooruzhennykh Sil SSSR*, p. 235.

20. Stalin to Hopkins, Sherwood, *The White House Papers*, Vol. 1, pp. 328–43.

21. Zhukov, *Vospominaniya i Razmyshleniya*, p. 250.

22. *Istoriya Velikoi Otechestvennoi Voiny Sovetskovo Soyuza*, Vol. 2, p. 21; Zhukov, *Vospominaniya i Razmyshleniya*, pp. 301–3; Shtemenko, *Generalnyi Shtab v Gody Voiny*, p. 29.

23. Compare, for example, Khrushchev's Secret Speech of 25 February 1956 and Zhukov, *Vospominaniya i Razmyshleniya*, p. 304.

24. See also Shtemenko, *Generalnyi Shtab v Gody Voiny*, pp. 112–45.

25. Voroshilov's speech to the 18th Party Congress of the CPSU (B), March 1939.

26. Sokolovsky, *Military Strategy*, p. 162; *50 Let Vooruzhennykh Sil SSSR*, p. 238; *Istoriya Velikoi Otechestvennoi Voiny Sovetskovo Soyuza*, Vol. 2, p. 62, and Vol. 3, p. 217.

27. Halder, *Kriegstagebuch*, Vol. 3, pp. 95 and 145.

28. Gorbatov, *Gody i Voiny*, *Novyi Mir*, May 1964.

29. Compare Halder, *Kriegstagebuch,* Vol. 3, p. 202.

30. For example, Baumann, *Die 35. Infanterie-Division im Zweiten Weltkrieg,* pp. 100–102.

Chapter Three

1. Guderian, *Panzer Leader,* p. 209.

2. Platonov, *Vtoraya Mirovaya Voina,* p. 218, contradicts *Kratkaya Istoriya Velikaya Otechestvennaya Voina Sovetskovo Soyuza,* p. 77, and *Istoriya Velikoi Otechestvennoi Voiny Sovetskovo Soyuza,* Vol. 2, p. 104.

3. *Ibid.,* pp. 106–10, and Zhukov, *Vospominaniya i Razmyshleniya,* pp. 317 and 321–23.

4. *Kriegstagebuch des Oberkommandos der Wehrmacht,* Vol. 1, p. 661, 26 September 1941.

5. Elisabeth Wagner, *Der Generalquartiermeister,* p. 206.

6. Warlimont, *Inside Hitler's Headquarters,* p. 186.

7. Von Leeb, *Tagebuch,* 21 July 1941.

8. These objectives were maintained even as late as 19 November. Halder, *Kriegstagebuch,* Vol. 3, p. 295.

9. *OKH Gen St d H Op Abt III Schematische Kriegsgliederung,* of 2 October 1941.

10. By mid-October the German High Command was still not aware that Timoshenko had left the West Front a month before.

11. *Wehrmachtführungstab Befehl Nr. 41 1675/41,* of 7 October 1941.

12. Von Bock, *Tagebuch,* 7 October 1941.

13. By 31 December 1941 the contemporary records of Army Group Center showed a tally of 1,912,376 Soviet prisoners of war. *Heeresgruppe Mitte H 3/158 Gefangene und Beutemeldung,* of 4 January 1942. As of 20 March 1942 the overall total of Soviet prisoners stood at 3,461,338. *Kriegstagebuch des Oberkommandos der Wehrmacht,* Vol. 1, p. 489.

14. Rendulic, *Gekämpft Gesiegt Geschlagen,* p. 50.

15. Sokolovsky, *Razgrom Nemetsko–Fashistskikh Voisk pod Moskvoi,* p. 30; Zhukov, *Vospominaniya i Razmyshleniya,* p. 346; *Istoriya Velikoi Otechestvennoi Voiny Sovetskovo Soyuza,* Vol. 2, p. 234. The total personnel strength of 800,000 given in these accounts does not tally with the later German figures for prisoners taken at Vyazma. *Voenno Istoricheskii Zhurnal,* 1963, No. 3, pp. 70 and 72, however, gives a total figure of 1,200,000, this including all the administrative troops of the Rear Services.

Chapter 4

1. Halder, *Kriegstagebuch*, Vol. 3, p. 220.

2. *Ibid.*, pp. 202–3; Guderian, *Panzer Leader*, p. 190; Mueller-Hillebrand, *Das Heer*, Vol. 3, Chapter 10.

3. Guderian, *Panzer Leader*, pp. 219, 227 and 230.

4. Gareis, *Kampf und Ende der Fränkisch–Sudetendeutschen 98. Division*, pp. 125–30.

5. Halder, *Kriegstagebuch*, Vol. 3, p. 260.

6. Shtemenko in *Generalnyi Shtab v Gody Voiny* has described how the General Staff sometimes used the civilian telephone network to gather information from village soviets. On occasions the network had not been broken by the German advance.

7. Halder, *Kriegstagebuch*, Vol. 3, p. 276.

8. Konev in *Nachalo Moskovskoi Bitvy, Voenno Istoricheskii Zhurnal*, 1966, No. 10, has subsequently maintained that he did have some prior air intelligence of the imminence of the offensive. Konev's article conflicts, however, with the German evidence and Telegin's long account (note 23).

9. *OKH Gen St d H Op Abt III Schematische Kriegsgliederung*, of 2 Octoer 1941.

10. Guderian, *Panzer Leader*, p. 227.

11. *Kriegstagebuch des Oberkommandos der Heeresgrugge Mitte, Nr. 1 Band*, 1 October 1941, p. 525.

12. *Ibid.*, 6 October, p. 559. The attempt the previous day failed.

13. *Ibid.*, 6 October, p. 562, and 10 October, p. 587; Guderian, *Panzer Leader*, p. 237.

14. Lelyushenko, *Zarya Pobedy*, p. 43.

15. Livshits, *Pervaya Gvardeiskaya Tankovaya Brigada v Boyakh za Moskvu*, pp. 34–68.

16. Guards designations were given to those formations which had distinguished themselves in battle. With the exception of tank armies a separate roll was maintained of guards formations so that, for example, when 64 Army was given a guards designation it was admitted to the rolls as 7 Guards Army.

17. Sokolovsky, *Razgrom Nemetsko–Fashistskikh Voisk pod Moskvoi*, pp. 67 footnote and 77.

18. Von Senger und Etterlin, *Die 1. Kavallerie-Division*, pp. 61–63.

19. Hoth, *Panzeroperationen*, p. 131.

20. *Kriegstagebuch des Oberkommandos der Heeresgruppe Mitte Nr. 1 Band*, 4 October 1941, p. 545.

21. "*2, 4 und 9 Armee melden übereinstimmend, dass der Angriff den Feind überraschend getroffen hat. Er leistet überall, wo er angegriffen wurde, zunächst nur*

geringen infanteristischen und artilleristischen Widerstand. . . ." *Ibid.,* 2 October 1941, p. 531.

22. *Istoriya Velikoi Otechestvennoi Voiny Sovetskovo Soyuza,* Vol. 2, pp. 235–36.

23. Telegin, *Moskva Frontovoi Gorod, Voprosy Istorii KPSS,* No. 9.

24. Zhukov, *Vospominaniya i Razmyshleniya,* pp. 344–52.

25. Gorbatov, *Gody i Voiny, Novyi Mir,* 1964; and Shtemenko, *Generalnyi Shtab v Gody Voiny,* p. 18.

26. *Kriegstagebuch des Oberkommandos der Wehrmacht,* Vol. 1, p. 702; von Bock, *Tagebuch,* 19 October 1941; *Kriegstagebuch des Oberkommandos der Heeresgruppe Mitte Nr. 1 Band,* 19 October 1941, pp. 642–48.

27. *Ibid.,* 15 and 16 October, pp. 614 and 622. These entries complain of the enormous delays due to the catastrophic condition of ground and roads and say that the difficulties of movement were a far stronger enemy than the Russian. Panzer and motorized divisions could not move. *"Die mot. Verbände sind so gut wie unbeweglich."*

28. *Ibid.,* 28 October, p. 703; Guderian, *Panzer Leader,* p. 244.

29. *Ibid.,* pp. 242–45.

30. Rendulic, *Gekämpft Gesiegt Geschlagen,* pp. 74–76.

31. Nitz, *Die 292. Infanterie-Division,* pp. 70–71.

32. Baumann, *Die 35. Infanterie-Division im Zweiten Weltkrieg,* pp. 114–17.

Chapter Five

1. *Istoriya Velikoi Otechestvennoi Voiny Sovetskovo Soyuza,* Vol. 2, p. 241.

2. Fedyuninsky, *Podnyatie po Trevoge,* p. 68.

3. Stalin's speech of 6 November 1941.

4. Werth, *Russia at War,* pp. 236–38; *Kratkaya Istoriya Velikaya Otechestvennaya Voina Sovetskovo Soyuza,* p. 115; Samsonov, *Die Grosse Schlacht vor Moskau,* p. 70.

5. Telegin, *Moskva Frontovoi Gorod, Voprosy Istorii KPSS,* 1966, No. 9, pp. 104–7.

6. Army Group Center noted the same problem in 161 Infantry Division, "forest fighting, the lack of experienced junior leaders and the unreliability of Russian maps giving rise to mounting casualties." *Kriegstagebuch des Oberkommandos der Heeresgruppe Mitte, Nr. 1 Band,* 31 October 1941, p. 720.

7. Gareis, *Kampf und Ende der Fränkisch–Sudetendeutschen 98. Division,* pp. 142–60.

8. *Gen St d H Org Abt (1) Nr 731/41g Kdos,* of 6 November 1941 (*Kriegstagebuch des Oberkommandos der Wehrmacht,* Vol. 2, pp. 1,074–75).

9. *Istoriya Velikoi Otechestvennoi Voiny Sovetskovo Soyuza,* Vol. 2, p. 257.

10. *Ibid.,* p. 274.

Chapter Six

1. Halder, *Kriegstagebuch,* Vol. 3, p. 279 *et seq.*
2. *Ibid.,* p. 280; *Kriegstagebuch des Oberkommandos der Heeresgruppe Süd,* 3 November 1941.
3. In fact, three Soviet armies (44, 47 and 53) were moving out of Iran into the Caucasus.
4. Halder, *Kriegstagebuch,* Vol. 3, p. 287.
5. Charles de Beaulieu, *Generaloberst Erich Hoepner.*
6. Halder, *Kriegstagebuch,* Vol. 3, p. 288; Guderian, *Panzer Leader,* p. 247; Blumentritt's account in Liddell Hart, *The Other Side of the Hill,* p. 285; Elisabeth Wagner, *Der Generalquartiermeister* (Eckstein), pp. 288–89.
7. *Die Kriegswehrmacht der UdSSR, OKH Gen St d H O Qu IV Abt Fremde Heere Ost (4) Nr. 100/41g,* of 1 January 1942, pp. 3–5 and 9; *OKH Qu IV Abt Fremde Heere Ost* Appreciation of 4 November 1941.
8. Birkenfeld, *Geschichte der deutschen Wehr- und Rüstungwirtschaft (1918–45),* p. 268.
9. Halder, *Kriegstagebuch,* Vol. 3, p. 309.
10. *Ibid.,* pp. 296–99.
11. Guderian, *Panzer Leader,* p. 248.
12. Schmidt, *Geschichte der 10. Division,* pp. 110–16.
13. Gareis, *Kampf und Ende der Fränkisch–Sudetendeutschen 98. Division,* pp. 162–64.
14. Grossman, *Geschichte der Rheinisch–Westfälischen 6. Infanterie-Division,* pp. 84–87.

Chapter Seven

1. Zhirin, *Parad sorok pervovo, Ogonek 1966,* No. 45.
2. Zhukov, *Vospominaniya i Razmyshleniya,* pp. 363–64.
3. Golikov, *V Moskovskoi Bitve,* pp. 11–28.
4. Lelyushenko, *Zarya Pobedy,* pp. 82 and 88–89.
5. Charles de Beaulieu, *Generaloberst Erich Hoepner,* pp. 209–14; Wagener, *Moskau 1941,* pp. 130–33.
6. Baumann, *Die 35. Infanterie-Division im Zweiten Weltkrieg,* pp. 117–20.
7. *Ibid.,* pp. 120–21.
8. Zhukov, *Vospominaniya i Razmyshleniya,* pp. 369–70.
9. Wagener, *Moskau 1941,* pp. 121–23; Guderian, *Panzer Leader,* p. 254.
10. *Ibid.,* pp. 252–55.
11. Halder, *Kriegstagebuch,* Vol. 3, p. 322.
12. Gschöpf, *Mein Weg mit der 45. Infanterie-Division,* pp. 196–202.
13. Von Bock, *Tagebuch,* 18 November 1941.

14. Gareis, *Kampf und Ende der Fränkisch-Sudetendeutschen 98. Division,* pp. 164–66.

15. Merker, *Das Buch der 78. Sturm Division,* pp. 117–22.

16. Nitz, *Die 292. Infanterie-Division,* pp. 75–77.

17. Dieckhoff, *Die 3. Infanterie-Division,* p. 137 *et seq.*

18. *OKH Lage Ost* map, of 6 December 1941.

19. *Kriegstagebuch des Oberkommandos der Heeresgruppe Mitte,* 3 December 1941, pp. 886–89.

Chapter Eight

1. *Kriegstagebuch des Oberkommandos der Heeresgruppe Süd,* 3 November 1941.

2. Pottgiesser, *Die Reichsbahn im Ostfeldzug,* pp. 33–40; Keitel, *Memoirs,* pp. 176–77.

3. Halder, *Kriegstagebuch,* Vol. 3, pp. 319–23; *Kriegstagebuch des Oberkommandos der Heeresgruppe Süd,* 30 November 1941.

4. Keitel, *Memoirs,* pp. 161–62.

5. *Istoriya Velikoi Otechestvennoi Voiny Sovetskovo Soyuza,* Vol. 2, p. 213.

6. Halder, *Kriegstagebuch,* Vol. 3, pp. 311 and 313.

7. *Ibid.,* p. 323.

8. *Ibid.,* p. 323.

9. *Ibid.,* p. 327.

10. Von Bock, *Tagebuch,* 30 November 1941.

11. *Ibid.,* 1 December 1941.

12. *Ibid.,* 3 December 1941; also *Kriegstagebuch des Oberkommandos der Wehrmacht,* Vol. 1, p. 790.

13. Halder, *Kriegstagebuch,* Vol. 3, pp. 329–31.

14. *Ibid.,* p. 332.

15. Hubatsch, *Hitlers Weisungen für die Kriegführung,* p. 171.

16. Von Bock, *Tagebuch,* 13 December 1941; Guderian, *Panzer Leader,* p. 262; Halder, *Kriegstagebuch,* Vol. 3, p. 348.

17. Von Bock, *Tagebuch,* 14–16 December 1941; also *Kriegstagebuch des Oberkommandos der Heeresgruppe Mitte,,* 16 December 1941, p. 999.

18. Keitel, *Memoirs,* p. 163.

19. *Goebbels' Diary,* 20 March 1942, p. 92.

20. Keitel, *Memoirs,* p. 164.

21. *Ibid.,* p. 164.

22. See also Mueller-Hillebrand, *Das Heer,* Vol. 3, Chapter 10.

23. Halder, *Hitler as War Lord,* p. 51.

24. Halder, *Kriegstagebuch,* Vol. 3, pp. 354–55.

Chapter Nine

1. Vasilevsky, *Bitva za Moskvu*, p. 24, and Zhukov, p. 77; Zhukov, *Vospominaniya i Razmyshleniya*, pp. 373–74.

2. *Bitva za Moskvu*, Zhukov, p. 81.

3. Zhukov, *Vospominaniya i Razmyshleniya*, pp. 375–76. There is some contradiction in Soviet accounts as to the dates, whether this happened on 30 November or 2 December. The difference is of only minor consequence.

4. *Ibid.*, p. 377.

5. *Istoriya Velikoi Otechestvennoi Voiny Sovetskovo Soyuza*, Vol. 2, p. 280 *et seq.*

6. *Bitva za Moskvu*, Timoshenko, p. 97.

7. *Ibid.*, p. 103; Sokolovsky, *Razgrom Nemetsko–Fashistskikh Voisk pod Moskvoi*, pp. 169, 170–72.

8. See also Shtemenko, *Generalinyi Shtab v Gody Voiny*, p. 40.

9. Halder, *Kriegstagebuch*, Vol. 3, p. 341.

10. *OKH Qu IV Abt Fremde Heere Ost* Appreciation of 4 November 1941.

11. *OKH Lage Ost* map, of 6 December 1941.

12. *Kriegstagebuch des Oberkommandos der Heeresgruppe Mitte*, p. 1,008.

13. *Inter alia, Op Abt (1M) Nr. 1725/41g. Kdos Chefs*, of 16 December, and *OKH Gen St d H Op Abt (111) Nr. 1736/41g. Kdos Chefs*, of 18 December 1941.

14. Von Bock, *Tagebuch*, 14 November 1941.

15. *Ibid.*, 7 December 1941.

Chapter Ten

1. Charles de Beaulieu, *Generaloberst Erich Hoepner*, pp. 212–13.

2. *Kriegstagebuch des Armee Oberkommandos 4. Pz AOK 4 (Pz Gp 4] III Teil*, 6 and 8 December, 1941.

3. *Ibid.*, 12 December.

4. Merker, *Das Buch der 78. Sturm Division*, pp. 122–42.

5. Charles de Beaulieu, *Generaloberst Erich Hoepner*, pp. 227–28.

6. *Geschichte der 56. Infanterie-Division 1938–1945*, p. 40 *et seq.*

7. Gschöpf, *Mein Weg mit der 45. Infanterie-Division*, p. 211.

8. Guderian, *Panzer Leader*, p. 262.

9. *Ibid.*, pp. 263–68.

10. *Ibid.*, p. 270; *Kriegstagebuch des Oberkommandos der Heeresgruppe Mitte*, p. 1,075.

11. Gareis, *Kampf und Ende der Fränkisch–Sudetendeutschen 98. Division*, pp. 169–92.

12. *Kriegstagebuch des Armee Oberkommandos 4 (AOK 4 KTB Nr. 11)*, 3 January 1942.

13. *Ibid.*, 5–6 January.

14. *Ibid.*, 7–8 January.
15. Nitz, *Die 292. Infanterie-Division*, p. 78.
16. Grossmann, *Geschichte der Rheinisch–Westfälischen 6. Infanterie-Division*, pp. 92–108.
17. From correspondence of Rudolf Schmidt, 27 January 1942.

Chapter Eleven

1. *Bitva za Moskvu*, pp. 77–89; Zhukov, *Vospominaniya i Razmyshleniya*, pp. 377–79.
2. *Ibid.*, pp. 380–81.
3. *Istoriya Velikoi Otechestvennoi Voiny Sovetskovo Soyuza*, Vol. 2, pp. 292–97.
4. Zhukov, *Vospominaniya i Razmyshleniya*, p. 383.
5. *Istoriya Velikoi Otechestvennoi Voiny Sovetskovo Soyuza*, Vol. 2, p. 321 *et seq.*
6. *Kriegstagebuch des Oberkommandos des Heeresgruppe Nord, 75128/50*, 17 January 1942, p. 1,810; Halder, *Kriegstagebuch*, Vol. 3, pp. 381–82.
7. *Ibid.*, p. 386.
8. *Istoriya Velikoi Otechestvennoi Voiny Sovetskovo Soyuza*, Vol. 2, p. 226–27.
9. Halder, *Kriegstagebuch*, Vol. 3, pp. 369 and 401; von Manstein, *Lost Victories*, pp. 225–27.
10. *Istoriya Velikoi Otechestvennoi Voiny Sovetskovo Soyuza*, Vol. 2, pp. 369–60.

Chapter Twelve

1. *OKW/WFStb/Qu (Verw) Nr. 8/42*, dated 4 January 1942.
2. Halder, *Kriegstagebuch*, Vol. 3, p. 371.
3. *Ibid.*, pp. 371–72.
4. *Ibid.*, pp. 373–74.
5. *Ibid.*, p. 373.
6. Charles de Beaulieu, *Generaloberst Erich Hoepner*, pp. 242–47.
7. Halder, *Kriegstagebuch*, Vol. 3, pp. 376–77; Guderian, *Panzer Leader*, p. 273; Keitel, *Memoirs*, pp. 165–67; Charles de Beaulieu, *Generaloberst Erich Hoepner*, p. 248.
8. *Ibid.*, pp. 249–53.
9. Jenner, *Die 216/272. Niedersächsische Infanterie-Division*, pp. 47–53.
10. Halder, *Kriegstagebuch*, Vol. 3, p. 392.
11. *Ibid.*, p. 378.
12. *Ibid.*, pp. 379–81.
13. *Ibid.*, p. 385.
14. *Ibid.*, p. 387.
15. *Istoriya Velikoi Otechestvennoi Voiny Sovetskovo Soyuza*, Vol. 2, pp. 324–28.
16. Baumann, *Die 35. Infanterie-Division im Zweiten Weltkrieg*, pp. 141–45.

17. Merker, *Das Buch der 78. Sturm Division*, pp. 145–54.
18. Gareis, *Kampf und Ende der Fränkisch–Sudetendeutschen 98. Division*, pp. 196–201.
19. Schmidt, *Geschichte der 10. Division*, p. 123 *et seq.*
20. Gareis, *Kampf und Ende der Fränkisch–Sudetendeutschen 98. Division*, pp. 202–12.
21. Schmidt, *Geschichte der 10. Division*, p. 132 *et seq.*
22. Zhukov, *Vospominaniya i Razmyshleniya*, pp. 383–85; *Istoriya Velikoi Otechestvennoi Voiny Sovetskovo Soyuza*, Vol. 2, p. 328 *et seq.*
23. In all, six German infantry divisions had been transferred from Western Europe during November and December and a further seventeen divisions arrived in the East between January and March in exchange for burnt-out formations leaving Russia.
24. *Kampfgruppe Scherer, Die Wehrmacht 1942*, pp. 38–50.

Chapter Thirteen

1. Halder, *Kriegstagebuch*, Vol. 3, p. 394.
2. *Ibid.*, p. 412.
3. Model committed suicide when his army group was surrounded by United States forces in the Ruhr in April 1945.
4. *OKH Gen St d H Op Abt III Schematische Kriegsgliederung*, of 7 January 1942.
5. *Istoriya Velikoi Otechestvennoi Voiny Sovetskovo Soyuza*, Vol. 2, pp. 328–29.
6. *Panzer Armeeoberkommando 3 Gefechtsbericht-Abschrift H 12-33/2 – Die Winterschlacht bei Rzhev 21 Januar–20 Februar.*
7. Gareis, *Kampf und Ende der Fränkisch–Sudetendeutschen 98. Division*, pp. 213–17.
8. Zhukov, *Vospominaniya i Razmyshleniya*, pp. 387–88.
9. *Ibid.*, p. 388; *Istoriya Velikoi Otechestvennoi Voiny Sovetskovo Soyuza*, Vol. 2, p. 331.
10. Gareis, *Kampf und Ende der Fränkisch–Sudetendeutschen 98. Division*, p. 217.
11. Dieckhoff, *Die 3. Infanterie-Division*, p. 157.
12. Gareis, *Kampf und Ende der Fränkisch–Sudetendeutschen 98. Division*, pp. 218–21.
13. Zhukov, *Vospominaniya i Razmyshleniya*, p. 385.
14. *Istoriya Velikoi Otechestvennoi Voiny Sovetskovo Soyuza*, Vol. 2, p. 331.
15. Zhukov, *Vospominaniya i Razmyshleniya*, p. 386.
16. Gareis, *Kampf und Ende der Fränkisch–Sudetendeutschen 98. Division*, pp. 222–26.

Chapter Fourteen

1. Hitler's statement to von Leeb; von Leeb, *Tagebuch,* 21 July 1941; *Kriegstagebuch des Oberkommandos der Wehrmacht,* Vol. 1, pp. 1,029–31.

2. Provided of course that the Führer would have permitted von Bock to have kept his armies concentrated; this would have been quite foreign to Hitler's mentality.

3. Of this Halder said, *"Wir laufen in die Breite, haben schliesslich keinen Schwerpunkt mehr."* *Kriegstagebuch,* Vol. 3, pp. 107 and 103, footnote 21.

4. Stalin is said to have told the British Ambassador, Sir Stafford Cripps, that if the worst came, he was prepared to withdraw eastwards and fight from the territory beyond the Volga. Compare also Deutscher, *Stalin,* p. 465.

5. Halder, *Kriegstagebuch,* Vol. 3, p. 318.

6. *Ibid.,* Vol. 3, pp. 430–32; see also *Kriegstagebuch des Oberkommandos der Wehrmacht,* Vol. 1, p. 489, which gives figures that are virtually the same as those noted by Halder. Mueller-Hillebrand, on the other hand, has a somewhat higher total for battle casualties, quoting as authority *Sämtliche Angaben nach Abt WVW des OKW.* He gives the total Wehrmacht and SS battle casualties from December to February as 127,000 dead and 24,000 missing, that is to say, 151,000 compared with Halder's 108,000. There is no known reason why Halder's figure should have been wrong, but assuming that Mueller-Hillebrand's figure is in fact accurate, even this higher total is not disproportionate to the summer and autumn casualty rate. See also Mueller-Hillebrand, *Das Heer,* Vol. 3, Table 65.

7. For example: Voroshilov, *Stalin i Krasnaya Armiya* (1938); Voroshilov, Mekhlis, Budenny and Stern, *The Red Army Today* (1939); Yaroslavsky, *Landmarks in the Life of Stalin* (1942); Voroshilov, *Stalin and the Armed Forces of the USSR* (1951).

8. Others, among whom was Vasilevsky, had been junior officers usually with wartime emergency or reserve commissions in the Tsarist Army.

9. Zhukov, *Vospominaniya i Razmyshleniya,* p. 381.

10. *Istoriya Velikoi Otechestvennoi Voiny Sovetskovo Soyuza,* Vol. 2, pp. 359–62.

SELECT BIBLIOGRAPHY

This list is not intended as a bibliography but merely to indicate the principal works to which reference has been made in the writing of this history.

I. Official and Semi-official Publications

Istoriya Velikoi Otechestvennoi Voiny Sovetskovo Soyuza (six volumes). Moscow.
Kratkaya Istoriya Velikaya Otechestvennaya Voina Sovetskovo Soyuza. Moscow 1965.
Nazi Conspiracy and Aggression (eight volumes). US Government Printing Office, 1946–1948.
Nazi–Soviet Relations 1939–1941. Department of State Publication 3023.
50 Let Vooruzhennykh Sil SSSR. Moscow 1968.
Die Wehrmacht 1941. Verlag "Die Wehrmacht," Berlin 1941.
Die Wehrmacht 1942. Verlag "Die Wehrmacht," Berlin 1942.

II. Edited or Collected Works

Anatomy of the SS State. Collins, London 1968.
Bitva za Moskvu. Moscow 1968.
Geschichte der 56. Infanterie-Division 1938–1945. Arbeitskreis der Division.
Kriegstagebuch des Oberkommandos der Wehrmacht (four volumes). Bernard and Graefe Verlag für Wehrwesen, Frankfurt am Main.

III. Books

Baumann, H. *Die 35. Infanterie-Division im Zweiten Weltkrieg.* G. Braun, Karlsruhe 1964.
Beloborodov, A. P. *Ratnyi Podvig.* Moscow 1965.
Beloff, M. *The Foreign Policy of Soviet Russia 1929–1941.* Oxford University Press, London 1949.
Belov, P. A. *Za nami Moskva.* Moscow 1963.
Benary, A. *Die Berliner Bären Division 257. Infanterie-Division.* Podzun, Bad Nauheim 1955.
Bezymensky, L. *Sonderakte Barbarossa.* Deutsche Verlags–Anstalt, Stuttgart 1968 (orig. Moscow).

Birkenfeld, W. *Geschichte der deutschen Wehr- und Rüstungwirtschaft (1918–1945)*. Harald Boldt, Boppard am Rhein 1966.

Biryuzov, S. S. *Surovye Gody*. Moscow 1966.

Blumentritt, G. *Von Rundstedt*. Odhams, London 1952.

Boldin, I. V. *Stranitsy Zhizni*. Moscow 1961.

Buxa, W. *11. Division*. Podzun, Kiel.

The Ciano Diaries 1939–1943. Doubleday, New York 1946.

de Beaulieu, Charles W. *Generaloberst Erich Hoepner*. Kurt Vowinckel, Neckargemünd 1969.

Deutscher, I. *Stalin*. Oxford University Press, London 1967.

Dieckhoff, G. *Die 3. Infanterie-Division*. Erich Börries, Göttingen 1960.

Eremenko, A. I. *V Nachale Voiny*. Moscoe 1964.

Fedyuninsky, I. I. *Podnyatie po Trevoge*. Moscow 1964.

Gareis, M. *Kampf und Ende der Fränkisch–Sudetendeutschen 98. Division*. Gareis, Tegernsee 1956.

Gilbert, F. *Hitler Directs His War*. Oxford University Press, New York 1950.

Goebbels, J. *Goebbels' Diaries 1942–43*. Doubleday, New York 1948.

Golikov, F. I. *V Moskovskoi Bitve*. Moscow 1967.

Gorbatov, A. V. *Gody i Voiny Novyi Mir*. Moscow 1964. (Published in English as *Years Off My Life*, Constable, London 1964.)

Greiner, H. *Die Oberste Wehrmachtführung 1939–1943*. Limes, Wiesbaden 1951.

Grossmann, H. *Geschichte der Rheinisch–Westfälischen 5. Infanterie-Division*. Podzun, Bad Nauheim 1958.

Gschöpf, R. *Mein Weg mit der 45. Infanterie-Division*. Oberösterreichischer Landesverlag 1955.

Guderian, H. *Panzer Leader*. Dutton, New York 1952.

Halder, F. *Kriegstagebuch* (three volumes). Kohlhammer, Stuttgart 1962.

———. *Hitler as War Lord*. Putnam, London 1950.

Haupt, W. *Heeresgruppe Mitte*. Podzun, Bad Nauheim 1968.

Heiber, H. von. *Hitlers Lagebesprechungen*. Deutsche Verlags–Anstalt, Stuttgart 1962.

Hillgruber, A. *Hitlers Strategie*. Bernard und Graefe, Frankfurt am Main 1965.

Hitler, A. *Mein Kampf*. Houghton Mifflin, Boston 1939.

Hofmann, R. von. *Die Schlacht von Moskau 1941. Entscheidungsschlachten des Zweiten Weltkrieges*. Bernard und Graefe, Frankfurt am Main 1960.

Hoth, H. *Panzeroperationen*. Vowinckel, Heidelberg 1956.

Hubatsch, W. *Hitlers Weisungen für die Kriegführung 1939–1945.* Bernard und Graefe, Frankfurt am Main 1962.

Jacobsen, H.-A. *Der Zweite Weltkrieg in Chronik und Dokumenten.* Wehr u. Wissen Verlagsgesellschaft, Darmstadt 1961.
_____ and Rohwer, J. *Entscheidungsschlachten des Zweiten Weltkrieges.* Bernard und Graefe, Frankfurt am Main 1960.
Janssen, G. *Das Ministerium Speer.* Ullstein, Berlin 1968.
Jenner, M. *Die 216/272. Niedersächsische Infanterie-Division.* Podzun, Bad Nauheim 1964.

Kazakov, V. I. *Na Perelome,* Moscow 1962.
Keilig, W. *Das Deutsche Heer 1939–1945* (three volumes). Podzun, Bad Nauheim.
Keitel, W. *Memoirs.* Stein and Day, New York 1966.
Kesselring, A. *Soldat bis zum letzten Tag.* Athenäum, Bonn 1953.
_____. *Gedanken zum Zweiten Weltkrieg.* Athenäum, Bonn 1955.
Klietmann, K. G. *Die Waffen SS.* Der Freiwillige, Osnabrück 1965.
Kolganov, K. S. *Razvitie Taktiki Sovetskoi Armii v Gody Velikoi Otechestvennoi Voiny.* Moscow 1958.
Konev, I. S. *Sorok Pyatyi God. Novyi Mir.* Moscow 1965.

Lelyushenko, D. D. *Zarya Pobedy.* Moscow 1966.
Lemelsen, J. *Die 29. Division.* Podzun, Bad Nauheim 1960.
Livshits, Ya. L. *Pervaya Gvardeiskaya Tankovaya Brigada v Boyakh za Moskvu.* Moscow 1968.
Lossberg, B. von. *Im Wehrmachtführungsstab.* Nölke, Hamburg 1950.

Manstein, E. von. *Lost Victories.* Regnery, New York 1958.
Merker, L. *Das Buch der 78. Sturm Division.* Kameradschaft der Division.
Meyer-Defring, W. *Die 137. Infanterie-Division.* Kameradschaft der Bergmann-Division 1962.
Morzik, F., and Hümmelchen, G. *Die Deutschen Transportflieger im Zweiten Weltkrieg.* Bernard und Graefe, Frankfurt am Main 1966.
Mueller-Hillebrand, B. *Das Heer 1939–1945* (three volumes). Mittler, Frankfurt am Main.

Nitz, G. *Die 292. Infanterie-Division.* Bernard und Graefe, Berlin 1957.

O'Neill, R. *The German Army and the Nazi Party.* Heineman, New York 1966.

Philippi, A. *Das Pripjetproblem*. Mittler, Frankfurt am Main 1955.

—— and Heim, F. *Der Feldzug gegen Sowjetrussland 1941–1945*. Kohlhammer, Stuttgart 1962.

Picker, H. *Hitlers Tischgespräche*. Seewald, Stuttgart 1963.

Platonov, S. P. *Vtoraya Mirovaya Voina*. Moscow 1958.

Pottgiesser, H. *Die Reichsbahn im Ostfeldzug*. Vowinckel, Neckargemünd 1960.

Rendulic, L. *Gekämpft Gesiegt Geschlagen*. "Welsermühl" Wels, München 1957.

Röhricht, E. *Probleme der Kesselschlacht*. Condor, Karlsruhe 1958.

Samsonov, A. M. *Die Grosse Schlacht vor Moskau*. Berlin 1959 (orig. Moscow).

Sandalov, L. M. *Perezhitoe*. Moscow 1966.

Schmidt, A. *Geschichte der 10. Division*. Podzun, Bad Nauheim 1963.

Schramm, P. E. *Hitler als militärischer Führer*. Athenäum, Frankfurt am Main 1962.

Seaton, A. *The Russo–German War 1941–1945*. Arthur Barker, London 1970.

Senger und Etterlin, F. M. von. *Die 24. Panzer-Division vormals 1. Kavallerie-Division*. Vowinckel, Neckargemünd 1962.

Sherwood, R. E. *Roosevelt and Hopkins: An Intimate History*. Harper, New York 1948.

Shtemenko, S. M. *Gereralnyi Shtab v Gody Voiny*. Moscow 1968.

Sokolovsky, V. D. *Razgrom Nemetsko–Fashistkikh Voisk pod Moskvoi*. Moscow 1964.

——. *Military Strategy*. Pall Mall Press, London 1963.

Souvarine, B. *Stalin*. Secker and Warburg, London 1939.

Telpukhovsky, B. S. *Die Sowjetische Geschichte des Grossen Vaterländischen Krieges 1941–1945*. Bernard und Graefe, Frankfurt am Main 1961 (orig. Moscow).

Teske, H. *Die Silbernen Spiegel*. Vowinckel, Heidelberg 1952.

——. *General Ernst Köstring*. Mittler, Frankfurt am Main 1966.

Tessin, G. *Verbände und Truppen der Deutschen Wehrmacht und Waffen SS 1939–1945* (Volumes 2 and 3). Mittler, Frankfurt am Main.

Trotsky, L. *Stalin*. Stein and Day, New York 1967.

Wagener, C. *Moskau 1941*. Podzun, Bad Nauheim 1965.

Wagner, E. *Der Generalquartiermeister*. Gunter Olzog, München 1963.

Waslimont, W. *Insider Hitler's Headquarters*. Weidenfeld and Nicolson, London 1964.

Werth, A. *Russia at War 1941–1945.* Dutton, New York 1964.
Westphal, S. *The Fatal Decisions.* Michael Joseph, London 1965.

Zhilin, P. A. *Die Wichtigsten Operationen des Grossen Vaterländischen Krieges 1941–1945.* Berlin 1958 (orig. Moscow).
Zhukov, G. K. *Vospominaniya i Razmyshleniya.* Macdonald, London 1969 (orig. Moscow).